The Architecture of Europe

The Middle Ages, 650–1550

Also by Doreen Yarwood

Published

English Costume
The English Home
The Architecture of England
The Outline of English Architecture
English Houses
The Outline of English Costume
The Architecture of Italy
Robert Adam
The Architecture of Europe
European Costume
The Architecture of Britain
Encyclopedia of World Costume
Costume of the Western World
The British Kitchen
Five Hundred Years of Technology in the Home
English Interiors
Encyclopedia of Architecture
Chronology of Western Architecture
Fashion in the Western World
The Architecture of Europe
Volume 1 The Ancient Classical and Byzantine
    World 3000 BC–AD 1453
Volume 2 The Middle Ages 650–1550
Volume 3 Classical Architecture 1420–1800
Volume 4 The 19th and 20th Centuries

The Architecture of Europe

The Middle Ages, 650–1550

Doreen Yarwood

Volume 2

B.T. Batsford Ltd, London

Doreen Yarwood 1992
First published 1992

Typeset by
Servis Filmsetting Ltd, Longsight, Manchester
and printed in Great Britain
by Courier International Ltd
East Kilbride, Scotland
for the publishers
B.T. Batsford Ltd
4 Fitzhardinge Street
London W1H 0AH

A CIP catalogue for this book is
available from the British Library

ISBN 0 7134 6963 3

Publishers' Note

The figure numbers run consecutively through Volumes 1 to 3.

Contents

Preface

There are many books available on the architecture of Europe. Most of these cover a specific area or period and a number present the subject in a general way. It is rare for one in the English language to deal with Europe as a whole; generally only western Europe is discussed and, within this context, a carefully chosen selection of western European countries. This is understandable, especially in the light of the older, academic approach to the subject, for it was long considered that only countries such as France, Italy and possibly Germany and the Low Countries had been instrumental in influencing and forming British architectural history.

Since 1945, with increasing leisure time, the expansion of higher education and, above all, a greater facility of travel, the whole of Europe has become opened up to tourists and students and academic study has broadened its base. There are still some difficulties and frustrations in visiting eastern Europe, but it is now easier for people to visit the Soviet Union and the satellite countries. In the light of these factors, the publishers and I decided that I should write a book which which would narrate simply and chronologically the history of European architecture within the geographical boundaries of modern Europe, showing the architectural development and interdependence of the 23 countries concerned from the time of Ancient Greece to the present day.

This is an immense canvas even for a work of this size and there can be no pretence of comprehensiveness or detail. The aim is to present as clear a picture as possible of the general evolution of style and taste in different areas, illustrating which trends—whether they be, for example, political, social or climatic—influenced certain areas at certain times. I have given greater space in each chapter to the countries which were of paramount importance in leading certain movements and which produced the finest work of that age. The areas concerned vary from century to century: Greece and Rome in the classical world, France in the Middle Ages, Italy in the Renaissance, Germany and Finland in the twentieth century. I have also given especial coverage to countries in eastern and northern Europe which tend to have been left out of books on European architecture. In this volume predominance is given to French, Italian and German Romanesque work and, in the Gothic style, to France, England and the Hanseatic area of the Baltic coastal regions.

Half the space is devoted to illustration, for architecture is a visual subject. My husband, John Yarwood, and I have travelled some 67,000 miles in Europe, mainly by car, visiting each of the countries, many of them several times. My husband has taken over 25,000 photographs from which the illustrations, both line drawings and photographic plates, have been made.

In Europe, as on a small scale in England, great buildings are constantly in process of demolition and alteration. Even today few of the books available on European architecture provide a reliable guide to the present state of such monuments. I hope that at least for a few years, this book will provide an up-to-date guide on the condition and existence of interesting architectural work. In our travels we have encountered many discrepancies from written descriptions; some buildings referred to as intact were totally destroyed in the Second World War, others have been demolished, adapted, restored or altered. This is a continuous process and only constant study can present an accurate overall picture.

I hope that one of the uses of this book may be to encourage readers to go to see buildings *in situ*. With this in mind, I have not followed the common tradition of naming buildings and places according to the time of their construction, but have referred to them by the names used currently in their present countries, names to be found readily in standard atlases and guide books.

I should like to express my appreciation to colleagues and friends who have provided me with data and photographs for areas which I was not able to visit. I should like to thank especially Professor Robert Clothier for his photographs of Aigues Mortes in France and Mr. Vjachaslav Orelski and his colleagues from the Union of Architects in Moscow, who assisted me greatly in that city and provided me with material on the more remote cities in the Soviet Union which lack of time made it impossible for me to visit. Most of all I wish to express my appreciation to my husband, Professor John Yarwood, not only for accompanying me on all the travels and taking the photographs, but for developing and printing them which was much more of a chore.

East Grinstead 1992   *Doreen Yarwood*

I
Pre-Romanesque and Romanesque: Seventh Century to Thirteenth Century

With the gradual emergence of Europe from the disorders and chaos of the Dark Ages and the establishment of a Medieval society the story of architecture becomes more complex. In the preceding three chapters the styles of work and the surviving examples discussed came from different parts of Europe, but, in Volume 1, only one basic source of inspiration and culture was affecting building design and function. Thus, in studying the baths, bridges and temples of Ancient Rome, the differences between those in the Imperial city and remains from France, for instance, are noteworthy but not very great. Similarly, in buildings from Ancient Greece and those of Byzantine origin, the fundamental characteristics remain the same even though Sicilian Byzantine churches differ in several respects from Greek or Serbian Byzantine ones.

With Romanesque architecture and with its preceding movements in Saxon England, Visigothic Spain and Carolingian Germany, the situation is quite different. The collapse first of the Roman Empire in the fifth century and consequent withdrawal of protection and influence from the states of the Empire—England, France, Germany, Spain—and, later, the phased withdrawals of the Eastern half of the Roman Empire eastwards to Byzantium, left behind chaos, disruption and the total collapse of Roman civilised life in the countries of western Europe. The Dark Ages, once thought to be of extensive duration lasting until Norman influence established itself or even beyond, are now becoming less 'dark'. Through archaeological and other studies, buildings and other remains are yielding up information of centuries which were not, as thought by our grandfathers, representative solely of barbarianism and the negation of culture. The fifth, sixth and early seventh centuries are still scantily represented in remains and knowledge, but from then onwards more and more is being learnt. From about 1000 A.D. the true

Romanesque style of architecture shows itself and, since it emerged in many different countries of Europe which were not in all these years under the influence and direction of one empire, as previously, it developed in different ways. Thus, German Romanesque has various characteristics which define and distinguish it from French or Italian, for example. Climate was a decisive factor in establishing these differences as was the availability of building materials, the degree of culture of the peoples, their beliefs and needs. For the student, therefore, the story becomes a more complicated one. Not only does he need to understand features basic to the Romanesque style—a pre-requisite—but he will want to trace the backgrounds leading to the differing crystallisation of one country's Romanesque from that of another.

The process of development of architectural style, however, is a continuous one. It will be noticed that the dates of buildings covered in Volume 1 overlap with those in Volume 2. Byzantine architecture indeed continued to expand and change in lands in Eastern Europe during the same centuries that Medieval architecture was spreading across western countries. There is no definite dividing line, either geographical or chronological, between Byzantine and Romanesque, pre-Romanesque and Romanesque or Romanesque and Gothic. These styles and modes of building merged and developed one into another at different dates in different countries. Thus, for instance, Italy begain building in a Romanesque style earlier than most nations—for its emergence from Roman work was a natural corollary— continued it later, produced little Gothic work and then burst forth into the Renaissance a century and more before the rest of Europe. England, on the other hand, had a comparatively short Romanesque period of development following an extensive Saxon one but a very long and a unique building period in Gothic architecture emerging into a tardy Renaissance, nearly the last in Europe except for that of the Iberian peninsula. Germany's Romanesque work is extensive, of long duration and outstanding quality but her Gothic work is more restricted. France, in contrast, had some fine Romanesque architecture, especially of Norman character, but established Gothic construction very early, producing probably the finest quality of building in this style to be found anywhere in the world. The story, therefore, from the seventh century onwards becomes an increasingly complex one as more countries sought out individual ways of satisfying their own needs, techniques, modes of living and religious beliefs. To endeavour to simplify this complexity, in each chapter from now onwards, a general description of the fundamentals and similarities of the style is given first and the contributions of each country are then dealt with individually. Also, a larger proportion both of text and drawings has been allocated to the countries whose contribution to that style has been most notable, for instance, France in Gothic architecture, Italy in Renaissance designs.

Pre-Romanesque *c.* 650–1050

Only some European countries possess remains of buildings, decoration, sculpture, pottery, burial and so on which enable us to trace the evolution of architecture during these centuries. This does not mean, of course, that the others did not have such buildings. They may have been of impermanent materials, such as wood, or the countries may have suffered greater devastation than their neighbours. Study and research into pre-Romanesque architecture is still comparatively recent and more is being found out each decade. At one time it was thought that the only inspiration for pre-Romanesque Europe was Ancient Rome and Byzantium. For Italy, Southern France and Dalmatia this is largely true. But in countries further west a stronger inspiration comes from indigenous sources. Examples of this tendency are the timber constructions of Scandinavia, Britain and Germany with their timber roofing (later leading to Romanesque stone vaults), the stone churches of Moravia and Croatia, and also the Visigothic churches of Spain displaying horseshoe arch forms long before the arrival of the Saracens. Influences are very mixed and, though travel was not easy, ideas spread with remarkable speed. Specific features such as the horseshoe arch, vault designs, interlacing in ornamental carving and the circular church design appear in widely separated places —Scandinavia, Britain, north Germany, Yugoslavia, Bohemia, for example—and are not Roman features so they would, one presumes, have percolated through from northern Europe rather than southern. Equally, in central Italy, as opposed to Lombard Italy which shows similar influences to northern Europe, and in southern France the Ancient Roman pattern reigned supreme. Pre-Romanesque Europe produced buildings of considerable interest and capability and created methods of construction certainly not all due either to Roman, Byzantine or later Romanesque knowledge as our forefathers believed. This study has yet far to go and it would be unwise to be too dogmatic about sources and influences at this stage.

By the sixth and early seventh century civilisation in Europe had declined to its lowest point. Urban communities gave place to rural ones and the Roman influence became attenuated though the language at least did not perish. Christianity and the emerging monastic orders began to be a civilising, educating influence and, even after the twelfth century, culture and learning were the monopoly of these orders and centres. At the same time, different peoples, sometimes referred to as barbarians, began to establish themselves in different parts of Europe and evolve their own culture, sometimes Christian, sometimes not, but the former was not necessarily more civilised than the latter. The Goths, who came from Gotland in the late third century divided and merged with other peoples. They established themselves as Visigoths in Spain, Ostrogoths in Italy and, in further movements of peoples, the Merovingians became paramount in modern France and the Vandals in north Africa. In so far as this affects the contemporary architecture, the Ostrogothic work in Italy has already been discussed (see Volume 1, Ravenna) but the Visigothic work in northern Spain was influential as was the effect of the Merovingian culture in northern France leading to the Carolingian dynasty in northern Europe under Charlemagne.

250 *Brixworth Church, England, seventh and tenth centuries, Saxon*

251 *Earl's Barton Church tower, England, early eleventh century, Saxon*

252 *Church of S. Donato, Zadar, Yugoslavia, early ninth century, Croatian*

253 *Interior, Church of S. Michael, Fulda, Germany, c. 820*

254 *Plan, S. Michael, Fulda*

255 *Plan, Palatine Chapel, Aachen Cathedral, Germany, begun 792*

Carolingian

In A.D. 800 Charlemagne (771–814) was crowned Holy Roman Emperor. Under his leadership northern Europe became more settled and a period of building activity was begun, though it was not of long duration. In style it owed much to Ancient Rome but was not only a copy of it; it showed Byzantine influence and also new ideas, adapting itself to its own period. Charlemagne himself was an energetic, cultured patron. Stone and brick buildings were initiated of which considerable portions exist. The *Monastery of Lorsch, Germany*, was begun in 774 (the three-arched gatehouse, 810, is extant); *S. Michael's Church* at *Fulda, Germany*, a monastic burial chapel, dates from *c.* 820 and is typical of its time, being a circular construction with ambulatory and based upon the Holy Sepulchre Church in Jerusalem. A strong Byzantine influence is visible here in the drilled hole capitals (**253** and **254**). Charlemagne's most famous building enterprise was the *Palatine Chapel* (part of the Cathedral) at *Aachen*, the seat of his court and site of his palace in *Germany*. Owing much in design to S. Vitale in Ravenna but on more elaborate lines, it was originally symmetrical and had a western entrance with atrium and two-storeyed gallery; the courtyard here was large and had a capacity of 7000. Apart from this it is not greatly altered, with its 16-sided exterior (105 feet in diameter) and octagonal interior. It is decorated in Italian mosaic and marbles and above has an octagonal, domical vault which, like much of the interior, is reminiscent of Rome at its most imperial. The cathedral has been enlarged in later times around this chapel which is now a central feature in the architectural mass (**255**).

Also a Palatine group was the lay-out at *Germigny-des-Prés* in *France*, near Orléans, where in 806 a palace and church was built. The palace has almost disappeared and the church has been poorly restored and does not give a good impression of the original. Other examples of French work of the ninth century showing particularly early examples of the French contribution in apse development towards later chevet designs are *S. Germain* at *Auxerre* (crypt, 859) and *S. Philibert-de-Gardlieu*, 847.

256 *The Island of Reichenau, in Lake Constance, Germany. S. George, Oberzell. Interior towards western apse, ninth century and c. 1000*

257

257 *The Minister, Mittelzell, ninth century to 1048 (later belfry)*

Reichenau, Lake Constance, Germany

Of slightly later date are the three basilican churches on this island, part of the monastic centre here first established in 724. The *Minster* at *Mittelzell* is the chief church, built first just after 800 but added to and altered a number of times since (**257**). The *Church* of *S. George* at *Oberzell* and that of *SS. Peter and Paul* at *Niederzell* have more remaining from the early work. At S. George, which was a small abbey founded in 840, most of the present church dates from the ninth to tenth century with the ninth century crypt as the earliest part. The western apse is of about the year 1000 and the narthex is later. The church, like the others on the island, is a three-aisled basilica with its western apse extending the full height of the church. The choir is still raised over the vaulted crypt which contains primitive, baseless columns (**399**). Inside, the roof is of the nineteenth century but the fresco painting on the walls is one of the oldest decorative schemes in Germany, dating from *c.* 1000. The nave arcade is also very old, with green sandstone columns and Tuscan bases (**256**). At *Niederzell* the *Church of SS. Peter and Paul* was begun in 799. It is also basilican and parts remain of the earlier work. The nave arcade, with its capitals and columns, is the most interesting and dates from the eleventh century (**401**).

Italy

Here the pre-Romanesque examples are not numerous and much of the work is Lombardic, in the north. The basilican *Church* of *S. Vincenzo in Prato* in *Milan* dates from *c.* 833. This is more an early Romanesque church than a pre-Romanesque example, has three parallel apses and is vaulted with brick wall supports. Outside are pilaster strips and there are also arched corbel tables. Further south is the interesting *Church* of *S. Pietro* at *Tuscánia*, deriving from Roman and Lombard sources. Here is a very early crypt dating from the seventh century and a five aisled nave with varied finely carved capitals (**420**).

Scandinavia, Croatia, Moravia

Occurring in many, widely separated places is the circular planned, stone church, like that already mentioned at Fulda. Other examples include several on the *Island of Bornholm* in

Scandinavia (see p. 5) and the outstanding one at Zadar. These churches have a circular exterior and interior plan with an interior row of columns supporting a dome; some versions have eastern semi-circular apses. *S. Donato* at *Zadar* in *Yugoslavia* is an early church of this type from *c.* 812–876. Its inner row of granite columns supports a circular inner wall which is pierced by eight narrow high arches. There are three apses at the east end (**252**) and these contain niche recesses. The nave is barrel vaulted and on its north side a staircase leads to the upper storey which has a round gallery. The high, conical cupola above the centre is lit by small windows in the drum. This is a particularly complete example, though the decoration has not survived. Square planned churches also exist in these areas, though both designs are in a more fragmentary state in the western Slavonic districts. All examples show similar characteristics; they are generally stone vaulted—an unusual feature in so early a period and rare in southern Europe—the majority have cupolas supported on squinches and/or intersecting barrel vaults; the stonework is solid but crude; ornament generally includes interlacing in bands of carving on stone borders and the patterns are made up from circles, diamonds or zig-zags—the interlacing is like a prototype of the later Romanesque basket work patterns. Animals and birds are sometimes included in the interlacing.

England

Much of the Saxon work was in timber and was destroyed in Viking raids. A number of stone churches survive in whole or in part and these date from two different periods of building: the seventh to eighth century and the tenth to eleventh. These buildings show characteristics different from later Romanesque work. Generally they have thinner walls and are unbuttressed, having pilaster strips and long-and-short work quoins. The windows and doorways are distinctive with their round and triangular heads and baluster shaft openings to the former. Some churches are of basilican plan with semi-circular eastern apse (though the altar might still be at the west end) and a western or central tower standing on the ground. Roofs were usually of timber. Among the surviving examples are *Brixworth Church* (where Roman bricks have been re-used but without radiating voussoir construction) (**250** and **392**), *Earl's Barton*, tower (**251**), *Sompting Church*, eleventh century tower, *S. Lawrence, Bradford-on-Avon*, tenth century, *Worth Church*, tenth century (**386**), also those at *Greensted, Barton-on-Humber, Escomb, Boarhunt* (**426**) and *Bradwell*.

Spain

It is ironic that the most interesting group of pre-Romanesque churches in Europe should be in a country largely taken over by the Moslems. In the eighth century the Moors moved rapidly over Spain from their base in North Africa and occupied the whole country except for a small area in the north-west, between the Cantabrian Mountains and the sea. The religious freedom of Christians in Spain, however, was not suppressed and they were permitted to retain their churches and worship in them. Moslem Spain was the most cultured society in Western Europe at the time. The peoples who survived in the north-west area gained greatly from the mixture of arts and race but retained their individuality also until the tide turned once more and the north-western island increased its influence eventually over the whole of Spain.

Visigothic architecture had established itself before the Moslem invasion and was flourishing from c. 450–720. A few examples are extant from this early period but most of these have been greatly altered. These include the *episcopal palace* at *Mérida* and the *baptistery* of the *Church of S. Miguel* at *Tarrasa*. The most interesting feature of Visigothic architecture is the use of the horseshoe arch, employed both construction-ally and decoratively. This early use shows that its introduction is owed here not to the Moslems, who arrived much later, but probably to Syria and Persia. (The Romans had used it also but only in decorative form.) Visigothic decoration is primarily Roman in character but in simplified form; cable borders, rosettes, circles, stars and types of Corinthian capitals were in general use. The finest Visigothic church extant is *S. Juan Bautista* at *Baños de Cerrato*, near Palencia, built in 661. (The date is inscribed over the sanctuary arch.) It is a three-aisled basilica of stone with a four-bay nave which has clerestory windows above the nave arcade and a timber roof. The sanctuary is covered by a horseshoe tunnel vault.

The columns and capitals are a mixture of genuine Visigothic versions of Corinthian capitals and of original antique capitals and columns taken from Roman building in the area (**258** and **393**). A later example is the remotely situated *S. Comba* at *Bande* of the eighth century, which is a granite church on Greek cross plan with a square chancel. It also has a horseshoe arch entrance to the sanctuary, but its decoration is poorer than that at S. Juan.

After the Moslem occupation was complete the small area left to Christian Spain consisted of the north-west mountain district in Galicia and Asturias. An interesting architectural style evolved here, generally called *Asturian*, which came from Visigothic designs but also embodied Carolingian features of construction. This small area was centred around Oviedo on the northern coast. Two particularly fine examples, very close together, are *S. Maria Naranco* (842–50) and *S. Miguel de Liño* (848). S. Maria was originally a church built adjacent to a palace and was part of it, which probably accounts for its extensive and unusual character. It consists of two rectangular halls one above the other, giving a lower and upper church. The lower one is barrel vaulted; the upper hall is approached via steps and lofty porches (the south one is now destroyed) and these porches gave a cruciform plan to the building. Inside, the upper part consists of a hall 35 by 14 feet, with a rectangular tribune at each end divided from the hall by double arcades—good examples of stilted arches and mixed piers and columns. The capitals are carved diversely with human figures, animals and dragons. Outside, buttresses decorate and support the double vaulted storeys and these extend the whole height of the building (**259**). S. Miguel, nearby, is also a fine example both in construction and decoration, but only the western end exists, consisting of a two-storeyed narthex and part of the nave. The decoration of windows, doorways, panels and nave capitals is exceptionally good (**260** and **381**). Both these churches illustrate the Asturian characteristics of the round-headed rather than the horseshoe arch construction (the Carolingian influence is evident), and Roman type decoration and capitals, though the Visigothic cable pattern is also used. Other nearby examples include *S. Julian de los Prados* (c. 830) (near Santullano), *S. Salvador de Priesca* (921)

258 *S. Juan Bautista, Baños de Cerrato, near Palencia.*
Interior towards chancel. Visigothic, 661
259 *S. Maria de Naranco, near Oviedo, Asturian,*
842–850

260 *S. Miguel de Liño, near Oviedo, Asturian, 842–850*
261 *S. Miguel de la Escalada, near Léon, Mozarabic,*
also Roman and Visigothic, 913

(**400**), and *S. Salvador de Fuentes* (1023), both near Villaviciosa.

Towards A.D. 900 refugees coming north from Moslem-occupied Spain settled near *León* and established in that area an architectural style part Christian and part Arabic, called *Mozarabic*. The buildings were based upon late Roman designs but also displayed Oriental features especially in decoration and their use of brickwork in constructional and ornamental forms. A very good example here is the Church of *S. Miguel de la Escalada*, built as part of a monastery in 912–13. This basilica, overlooking the river Esla, is 70 feet long and has a five bay nave separated from the aisles by marble columns with mixed capitals —Roman, Visigothic and tenth century Mozarabic (these last-named are palm leaf designs as in the Cordovan Mosque). The nave has a wooden roof. It terminates in a magnificent chancel arcade of horseshoe arches. Outside, the beautiful 12-bay portico was added *c.* 930–40 (**261, 380** and **403**).

Romanesque *c.* 1050–1250

Although the regional and racial interpretations of the true, mature Romanesque style were varied, there are a number of basic features common to all Romanesque buildings. Those which have survived have, not unnaturally, been altered and added to in a greater or lesser degree and entirely Romanesque examples are not numerous. Nevertheless, in Europe as a whole, there is a great quantity of Romanesque work and much of it in buildings where a considerable portion is in the original style, though perhaps restored. The greater part of building in this period was, of course, wholly or partly in timber and little of this exists. Our knowledge is derived from work constructed in more permanent materials—stone, marble, mosaic, brick—and such buildings were naturally the more important ones and not necessarily typical of the whole. The overriding influence in the Middle Ages was a religious one and, in Europe, the religion was Christianity. The Church, both as an organisation and in its buildings, was of supreme importance to all European communities, not only for the spiritual but physical and intellectual succour which it provided. In return for this support in times of need, it demanded contributions from everyone, in labour and in wealth, although the latter was often payment in kind. The Church gave to every community, large or small, refuge from persecution and pillage, provided education and learning, medical aid and a basis for life by which were allayed the superstitious fears of the individual, which stemmed from his lack of experience and knowledge of health, life and death, understanding of the world and of man himself.

Appreciation of the vital place which the Church had in Medieval life is necessary to an understanding of the buildings which we have inherited from this time. In the eleventh and twelfth centuries to build in stone, granite or marble was a prodigious undertaking, particularly if the area concerned did not possess the materials close to hand. Early Medieval peoples were not, as the Empires which had preceded them had been, living in slave states (though one people might be in subjugation to another). The vast constructions built up on slave labour by the Ancient Egyptians or Romans were therefore not possible in Romanesque Europe. Yet, with only a slowly emerging technical understanding of how to build on the large scale in durable materials and with immense difficulties of transport, lack of communications and inadequacy of power, vast buildings were erected and these cathedrals and churches of Romanesque Europe still stand as testimony to the determination of man when his spirit is sufficiently aroused.

From this period of time the great majority of extant work is ecclesiastical. These churches were built in honour of God and to provide shelter and succour in times of need. Everyone contributed to their building. The churches also carried out the function of education in spiritual guidance to a population largely illiterate. Though the extensive story telling of the Bible and Gospels was developed especially in Gothic architecture, in the great portals and walls, Romanesque work too tells this story. It is, however, not only a story of what happened in the Old and New Testament but also provides guidance on how to live, tells of the life to come and gives protection against spirits and devils. Romanesque capitals, in particular, abound with terrifying monsters devouring hapless victims—animal and human— and the different animals: lions, dragons, oxen, etc., all have their appointed place and meaning in this mythology and language.

Plate 41
The prophet Isaiah. Church of S. Mary,
Souillac, France, c. 1130

Plate 42
Apostles. Portico de la Gloria, Cathedral of
Santiago de Compostela, Spain. 1166–88, Mateo

The differences in Romanesque style of various nations will be dealt with individually; the main reasons for the differences are climate and availability of materials. In general, in the north, roofs slope more steeply to throw off rain and snow, windows and doorways are larger to let in available light and walls thick to keep out the cold. In Mediterranean areas the openings are small to exclude the sun and roofs are flatter as a steep pitch is superfluous. Stone buildings abound in much of France, especially Normandy, also in England, the German Rhineland and southern Italy; in Sicily and central France volcanic materials are much in evidence; along the whole Baltic coastal plain, brick is the predominant material as building knowledge developed, and elsewhere timber was in prime use. The traditional building in these materials led to variations in style and construction. All areas have a few stone buildings which were of vital importance but, in a district like northern England or Normandy, where stone is easily accessible and in abundance, understanding of construction in masonry developed much earlier.

The dominant power behind the movement in church building lay with the *monastic orders* who developed their own individual style (on Romanesque patterns) to suit the needs of the order. These styles transcended frontiers and thus one Benedictine church is much like another whether in France, England or Italy. The *Abbey Church* evolved from the early Christian basilica and early examples still had the altar at the west end. Churches in southern Europe continued to be influenced by Roman methods of construction in style and even used parts of Roman buildings— capitals, columns, decoration, etc.—but further north a newer style was produced which was monumental, austere and strong. The plan was generally based on the Latin cross and roofing was of timber. The fire hazards of such roofs led to the rediscovery of how to vault in stone. Barrel vaults were developed first and remained satisfactory in the south where their immense thrust on the walls could be borne by the use of small windows to avoid weakening the structure. In the north, however, where larger windows were essential, the intersecting and later the groined and ribbed vaults were evolved at a comparatively early date and walls were thickened to solve this problem. Domical vaults developed in parts of southern France and in Italy and the crossing was covered by a dome or tower. Bell towers were important features of most churches, serving as places of refuge, means of raising the alarm and giving notice of events.

Knowledge of architectural features of style was dispersed partly by the monastic orders and partly by the great pilgrimages. The cult of relics was important and great churches were built to house such relics. Pilgrims then came on foot and horseback for hundreds of miles across many countries to pay homage to these relics and churches were erected along the routes to such pilgrimage centres. The most famous instance is the great Church of *S. James* at *Santiago de Compostela* in north-west Spain, said to contain the remains of the apostle. Pilgrims to Santiago came from France, Germany, England, Italy and even further afield, from the tenth century onwards, along established pilgrimage routes across the Pyrenees. As a result there are pilgrimage churches right across northern Spain and on the main routes traversing France, Germany and Italy. Such *pilgrimage churches* tended to follow similar architectural patterns due to their similar needs. They are generally large to accommodate the pilgrims and resemble the church which was the pilgrimage goal. The richness of such churches, their decoration and sculpture, particularly the portals, is tribute to their important position on the routes. Famous *French* examples include such churches as *S. Trophîme* at *Arles* (**389**) or *S. Front* at *Périgueux* (Vol. 1). The typical pilgrimage church has a long, aisled and galleried nave, wide transepts and a large sanctuary. Commonly the whole church is barrel vaulted at one height throughout and these vaults have transverse arches carried on piers. The aisles and galleries continue round the whole building. The crossing is covered by a dome or lantern. The use of the choir (if the church is monastic) is retained for the clergy while the pilgrims occupy the nave and transepts. The exterior is large, forceful in design and has an impressive façade with tall towers. The *Church at Santiago* itself, the pattern for the rest, is shown in Fig. **319** and *S. Madeleine* at *Vézelay* in **267**.

Apart from pilgrimage churches, most examples follow certain general lines. The nave is lofty and divided into nave arcade, triforium and clerestory. The middle stage is often arcaded but not often lit (its alternative name is the blind storey which is more descriptive). On each side of the nave is a single aisle (though this may be double in larger churches) and the divisions are made by arcades of piers or columns. The aisle is roofed at a lower level than the nave and the triforia have the function of masking the lean-to roofs which cover these vaults. In Mediterranean countries, particularly southern Italy, the triforium is omitted and replaced by solid wall decorated in mosaic or fresco painting. From the eleventh century onward the eastern arm was developed and extended, partly to provide more space for chapels and relics and partly to seclude the clergy from the laity. Such arms were generally apsidal in one or three apses and these designs led to the later development of the chevet, particularly seen in France; also, in order to retain their privacy, the monks re-established the nave altars east of the crossing, so confirming the eastern altar position. An ambulatory generally circumnavigates the whole of the east end of such churches, providing communication throughout the building with access to the nave aisles.

France

Alone of the countries of Europe during this time England presented a more or less single, unified group. Elsewhere, the modern names and regions are difficult to reconcile with the Romanesque ones. The area that is modern France displayed within its boundaries a great variation on the Romanesque architectural theme, since it was not one nation but a number of states whose buildings were influenced by climate, materials and purpose. Even with drastic simplification it is necessary to sub-divide the country.

Northern France

Taking the river Loire as a boundary the lands north of this reflected the *Norman* influence— that same influence which produced England's Norman architecture also that of Sicily and southern Italy. Here, in modern Normandy and Brittany, Roman remains were scanty and a new Romanesque style evolved. Stone, particularly of the Caen neighbourhood, enabled the techniques of masonry to be understood early. Churches are tall, monumental and austere. Norman architecture, owing something to Lom-

bardic influences, was the earliest to develop the true Romanesque—as opposed to Roman—style. The Northmen (Norsemen) settled here and by the early tenth century were converted to Christianity and began to build churches. Little of the early work—such as the original Abbey of Jumièges—survives, but in *Caen* itself exist among other work, the two famous churches of William I of Normandy (William the Conqueror of England). These are the *Church of S. Etienne* (L'Abbaye-aux-Hommes) and the *Church of La Trinité* (L'Abbaye-aux-Dames). *S. Etienne*, built originally 1066–77, has a magnificent exterior illustrating the best of Northern Romanesque grouping in masses and towers. The west front is vertical in emphasis with two tall towers capped by Gothic spires and with a plain façade decorated only by round-headed windows and doorways (**265** and **398**). The east end was altered in mid-twelfth century by an early chevet design with turrets and flying buttresses which blends admirably with the earlier work (**264**). Inside, the long nave is vaulted in sexpartite fashion in the typically French vaulting manner, comprising one nave bay to two aisle bays, retaining the square compartment and with an intermediate transverse rib introduced to the springing from the aisle vaulting shaft, thus giving extra support to the vault. The church is lofty, with three stages and, over the crossing, has a lantern with its octopartite rib vault. *La Trinité*, founded in 1062 by William's Queen, Matilda, of Bayeux Tapestry fame, has retained its original pattern better. It is a massive, very Romanesque building with a monumental façade of twin western towers in arcaded stages and, between, a gabled centrepiece with deeply recessed round-headed doorway below; there is a square tower over the crossing with stumpy spire. The interior is finely preserved (**263**) and has a long nave, with barrel vaulted aisles, broad transepts and a fine apse with groined vault. In the nave, the upper part above the ground arcade is a little later and has a decorative triforium and arcaded clerestory. The sexpartite styled vault is of twelfth century construction. Fig. **262** shows the existing Romanesque parts of the nave of the *Abbey Church* of *Mont S. Michel*, not far away. The eastern part of this church is Gothic but this portion illustrates clearly the typical Romanesque wall pattern divided into its three parts of nave arcade, tri-

262 *Abbey Church of Mont S. Michel, nave, 1022–1135*
263 *Abbaye-aux-Dames (La Trinité), Caen, looking
east, 1063–1125*
264 *Abbaye-aux Hommes (S. Étienne), Caen, from the
east, 1066–1166*
265 *Abbaye-aux-Hommes, west front*

forium and clerestory with wooden roof above. The piers, arches, aisles and proportions present here a good guide to the classic pattern of such interiors.

Burgundy

In Romanesque times this was a very large, flourishing province with a strong monastic influence in its ruling house. The Burgundians were great church builders, in varied style, but chiefly based on the design of the great *Abbey of Cluny*. The third building on the site was begun in 1089 but has been largely demolished. Churches on this pattern have barrel vaults and particularly fine nave porches with narthex in front. Two particular examples are Autun Cathedral and the Abbey Church of S. Madeleine at Vézelay. The *Cathedral* at *Autun* was begun in 1120 and considerable parts of the Romanesque building remain. The two finest parts of these are the narthex and the nave interior. The west façade, flanked by two towers, is approached up a flight of steep steps into a magnificent, open narthex (1178) where is situated the west portal. This portal is famed for its rich, vivid sculpture by *Gislebertus*. The tympanum is exceptionally large and, with the lintel below, depicts the Last Judgement. In the centrepiece is Christ, seated on a throne, and the remainder illustrates with extraordinary clarity and detail the Romanesque conception of heaven and hell, with the celestial delights for the fortunate and the demons clawing upwards to capture the souls of the damned. Inside, the cathedral is barrel vaulted with transverse arches and the east end is triapsidal. The nave, still a fine example of Burgundian Romanesque, shows the influence of Ancient Rome on its classically fluted pilasters and piers (**266**). Many of the famous capitals, decorated by animals, biblical scenes, demons, etc., have been removed for safety from the vibration of the bells to an upstairs museum where they can be studied at leisure and at a more accessible height. Copies have replaced them in the cathedral nave.

Like Autun, the *Abbey Church* of *S. Madeleine* at *Vézelay*, has a magnificent narthex and western porch. The exterior portal has been restored with modern sculptural decoration but inside the narthex the original work of 1128–32 survives; this has three bays and is a very early, typically Burgundian example. This church is

situated on the summit of a hill; its façade has only one western tower complete and, between, is a gable containing a fine, five light, sculptured window with portal below. Inside is a palely polychrome effect with the striped semi-circular transverse arches separating the quadripartite vaulting bays. The church is high and light so that the vista from narthex to eastern apse is clear and uninterrupted. The capitals display amazing vividness and variety in subject and handling: neo-Corinthian, animal, bird and human subjects (**267, 411** and **412**).

Central France

In this broad extent a number of influences are apparent from the domed churches of Périgord with their Byzantine inspiration to the richly coloured buildings in volcanic materials in the Auvergne. In the northern part of the region the *Abbey of Fleury*, now *S. Benoît-sur-Loire*, presents a fine, mature example. This large monastery was begun about 1070 and, though the abbey buildings have gone, the church remains. It

266 Interior, Autun Cathedral, France, 1120–1140

266

267 *Abbey Church of S. Madeleine, Vézelay, Burgundy, nave, c. 1104*
268 *Basilica of S. Benoît-sur-Loire, choir, 1070–1130*
269 *Pilgrimage Church of S. Sernin, Toulouse, from the north-west, 1080–1150. Tower and spire 1250–1435*

possesses a most interesting tower porch (*clocher-porche*) originally three-storeyed but now only two as the bell chamber has disappeared. The upper storey is now a disused chapel but below is an unusual and magnificent entrance porch. It has four rows of four columns and piers, each with different capitals, representing biblical scenes with human figures, monsters, demons and a type of Corinthian design. The original purpose of this large porch was to shelter pilgrims. The church itself, now partly restored, is cruciform with a quadripartite nave vault (Gothic) and barrel vaulted choir. There is no triforium to the nave but in the eastern arm is a stubby triforium arcade and a fine apse with ambulatory and radiating chapels. The clerestory continues all round the church. The central dome is raised on squinches above the wide pointed crossing arches (**268**). The *Cathedral* at *Angers* is a good example of the massive, domical building of Anjou, though parts of it were rebuilt in Gothic times. It retains, however, its Roman simplicity, particularly in the interior which is large scale and spacious. The cathedral was begun in the eleventh century and completed in the thirteenth. It is aisleless, cruciform and the nave is of the twelfth century with three large domical vaulted square bays in ashlar construction and is very wide, having a vault spanning 54 feet and which is 80 feet high—a remarkable achievement for so early an example. The transept and crossing have Angevin rib vaults in octopartite divisions.

Further west in the area from the Loire down to Périgueux are a number of well-known churches and cathedrals of the domed and domical vault type. Still on the Loire is the impressive *Abbey of Fontevrault*, founded in 1098 and originally covering a tremendous area with four convents and supporting buildings of which a number remain. The abbey church is a magnificent example of these domed churches; it is 275 feet long. Like most other examples of this type it has no aisles but a short, wide nave, covered by four domes. These are replacements but are still carried on the original pendentives. At the crossing is a domed covering under the tower, supported on high piers. The transepts have barrel vaults and the east end a semi-circular vault. Round the eastern end is an ambulatory with radiating chapels. Though further north than the other churches of this type, it is a perfect

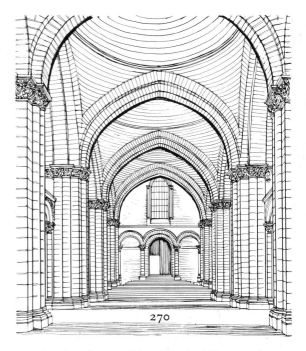

270 *Interior of nave, Abbey Church of Fontevrault, France, 1104–1150*

example of the style (**270**). Probably of greater renown than the church is the great *kitchen* here with its eight oven shelters each containing a central fireplace and with a great vault in the middle. On the exterior (**276**) is the high pyramid surrounded by smaller ones all covered with the scaled roofing tiles so typical of the region. In *Poitiers* are two churches in particular: *S. Hilaire* begun 1025 and rebuilt 1165 and the more famous *Notre Dame La Grande* (**271**) which dates from 1130. This is the richest of the indigenous churches of the district where limestone is plentiful and masonry developed early. The façade is decorated all over with carving and sculpture; the recessed doorway is enclosed in four orders of short columns and the arches have carved, decorative voussoirs. On either side are arcades capped by a sculptured corbel table and above is a further arcading and a central window. The other regional feature of the exterior displayed here is the fish-tail roofing of turrets and lantern, which has an oriental appearance and is like that at Fontevrault kitchen (**276**) and Angoulême Cathedral (**273** and **376**), also the Spanish Cathedral of Zamora (**316**). Poitiers was on one of the pilgrimage routes to Santiago and the interior of Notre Dame shows this in its

271 *Church of Notre Dame La Grande, Poitiers, from the south-west, eleventh and twelfth centuries*
272 *Abbey Church of Solignac, near Limoges, c. 1145*
273 *Angoulême Cathedral from the east, 1100–1128 (restored nineteenth century)*

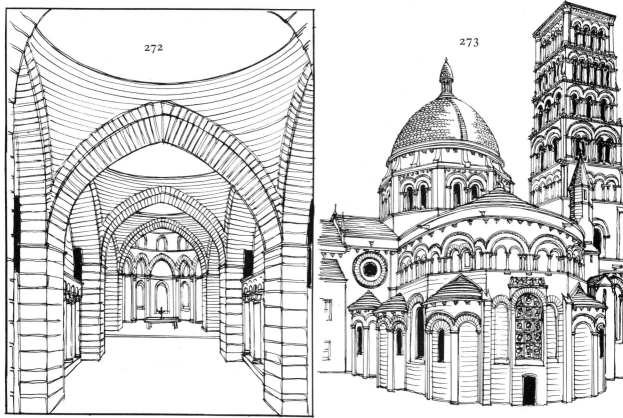

layout and barrel vaulted roofs. There is neither triforium nor clerestory; the crossing dome is conical and unusual.

Further south are some of the outstanding examples of the Byzantine influenced Romanesque churches of France. *S. Front* at Périgueux has already been described (Volume 1, p. 122), but at Angoulême and Solignac is further work. The *Abbey Church of Solignac* is a large building in a small village; it was also on one of the pilgrimage routes. Built on Latin cross plan, it has a polygonal eastern apse with three smaller apses and there are two more on the transepts. The interior, built of large blocks of reddish stone, is wide and spacious, its nave covered by two plastered domes and others over the crossing and one transept (while a barrel vault covers the other). The domes are carried on pendentives and below are rectangular piers without capitals. The wide pointed arches have no mouldings. There are no aisles or triforium (**272**). The *Abbey Church of Souillac*, now chiefly famous for its magnificent Romanesque sculpture, is nearer to Périgueux. The best of these are now set on the interior of the west wall (PLATE 41). The *Priory of Moissac* (further south still) is likewise best known for its beautiful sculpture in figures and carved decoration, chiefly on the portal. The *Cathedral* at *Cahors* is also a domed, Byzantine type structure with its domes supported on pendentives, but the building in general is now a mixture of styles with a largely Gothic façade. The north doorway has a remarkable tympanum deeply set in the porch like that at Autun.

The two most outstanding examples of this Byzantine-Romanesque style are *S. Front* at *Périgueux* and *Angoulême Cathedral*. The former is based on Greek cross plan and has been included in Volume 1 but *Angoulême*, despite its layout and domes, is fundamentally Romanesque. The domes, like the others of this area already mentioned, are pointed in form and are supported on pendentives. The construction and the pointed shape are Byzantine, but the Aquitaine versions possess a type of curved silhouette indigenous to the region. The cathedral is on Latin cross plan with projecting transepts; these are square ended with towers over them (though the upper part of one of these was destroyed in the sixteenth century). The east end is apsidal with four smaller apses grouped round the centre one (**273**). The

church is domed over the nave and crossing (though only the latter dome can be seen from the exterior as the others are covered by timber roofing) and the chancel and transepts have barrel vaults. The façade is beautifully decorated all over with Romanesque carving, representing the Ascension and Second Coming in arcading and sculpture, and the remaining tower is similarly decorated (**376** and **422**). Inside, the nave has no aisles; it is covered by three stone domes and the crossing dome is raised on a drum which has 16 windows. The cathedral, which stands in a commanding position on a hill overlooking the wide valley below, was begun in the early twelfth century. It has been extensively restored but retains much of its original form (**273** and **384**).

Auvergne Churches

In this volcanic region the Byzantine influence is shown not so much in construction as in decoration, which displays diaper designs and striped polychrome inlaid in lava and red and white stone. Like the southern Italian and Sicilian Norman churches, there is also an eastern influence seen in the use of horseshoe arches often with trefoil and cinquefoil cusping. Two interesting examples are the cathedrals at Issoire and Le Puy. *S. Austremoine*, the *Cathedral* at *Issoire*, is, like a number of churches in the area, based on hall pattern (with nave and aisles of equal height). There is a tall nave arcade and no clerestory. Round arches are used throughout, as are barrel vaults. The interior is simple, its chief decoration being in colour and in variation of capitals like those at *S. Pierre* in *Chauvigny* (PLATE 43). These capitals at Issoire are also very large, painted all over and represent animals, human figures and foliage. The columns and arches are painted in diaper and other patterns in indian red, black and white. The east end is apsidal and the church is blockish, building up in an impressive composition to an octagonal tower (**275**). The *Cathedral* of *Le Puy* is unusual in its setting and layout and reflects Moorish influence strongly. The volcanic area is formed into steep cliffs with outcrops of rock and the cathedral is perched on a ledge near the top of one of these, above the town, which clings to platforms on the hillside (**274**). One approaches the west façade of the cathedral up steep flights of steps and the triple

Plate 46
Wheel window of marble plates
Troia Cathedral, Italy

Plate 47
Doorway capital detail, Bitonto Cathedral, Italy,
1175–1200

Plate 48
Column support, west doorway. Church of
S. Nicola, Bari, Italy, 11th century

ROMANESQUE IN FRANCE: LOIRE, PUY-DE-DÔME, AUVERGNE

274 *Le Puy Cathedral from the south-west,
twelfth century*
275 *Cathedral of S. Austremoine, Issoire,
twelfth century*
276 *The kitchen, Abbey of Fontevrault, from
the eleventh century*
277 *The cloisters, Le Puy Cathedral*

entrance porch leads, not into the nave due to the steepness of the hillside, but below it and one must ascend further steps inside to reach the nave above the porch. The façade, like the rest of the building, is built of red and black granite and decorated in lava and coloured stone in shades of pink, grey and black. Inside, the nave vaults are octagonal domical shape and the central dome is carried on pseudo-pendentives rather like squinches. On the south-east side of the cathedral is a fine porch (*porche du For*) of Transitional design with the same polychrome decoration and interesting capitals. On the north side is an exceptional cloister in black and white stone with walls above the arcade decorated in lozenge mosaic patterns in red, black and white. The capitals are mainly foliated and are varied (**277**). The cathedral, which was begun in the eleventh century, shows clearly its Moorish influence throughout in its zebra striped patterns, lozenge and diamond inlay and cusped arches. Nearby is the unusually situated *Chapel* of *S. Michel de l'Aiguilhe* on top of its pinnacle of rock. It is built of the same materials and shows the same Moorish features of decoration and construction (**415**). The interior is unusual with columns set on circular plan but with flatter, straight sides to the exterior walls. It is reminiscent of circular interiors like S. Michael at Fulda in Germany.

Southern France

At *Toulouse*, towards the Pyrenees, is the famous pilgrimage church of *S. Sernin*, which is one of France's largest, barrel vaulted churches. It was begun about 1077, the first construction being at the east end, so that the nave is early twelfth century and the façade a little later. It is cruciform with a long, double-aisled nave, aisled transepts and a central, octagonal tower over the crossing; the steeple is mainly thirteenth century with a spire, 215 feet high, built in 1475 (**269**).

In *Provence* the Romanesque architecture is different from that in most other parts of France. Here, the influence is from Ancient Rome not Normandy or Byzantium. The classical tradition, as in Italy itself, never died and the churches of this region, though indubitably Romanesque, have a classical interpretation of the style and use classical columns, capitals, mouldings and decoration often, as in Italy, incorporating actual Roman fragments from ruined buildings. The façades, especially the entrance porches, and the cloisters show the magnificent decoration of such churches at its best. Two particular examples are *S. Trophîme* at *Arles* and *S. Gilles* nearby. At S. Trophîme the Roman influence is very strong in the west porch, which is based on a Roman triumphal arch. The Romanesque development shows, however, in the deeply recessed mouldings and jambs and in the columns which stand on lions' backs. The sculptural decoration here is very rich in figures and picture carving. The tympanum represents Christ as Judge of the World and, below, the architrave has a row of sculptured figures above the larger figures of saints which alternate with the columns (**389** and **419**). The cloisters are equally fine and on the north side date from 1170 like the portal. They have round arches and varied, beautiful carved capitals. The *Church* at *S. Gilles-du-Gard*, near Arles, possesses the most impressive of these portal entrances in Provence, this time in triple

278 *Le Pont du Benezet, bridge over the Rhône at Avignon, 1177–1185 (originally 22 arches now only 4)*

arched design, connected by colonnades. The church was part of a great Cluniac priory and a pilgrimage centre. The façade dates from 1140 (**391**).

Among the few secular constructions of the Romanesque period in France is the famous *bridge* in Provence at *Avignon*, the *Pont S. Bénézet*, built in 1177–85 by the Sacred Guild of Bridge Builders across the river Rhône. It is a good example of construction in masonry though it now possesses only four of the original 22 arches which spanned the river. S. Nicholas' Chapel still remains at the end of the existing structure (**278**).

Italy

Even more than French, Italian Romanesque architecture was subjected to varied influences in different parts of the peninsula. In the north, building design had much in common with northern Europe and primarily evolved from Lombard styles; in central Italy, particularly Tuscany, coloured marbles were used as veneers in decoration both on the outside and inside of the buildings giving a colourful rather than plastic effect to the decoration. Southern Italy was under Norman domination and architecture here has much in common with Norman buildings in France and England, taking into account the different climatic conditions and needs of the area. Sicily is, like southern Italy, especially rich in Romanesque work, but in this region the Norman style, which was dominant, was tempered by the mixed heritage of the island— Saracenic and Byzantine, in particular—and the architecture is an exciting and enchanting amalgam of these influences and a unique study in its own right.

In general, however, Italian Romanesque architecture has, as in other European countries, common features. As in Provence in southern France, links with the Roman tradition were never wholly severed so that arches, arcades, entablatures, columns and capitals tend to approach the classical form more than the Medieval. In churches, the basilican plan is most common while stone vaulting is the rarity rather than the rule. The Roman technique of timber roofing to nave and choir, with lower, sloping, timber coverings to the aisles, was commonly

adhered to. Likewise, the early Christian ground plans and arrangements had a strong influence. The altar remained at the west end in a number of cases. Separate baptisteries continued to be built for many years and separate, free-standing campaniles were the general rule; these features acted as watch towers and were symbols of local importance. Many examples were very tall—up to 250 feet high. In a constructional sense the arch never dominated Italian Romanesque work as it did in northern Europe; it remained as in Roman times, more decorative than constructional in its purpose. It is simple and rarely deeply moulded. Arcading, using round arches, is a popular feature in Italian Romanesque buildings but it is always decorative in its application except in a number of instances in northern Italy. The elevation of Italian churches, unlike those of northern Europe, is low, with the emphasis on the horizontal lines. Inside, the triforium is often omitted or is just a decorative band, while the nave arcade is of great importance. Over the crossing, a cupola raised on a drum is more usual than a tower, particularly in Lombardy and Tuscany. Italian Romanesque architecture is of a very high standard of craftmanship and beauty, differing from French, English or German examples but in general, ahead of these on contemporary development. Churches such as S. Miniato in Florence, built in 1013, show a sophistication unknown at this early date in northern Europe.

Northern Italy

The Lombard Plain is a natural corridor flanking the river Po at the foot of the Alps. The Teutonic race of Langobards (Lombards) were conquered by Charlemagne in 774. They were then unskilled builders but quickly developed in technique and understanding. Most of the existing remains are of the eleventh and twelfth centuries though built on sites of earlier buildings from the eighth century onwards. The natural communications of the region, the navigable Po and the Alpine passes, made this a suitable area for an exchange of ideas with Germany, France and Spain; architecturally a movement was established here which led the way for other regions. By the eleventh century a number of towns existed along the valley and important civic and ecclesiastical buildings were erected. *Milan* was

ITALIAN ROMANESQUE

279 *Trani Cathedral, Apulia, from the south-east, begun 1094*

280 *The Baptistery, Parma, 1196–1296*

281 *Church of S. Miniato al Monte, Florence, 1013 to thirteenth century*

282 *Old Cathedral of S. Corrada, Molfetta, Apulia, twelfth century*

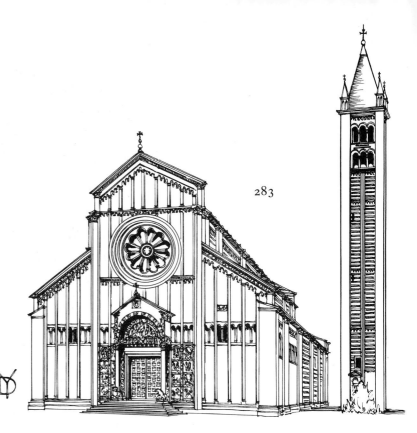

283

283 *Church of S. Zeno,*
Verona, Italy, from the
west, c. *1140*

one such centre; others included *Parma, Cremona, Como, Pavia* and *Ferrara*. Brick was the regional building material, with stone or marble facing, though a few buildings were entirely of stone. Two particular characteristics of regional building style were the tall towers—either for churches or civic buildings—and the development of the rib vault which, in Italy, was unusual. The towers were very tall, unbuttressed and were decorated by pilaster strips and corbel tables. Usually, as in most Italian towers, the window and belfry openings increased in number of lights as the stages ascended—commonly from one to five. Good examples exist at *Pomposa Church* 1063 and at the *Cathedrals* of *Ivrea* and *Aosta*. Twin towered churches in German style are found in the lower Alpine areas, as at *S. Abbondio* in *Como* which is an outstanding specimen of a stone church begun in 1063.

Vaulting was being developed all over Europe by the later eleventh century, but in Italy the wooden roof and/or the domical covering were the usual method. In Lombardy, however, the rib vault was experimented with and a number of examples were built. The usual church design had aisles which were half the nave width and there was an intermediate column between each pier. Thus, nave and aisles could be vaulted on

square bay pattern. Generally the vaults have replaced the original wooden roofs in the churches here and so are later than the rest of the building. Octagonal cupolas covered by flat pitched roofs were still normal crossing space covering.

A particular feature of northern Italian churches was the façade projecting porch built in two or three stages. It was vaulted and this vault was carried on columns which in turn were supported on the backs of animals—lions or oxen. Above the porch was usually a decorative circular window in the façade gable which lit the nave behind.

One of the best of early Romanesque churches in this region is *S. Ambrogio* in *Milan*, which set a pattern for Lombard churches. It was built in brick over a long period; the east end dates from the ninth century and the west from the tenth and eleventh while the vaults are mainly twelfth century. In front of the west façade is a large cloistered atrium and the narthex is flanked by towers, an older one on the south and a typical twelfth century pilaster strip one on the north side. Inside, the building is well lit by the ring of windows in the later, central, octagonal lantern. The nave is covered in double bays of domical rib vaults supported on piers while the aisles have groined vaults.

There are a number of *cathedrals* along the Po

284

284 *Palazzo Loredan, Venice, Italy, twelfth century*

valley with similar characteristics to one another, particularly those at *Parma* and *Cremona* which each comprise the basic threefold group of buildings—campanile, baptistery and cathedral —all separate. At Parma, the twelfth century cathedral exterior is of brick in simple design. It has continuous loggias all round the building and panelled walls and apses; there is a low octagonal cupola with small lantern. The façade is gabled with towers (only one completed) and three open loggias. The campanile, nearly 200 feet high, is later, 1284, and is of brick with stone faced pilasters at the corners. It is topped by a cone. The baptistery stands separately at the south-west corner of the cathedral and was begun in 1196. It is faced with stone on the outside and red marble inside. It is octagonal (16-sided on the interior) and has fine, carved sculpture and decorative doorways by *Benedetto Antelami* (**280**). At *Ferrara* the cathedral has been much altered, but the façade remains with its lower part Romanesque and the upper stages Gothic. The three Romanesque doorways are magnificently carved and the centre one has a typical projecting

porch of the twelfth century with infedels supporting the columns and vault. *Modena Cathedral* also has an impressive façade with wheel window in the gable (**383**) and porch below, on either side of which are four panels by *Guglielmo* depicting the Bible story from the Creation to the Flood (**390**). The magnificent 300 feet campanile—the *Torre Ghirlandina*—dates from the thirteenth century. The interior is in simple, brick design with high vaults and brick piers and marble columns. The pulpit and gallery are beautifully sculptured; the columns are supported on infedels and lions—the latter devouring their prey and possessing a sad but demoniac appearance. *Piacenza* is another interesting Cathedral.

Among the churches of the region, *S. Zeno* at *Verona* and *S. Michele* at *Pavia* are exceptional. At *S. Zeno Maggiore* the façade is simple but very impressive. It is beautifully proportioned with central, projecting porch, its columns supported on the backs of crouching lions, and with marble, sculptured panels on either side of the magnificent bronze doors by *Niccolo* and *Gugliemo*. Above is the gable wheel window which lights the nave. The whole façade is decorated by pilaster strips connected by corbel tables. Beside the church is the free-standing, lofty campanile, also beautifully proportioned. It has no buttresses and has alternate courses of marble and brick. The bellchamber provides the only openings near the top which is surmounted by a high, pitched roof (**283**). The interior of the church has no triforium and only a small clerestory. The choir is raised high above the crypt in which, according to the early Christian custom, the saint's tomb is placed immediately underneath the altar in the choir above. *S. Michele* at *Pavia* (**424**) shows Byzantine influence in its east end and central cupola, but the façade is a cliff-like gable wall with fine Romanesque carving on three doorways (**408**) though, unfortunately, this is now somewhat weathered. The gable is wide and typically Italian in its stepped arcade following the gable angle. Below are shafts and dosserets which form shallow buttresses.

Venice

Venetian Romanesque architecture was dominated by the city's eastern contacts and Byzantium continued to have more influence than Lombardy or Pisa. Mosaic decoration was more usual than carved stonework and this type of ornament was still carried out predominantly by Byzantine Greek craftsmen. Not many buildings of this period survive unaltered; the *palace* in Fig. **284** shows a Grand Canal façade of the time with cubiform capitals and stilted as well as semicircular arches, while the finest complete example is the *Cathedral* of *SS. Mary and Donato* on the *Island* of *Murano* in the Venetian Lagoon. This building is more Romanesque than other works; it is cruciform and has a particularly fine galleried and arcaded apse dating from about 1140.

Central Italy

In this region exists the finest Romanesque architecture in Italy in quality and development. It is also an area which produced several variations in style from the Pisan school centred on Pisa and Lucca to the work in Florence with its coloured marble facings and the districts further south in Assisi and Rome where contacts with the Lombard style are notable. There was no shortage of excellent building materials from varied marbles to stone, brick and volcanic substances.

The climate is good, not too hot but with brilliant sunshine to set off the vivid colouring and give shade and modelling to the arcaded treatment of façades. Vaulting is unusual, most roofs are timber spanned, windows are not large, walls unbuttressed and roof pitches shallow. The influence of Papal Rome largely prevailed and the basilican church plan was usual. The campaniles were separate but not generally as tall as Lombard ones.

The Pisan School

Here developed in the eleventh and twelfth centuries a centre for the arts which attracted artists and craftsmen from all over Italy. The typical Tuscan church of the region has exterior arcading and open galleries over its façades, often all round the building. The arches spring from low projection pilasters and engaged shafts. The façades are rarely, as in Lombardy, divided into bays and masses but are evenly decorated all over with arcading, up to four or five rows on the west side.

The most outstanding example of this type of work is the Pisan complex, the *Piazza dei Miracoli* in the city (**285** and **286**). This consists of four separate buildings: the baptistery, the cathedral, the campanile and the cemetery (this last, the *Camposanto*, was badly damaged in the Second World War but is now largely rebuilt apart from the beautiful frescoes which were for the most part beyond repair). The building of the complex spanned a long period, from the foundation of the cathedral in 1063 to the completion of the campanile in 1350, but the whole group is one stylistic unit. All the buildings are faced with marble panelling and decorated with arcading which still gleams white and sparkling in the sunshine. The basilican *Cathedral* has a double-aisled nave, transepts and apsidal east end. The oval dome over the crossing is supported on squinches and shallow pendentives. Apart from the interior triumphal arch, which is pointed, the other arches are semi-circular. The façade is very fine, with typical Tuscan arcading in four rows to the top of gable while below are three doorways set in a marble panelled and inlaid front. The columns and capitals derive from classical rather than Romanesque sources. The original doors of 1180 by *Bonanno* were replaced

ITALIAN ROMANESQUE: PIAZZA DEI MIRACOLI, PISA

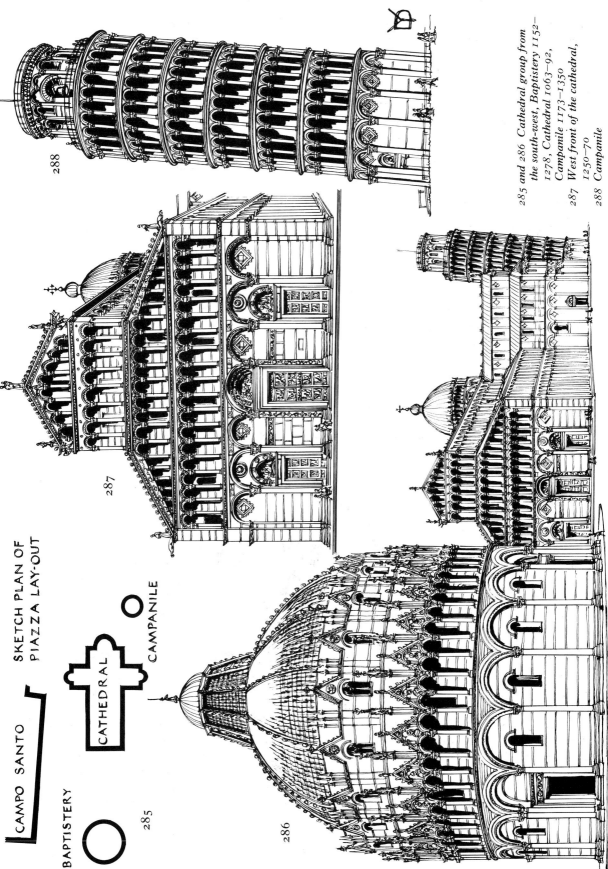

285 and 286 *Cathedral group from the south-west, Baptistery 1152–1278, Cathedral 1063–92, Campanile 1173–1350*
287 *West front of the cathedral, 1250–70*
288 *Campanile*

288

287

SKETCH PLAN OF
PIAZZA LAY-OUT

CAMPO SANTO

BAPTISTERY

CATHEDRAL

CAMPANILE

285

286

in the seventeenth century. His work on the transept doorway is, however, still extant (**287**).

The *baptistery* is circular, 114 feet in diameter, and is covered by a later cupola. The truncated cone, which extends upwards through this cupola, is the original roof. The interior consists of two concentric, circular forms, the outer walls in white marble, banded in grey and black and, inside these, an inner circle of Corinthian columns and piers. The classical influence is even more marked here (**414**). The pulpit of 1260 by Nicola Pisano is a masterpiece. It is hexagonal and stands on seven columns; the central one has a base of human figures and animals while the others are supported on the backs of lions.

The *campanile*, the famous leaning tower, is cylindrical, 52 feet in diameter and, like the cathedral, is marble faced and arcaded up to six storeys. It settled even while building was in progress and the fourteenth century bellchamber was differently angled in an attempt to right the inclination. The tower is nearly 180 feet high and over 13 feet from the vertical at the top (**288**).

The Pisa group is so superb that it overshadows the rest of the work in this district. Also, it is so situated, in a piazza on the fringe of the town,

that it can be appreciated without the distraction of heavy traffic and commercial buildings. The very fine work in this same style at *Lucca*, for example, should not be missed, for it is of high quality and is equally typical Tuscan Romanesque. There are three outstanding churches in the city: the cathedral of S. Martino and the churches of S. Michele and S. Frediano. The *Cathedral*, begun 1160, has a beautiful Romanesque façade (1196–1204) with a narthex, galleried and arcaded with screen gable and, beside it, a tall bell tower with typical Italian openings, increasing in number of lights towards the top. There is some fine carving and inlay decoration on this façade. Inside, the cathedral is Gothic. *S. Michele* (**289**) is the best of the three. It was begun *c.* 1140, but the impressive arcaded façade dates from the early thirteenth century. Like the others, it is covered with white and coloured marble sheathing with marble carving and decoration. *S. Frediano*, 1112–47, which is similar, is noted for its striking mosaic on the gable façade; the church shows a Byzantine and Roman influence.

Further south the Romanesque architecture is traditional but strongly tinged with classical

289 Church of S. Michele, Lucca, Italy, begun c. 1140, façade c. 1239

forms from Rome. The *Cathedral* of *S. Rufino* at *Assisi*, begun 1144 (now overshadowed by S. Francesco) has a beautiful façade, very simple and dominated by its circular windows and sculptured doorways. Of the three windows, the large central one is carried on carved figures, an unusual design, which has much in common with the façade at *Spoleto Cathedral*, of similar date, but with a later porch in front. *S. Maria in Cosmedin* in *Rome* still has its elegant tower of *c.* 1200 in seven storeys, each of which is arcaded, and has a brick cornice. The tower is the least altered part of the church where the interior, especially, has been much restored, but it is still interesting and retains its ancient atmosphere. It is a basilican church which incorporates the original building on the site—a Roman corn hall. Like most Roman churches, the building is of brick and is fronted by a porch and open narthex. South, on the coast, are two interesting cathedrals

at Amalfi and Salerno. *Amalfi Cathedral* has been partly rebuilt but still has its beautiful campanile and eleventh century façade doors (**377**). At *Salerno* the original rectangular atrium fronts the cathedral with its Saracenic styled arches and Roman capitals and columns. The Porta dei Leoni, the eleventh century entrance, is still intact.

The Tuscan work of the *Florence* School is a separate study because its characteristics are so different from those of Pisa or Rome despite its geographical nearness. The *Church* of *S. Miniato al Monte*, perched on a hill above the city is an early but mature and perfect example. It incorporates three influences: Roman, Byzantine and Romanesque. Antique Roman columns and capitals have been used, in some cases of ill-matching sizes, in the nave. The Byzantine influence is seen in the mosaic decoration inside and out and in the marble facing patterns while

*290 The Baptistery, Florence Cathedral,
viewed from campanile—black and white
marble, fifth-thirteenth century*

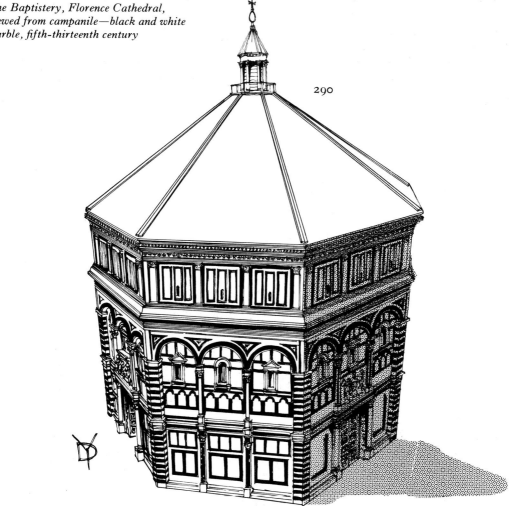

290

the Romanesque provides the general constructional layout. The façade, begun in 1013, is faced in white and green marble, with five arches on the lower part supported on composite columns. Above is a gable with window and mosaic decoration. The whole façade is faced with coloured marbles. Inside, the same vivid colour treatment is used on walls, columns, roof and pavement. The apse is mosaic-covered in its semi-dome above the decorative arcade. There is a beautiful, marble pulpit (**281**). The *baptistery* of *Florence Cathedral* shows the same marble decorative treatment. Partly Byzantine and partly Romanesque, it was altered in the Gothic period by Arnolfo di Cambio when he was working on the cathedral. The exterior view (**290**) is still primarily Romanesque; it is octagonal, 90 feet in diameter, and covered by an internal dome, 103 feet high. The façades are in three stages in black and white marble, surmounted by a low roof and lantern.

Apart from the ecclesiastical buildings of northern and central Italy, there are many *towers* surviving from the Romanesque and Medieval periods when they were places of refuge, fortresses and, later, status symbols. Many towns were a forest of such towers but most of these have now been demolished. S. Gimignano, near Siena, is the outstanding instance where a number of towers still survive and these date from the twelfth and thirteenth centuries. They are square in plan and rise sheer to varying heights without ornament, abutment and with few openings. Two particular towers remain in Bologna, the *Asinelli Tower* of 1109, 320 feet high and the *Garisenda Tower* of 1110. Both of these are inclined, from four to ten feet out of plumb, but they remain intact, the city traffic milling round them. They are survivors of about 180 such towers in Medieval Bologna.

Southern Italy

Although Calabria has always been a poor region, *Apulia*, in the years from the ninth to twelfth century, was rich. It was a large area, with its capital at Bari. From 870 to the mid-eleventh century it was a Byzantine colony where the Eastern Emperors held power despite Saracen attacks. In 1040 the Normans took over the area and its great cathedral churches date from the succeeding 100 years. Apulian Romanesque architecture is individual; it has the Norman characteristics of power and solidity but also Saracenic arch construction and Byzantine decoration. Because of the brilliant hot sun, windows are small, roofs flat and walls thick. Buildings are of the plentiful stone from the district and the sculpture is of as high quality as in the north of Italy at this time. The churches have short naves with high clerestory but (no triforium), single aisles, triapsidal east end, timber roofs and, on the exterior, large twin towers and one or more cupolas over the crossing, nave and transepts. The eastern and Byzantine influence is also noticeable in the lack of portrayal of the human figure in decoration; façades are ornamented with plant and geometrical forms. The great stone Cathedrals of Apulia have suffered from neglect over the centuries of impoverishment since the Norman civilisation crumbled, also from alterations and additions in eighteenth century Baroque work. In a number of cases, though, their magnificent bronze doors remain. These are often of solid cast bronze rather than bronze plates fixed to wooden doors as was more common in the north. Among such examples are those at Trani, Troia and Ravello, all of late twelfth century date and still in good condition.

Trani Cathedral was a large pilgrimage church built by the edge of the sea in a setting which appears to have changed little over the centuries. It was begun in 1084 and built over a seventh century church which now forms a crypt. It is tall, of golden stone and has a powerful, lofty eastern central apse with two smaller ones on either side of it, all lit by high windows (**382**). The transepts have large circular windows. There is only one tower (recently restored) at the southwest corner; the façade is arcaded and has three doorways, the central one finely sculptured. The bronze doors are by *Barisano da Trani* and have 33 panels decorated with foliage, animals and figures, depicting mythological and biblical scenes (**279**). *Troia Cathedral*, begun in 1093, is built high up in the small hill town and is visible for miles as it stands out of the surrounding flat plain. It is not large but is of high quality. One of its unusual features is the later window in the façade which is filled with decorative marble plates instead of glass (PLATE 46). The sculpture here, inside and out, is very fine and vigorous;

the bronze doors are unusual and interesting. At the east end the main apse is decorated by two rows of free-standing columns.

Other noteworthy cathedrals in Apulia include that at *Canosa* (now unfortunately somewhat derelict), the Old Cathedral at Molfetta (so-called to distinguish it from the Baroque one) and Bitonto Cathedral. *Molfetta Cathedral* has a fine site on the edge of the harbour. It has two tall Lombardic towers and three domes over the nave. It dates from the twelfth century and reflects the essence of Norman power and strength in architecture (**282**). *Bitonto* is different but equally massive. It has a gabled façade with wheel window at the top and two-light windows below. The central of the three portals is sculptured in a masterly manner with birds above the capitals (**417** and PLATE 47) and with columns supported on the backs of crouching (rather worn) lions. The nave is long and aisled with the aisles projecting to transept width. The interior is most noteworthy. The stone church of *S. Nicola* at *Bari* is one of the few ancient buildings in the city to survive. It is the oldest important church in southern Italy and was the prototype for many others. It was planned as a pilgrimage church with a large crypt for the relics and with stairways leading to it from the aisles. It was built mainly between the late eleventh century and 1197. The gable façade has three portals, the centre one of which (**388**) has columns supported on the backs of oxen (PLATE 48). Inside, the transept opens behind a triumphal arch which frames the apse with its altar. The famous Bari (Bishop's) throne is here; this is a magnificent piece of sculpture, 1098, by *Guglielmo* (**425**).

Sicily

The great cathedrals here, particularly those at Cefalù, Palermo and Monreale, are also of Norman origin but, owing to the mixed ancestry of the island's peoples, illustrate varied influences. Both Byzantine and Saracenic civilisations left their mark here, the former in decorative mosaics and carvings and the latter in the construction of stilted, horseshoe and pointed* arches and stalactite vaulting. The standard of craftmanship in these fields was high especially in glass mosaic design and application. Some of the Sicilian interiors glow with rich colour like

the greatest of the Byzantine ones. A favourite exterior wall decoration here is with lava and coloured stone inlay giving a cream, red and black scheme in geometrical shapes of lozenges and zig-zags like the volcanic decoration influenced by Byzantine work at Le Puy in France. Decorative motifs in Sicily, however, were immensely varied from Byzantine lozenges to Norman billet, Roman acanthus and Greek key patterns. The important cathedral foundations on the coast were begun between 1130 and 1200. *Palermo Cathedral*, begun in 1135, is the largest of the Norman royal buildings on the island but it has since been much altered. The façade and south porch are now Gothic and the interior and cupola were transformed in the eighteenth century. Only the east end remains typical of Sicilian Romanesque work, with interlaced arcading on the apses decorated ornately in inlaid lava and coloured stone. At *Cefalù* the *Cathedral*, built 1131–48, is impressively sited on the side of a mountain overlooking the sea; it appears to be growing out of the mountainside (**292**). Like Apulian cathedrals, it has a massive, stone exterior with apsidal east end and tiny windows, also western towers. The choir and transepts are immensely lofty with the main apse rising to the full height of the building but the nave is considerably lower. The façade is fronted by a narthex which is supported on Norman columns and capitals. Inside, the most spectacular part is at the east, where the apse and vault are covered by high quality Byzantine mosaic pictures, showing the form of the Pantocrator with angels above and the Virgin, archangels and apostles below. The cloisters are fine and have varied and original carved columns and capitals.

Monreale is the most notable of the Norman monuments in Sicily, situated in the hills above Palermo. It is a mixture of influences: Norman Christian, Byzantine, and Oriental Saracenic. The cloisters (1172–89) of the abbey church are beautiful; they are enclosed on four sides by coupled columns of stone and marble, inlaid with brilliantly coloured glass mosaic in patterns on the shafts and have richly varied carved capitals. The main doors of the cathedral are the original bronze ones, 1186, by *Bonanno of Pisa*, which have 42 sculptured panels depicting the Old and New Testament; they are similar to the

* *The pointed arch was used here long before it appeared in early Gothic buildings in Europe.*

ROMANESQUE CATHEDRALS IN SICILY

291 Monreale Cathedral, begun 1174. Apsidal east end.
Limestone inlaid with black lava, marble shafts
292 Cefalù Cathedral from the south-east, begun 1131

ones which he did later on Pisa Cathedral (p. 149). The exterior of the cathedral, particularly the apses of the east end, are incredibly decorated in coloured stone and inlaid lava in arcades, rosettes, strips and lozenges (**291**). The interior, which presents the most striking Sicilian example in Romanesque church building, is decorated largely by mosaic pictures on walls, apse vault, capitals and columns. The lower part of the walls is marble faced and the open roof is of painted and gilded wood. The mosaics cover an enormous area and tell the Bible stories in detail and at length.

England

English Romanesque architecture is generally called '*Norman*' after the dynasty established by William I of Normandy in 1066. English Norman architecture has much in common with its proto-type in Normandy but, as the child will often outpace his father, so the English branch reached greater heights than its progenitor. No other European country produced such magnificent and varied Romanesque architecture and none other possesses such a quantity of that heritage extant. These remains are not only in large cathedrals; all over the country exist many parish churches, abbey ruins and remains of fortifications and castles. Most of the cathedrals and churches have later alterations and additions but, in many cases, Romanesque work is present in quantity; perhaps due to the depredations of Henry VIII, English abbeys and priories, instead of being given Baroque face-lifts, have survived, more or less, as ruins from the Medieval period (PLATE 50).

English Norman architecture was, in the case of important buildings, constructed from stone, often Caen stone imported by William from Normandy. The style is massive, austere, finely proportioned and intensely durable. Builders tended to underestimate the strength of their work and walls, in particular, are of tremendous thickness as at, for example, the Keep of the Tower of London. In cathedral building the pattern developed differently from the Conti-nental one. The nave is often very long, as at Norwich with 14 bays and Ely with 13, while Continental examples are much shorter. In distinction, the eastern arm in England is shorter and, after the earlier Norman work, terminated more often in a square rather than an apsidal end. The cruciform pattern on Latin cross plan was retained, with much lower vaults than on the Continent. This led to the ability to span roofs with stone vaulting at an early date—a field in which England led the way—and, also, to provide a sound basis for supporting a massive central tower which, in later times, also carried a spire. On the Continent a central cupola was more common or, if a tower were intended, it was usually never built as the high vaults would not bear it. Few English cathedrals still have Norman vaults; they either retain a timber roof as at Ely, or more commonly were re-vaulted in the Gothic period; there are, however, numerous examples of Romanesque arcades supporting later vaults—a tribute to Norman constructional ability.

England is the only country of Europe where Romanesque building does not vary greatly in style from district to district. This is due to William of Normandy who created the founda-tion of a nation—the first in Europe. Of course, certain differences occur, due to varied needs and the availability of materials. Timber was used for building where stone was rare or expensive to transport but, for important building in abbeys, cathedrals and castles, the same style and stone material was employed whether in London or elsewhere.

Cathedrals

The English heritage is rich and, of these build-ings standing all over the country, many retain a considerable Romanesque portion. One cathedral is paramount in this respect: *Durham*. Sited magnificently on steep rocks overlooking the river Wear, it was built in this commanding situation not only as a monastic centre but as a fortification (**294**). The exterior has been altered many times and now only the lower parts of the western towers and the main nave and choir show Romanesque work. Inside, though, the whole interior is of one Romanesque scheme. Durham was a very early example in Europe to be stone vaulted over such a wide span. The choir has since been re-covered, but the nave high vault survives in its original form, which was completed in 1133. The Durham vaults are quadripartite ribbed constructions—a great ad-vance over the more usual barrel and domical

ENGLISH ROMANESQUE: DURHAM CATHEDRAL

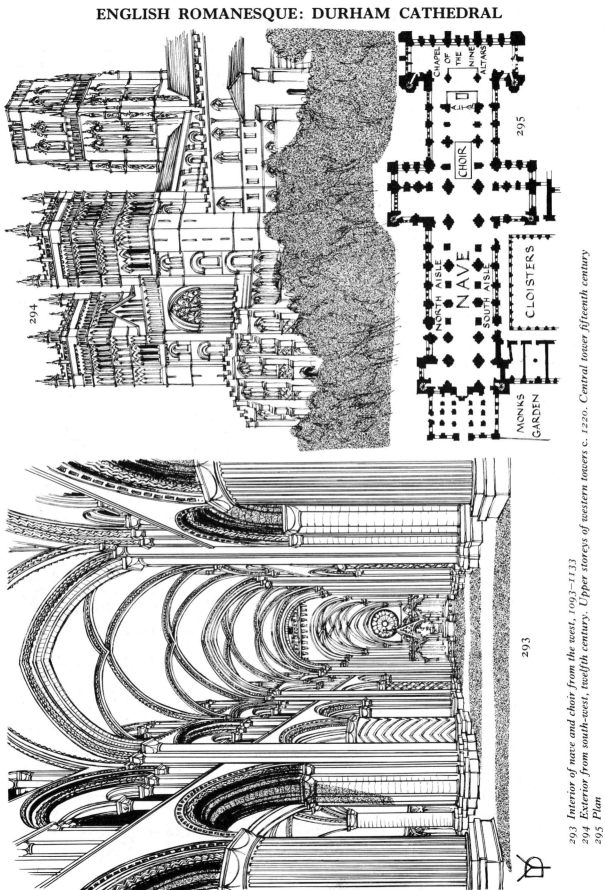

293 *Interior of nave and choir from the west, 1093–1133*
294 *Exterior from south-west, twelfth century. Upper storeys of western towers c. 1220. Central tower fifteenth century*
295 *Plan*

designs of France or Italy. The ribbed vault is a lighter construction and so does not place the same enormous stress upon the walls and arcades supporting it. At Durham also, flying buttresses were put in to take some of the thrust of the vault but these are not visible, being hidden under the triforium sloping roofs (**293**). Durham Cathedral was begun in 1093 on cruciform plan (**295**) with a low, central tower (since rebuilt) and two western towers. The great columns of the nave, with their varied chevron and fluted decoration and their cushion capitals, alternate with piers which have shafts extending upwards to support the vault. The aisles are also rib vaulted as can be seen in Fig. **293.** The cathedral has the traditional triforium arcade with two round arches under one larger one per bay and clerestory windows above. Durham is one of the very few ecclesiastical buildings in England to retain its original clerestory windows (as can be seen in Fig. **294** of the exterior). Most churches had larger windows inserted later to give greater light to the interior, but the Durham examples were not so small as usual. The interior certainly does look light, though it is assisted in this respect by the Cathedral eastern Gothic rose.

A good idea of how the great Norman towers looked when they were built is provided by the large, pilgrimage church at *Southwell* (**296**). The

stubby spires here which surmount the western towers are not ancient, but they replace the originals in the earlier style and are the type which Durham would have had in the eleventh and twelfth centuries. Southwell Minster is a very beautiful building, much of its exterior unchanged from Norman times but also with its unique thirteenth century interior work (Chapter 2).

The eastern end of *Norwich Cathedral* (**298** and **299**) is one of the few English examples which retains the apsidal termination—in this case, tri-apsidal. As indicated in the drawing, the spire, Lady Chapel and clerestory of the choir are later work in Gothic style but the remainder, giving a basis of design and construction, is Romanesque. Among the many cathedrals with Norman remains, it is most usual for the nave to

296 Southwell Minster from the north-west. West front c. 1130, later perpendicular windows. Chapter House c. 1290

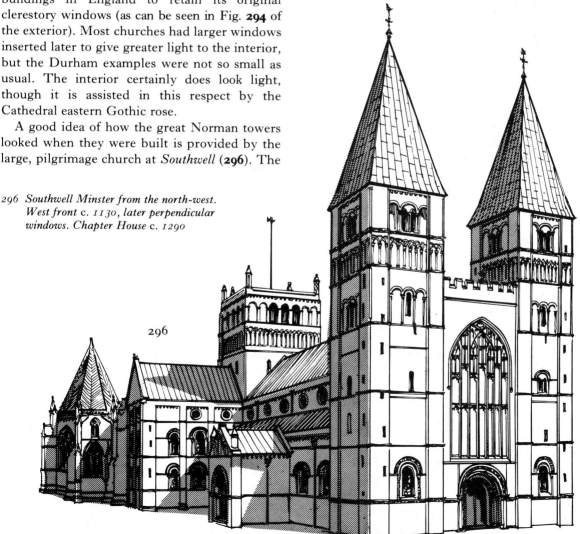

296

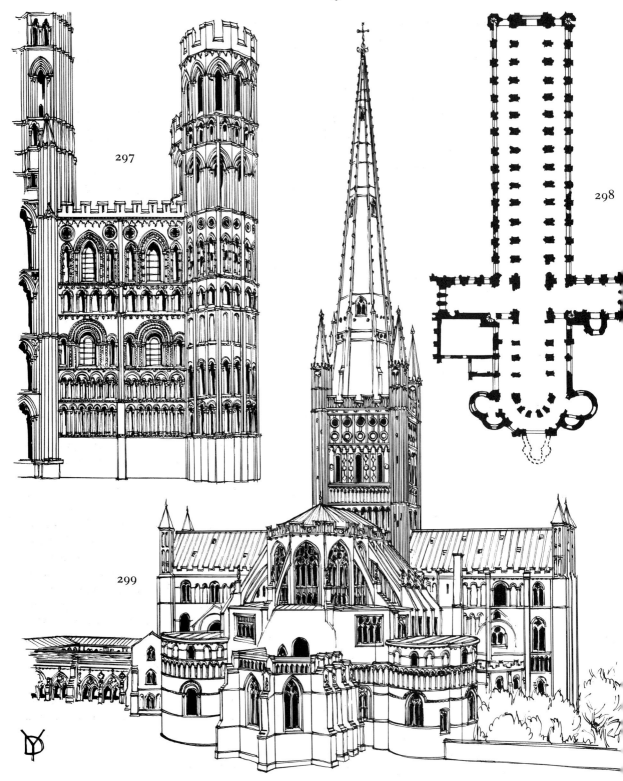

297 *Ely Cathedral, towered transept, begun 1083*
298 *Norwich Cathedral, plan (dotted line represents original Lady Chapel)*

299 *Norwich Cathedral from the east, 1096–1120, clerestory 1362–9, spire c. 1464–72, Lady Chapel c. 1930*

be unaltered—the eastern arm and transepts were generally enlarged later to provide more accommodation. Outstanding *cathedrals* still possessing such naves include *Ely, Rochester, Gloucester, Peterborough, Hereford* and *S. Albans,* also the *Abbey Churches* of *Tewkesbury* and *Waltham,* though most of these have undergone one or more restorations since the original building. *Lincoln Cathedral* still retains a Romanesque lower section to its west front with a remarkable portal (**395**). *Exeter* has Norman transeptal towers (an unusual design) and many cathedrals have Romanesque *central towers*—*Winchester, S. Albans* and *Tewkesbury*—while a number of *abbeys,* ruined and in use, have Norman remains, for example *Fountains, Buildwas, Leominster* (**405**) and *Malmesbury* (**413**). At *Ely* (**297**) is a particularly fine example of Transitional work, that is, the style which evolved from Romanesque and preceded a complete transference into Gothic. This is in the surviving transept and towers. Another instance of the type of work which generally includes both round and pointed arches in one building is in the *Church* at *New Shoreham.* Here, the round arches are predominant on the lower storey of both nave and tower and pointed arches above.

Parish Churches

Norman work surviving among these is too numerous to list. Every county has many such churches with a Norman nave, tower, west doorway or south porch, sculptural decoration and other features. *Iffley Church,* illustrated in Fig. **301** is a good example with typical, beautifully carved doorways and window openings showing Norman ornament of chevron, billet and dentil. Of particular interest, in sculpture, is the Herefordshire School, of whose work *Kilpeck Church* is the outstanding example. The south doorway here, for instance, of reddish sandstone, is beautifully carved (**407** and PLATE 45). *Barfreston Church* in *Kent* also has a richly carved doorway and corbels and a number of churches like *Eardisley,* also *Herefordshire,* have interesting Romanesque basket plaited fonts. In general, though, English Romanesque was not noted for its sculpture. The decoration is often rich, but more commonly of geometrical or plant form as at Lincoln (**395**).

Castles and Fortifications

William I of Normandy took over a new country and, to unite it and to bring peace and prosperity to it in accordance with his ideas, he had to show strength. To this end he built many castles. At first these were of timber, on motte and bailey pattern, but gradually during the eleventh and twelfth centuries the wooden keeps were replaced, in important places, by stone ones. Many such keeps survive, in a ruined condition, as at *Rochester, Colchester* or *Castle Hedingham* or, still in use as at *Dover* and *London.* The *Tower of London* was William's first and most important care and in 1080 he built the stone keep now called the *White Tower.* This is a classic example of the Norman design. It has four storeys and rises to over 90 feet in height. Its walls are massive (up to 20 feet thick at base) and its openings are small and well protected (**302**). Of particular interest in the White Tower is the surviving *Chapel of S. John,* which presents an excellent impression of Norman work. It has a simple nave with aisles in the wall thickness and continued round the east end with an ambulatory behind the altar. The columns are circular, very thick and have cubiform capitals. Above the nave arcade is a clerestory but no triforium (**300**). The keep of *Rochester Castle,* though ruined and with its floors missing, still gives a clear impression of what living in such keeps was like. This castle, built *c.* 1130, is of stone and is about 125 feet high and based on a plan 70 feet square. The walls are 12 feet thick and have passages, garderobes and bedchambers in them. The arrangement of accommodation is typical; the floors, of timber, were divided vertically by walls giving two rooms per floor. The second floor is the principal one, comprising the great hall and the dividing wall here is pierced by arches and piers to make one large room. Each of these parts has its own fireplace. Among the smaller examples *Oakham Castle* in Rutland still possesses its Great Hall which is famous for its windows, doorways and Transitional style capitals; it dates from 1190 and is now used for Assize Court sittings.

Spain and Portugal

It is sometimes stated that, due to the occupation of the Iberian Peninsula by the Moors until 1453, there is almost no Romanesque architecture here.

300 *S. John's Chapel, White Tower, Tower of London,*
 c. 1080
301 *West front, Iffley Church, Oxfordshire, c. 1170*
302 *White Tower, plan of third floor of keep*
303 *Gloucester Cathedral, nave looking east, c. 1100–60,*
 vault c. 1242

38

Anyone who takes the pilgrimage route to Santiago de Compostela from the Pyrenees and along the northern route via Pamplona, Logroño, Santo Domingo de la Calzada, Frómista and León will find that almost the opposite is true. It is a fact that, due to Moorish occupation, Christian buildings exist mainly in the northern half of the country in a broad band stretching from the Pyrenees down the Mediterranean coast to Tarragona and across to the west coast at Santiago, but, because of the Moslem domination, the Christian opposition in Spain was warlike and strong and Romanesque architecture reflects this spirit. The war of reconquest against the Moors got under way in 718 in the north-west near Oviedo and, over the years, Christian Spain forced a Moslem retreat southeastwards, reaching Toledo by 1085. Because of its remoteness behind the Pyrenean mountain barrier and because of Moslem dominance, architectural ideas were slower to reach Spain and develop there. As a result, Romanesque architecture lasted much longer than in Italy or France or England, indeed it was more on a par with Germany in this respect, but, equally, Gothic architecture when it arrived, also lasted much longer, delaying the Renaissance till the late sixteenth or early seventeenth century.

Indicative of its militarism was the Christian forcefulness and enthusiasm for the *pilgrimage* to *Santiago*. The Apostle S. James was made Spain's patron saint and according to legend, was brought by sea from Palestine and died martyred. After burial at Santiago, a church was built over the relics. Later, in 1077, the great pilgrimage church was begun and, all along the route from the French frontier, Romanesque pilgrimage churches were built to give shelter and succour to the thousands of pilgrims. Today, the pilgrimage still takes place, now by air or car for many and, for the 1965 pilgrimage year, the Spanish government made strenuous and successful efforts to restore and clean these famous churches (and also provide hotels for tourists) on this traditional route.

Spanish Romanesque architecture is subject to a number of influences, in particular, the mixture of Christian and Mohammedan sources —the basis of the country and its people for hundreds of years—and European sources, especially from France and Lombardy. At this time the Moors had a higher standard of culture which included art and architecture. Their buildings were more finely finished and decorated and were certainly more beautiful. In contrast, the Spanish Romanesque is rougher, more austere, more solemn than not only Mohammedan architecture but also Romanesque work from elsewhere in Europe. There are two periods of Romanesque in Spain: the basic Spanish product, of buildings erected before the great southward expansion in the late eleventh century and a transitional style of Late Romanesque of twelfth and thirteenth century work, resulting both from this expansion and from the French influence coming in from the north-east.

From the tenth and eleventh centuries, as the church established itself in northern Spain, the French seized the opportunity and set up monastic centres in the region under the Cluniac Order. In the twelfth century came a wave of Cistercian expansion to add to and replace the earlier foundations. Thus, in the northern coastal districts and also particularly in Aragon, Navarre, Castile and across to Galicia, French influence on Romanesque architecture was paramount. In the central regions the Mohammedan and Mujédar example was stronger and resulted in beautiful construction and decoration in brick, while in Catalonia, with its Mediterranean mercantile trade, the Lombard ideas percolated most strongly. In Portugal the French influence was strongest, led by Burgundy, and craftsmen and artisans had reached as far south as Lisbon by the mid-twelfth century. Despite all these outside influences, Spanish Romanesque architecture remains individual and nationalistic, being fundamentally a marriage of the two parts of the population: Spanish Christian and Spanish Moslem.

Catalonia and the North-East

In this area, due to the maritime trade with Italy from the Catalonian ports, Lombard Romanesque had the strongest effect. Many churches were built, generally small but stone, barrel vaulted and with Roman detail in ornament, columns and capitals, many probably taken from ruined Roman buildings. The layout is a solid one with thick, cellular walls and tall buttresses with chapels between. The whole exterior has a blockish appearance and the

SPANISH AND PORTUGUESE ROMANESQUE

304 Monastery
Church of S. Maria,
Ripoll, Spain, façade
c. 1160, restored
nineteenth century
305 The Old
Cathedral (Sé Velha)
Coimbra, Portugal,
east apsidal end,
1162–1300
306 Meira Abbey
Church, Spain,
interior looking east,
twelfth century to 1258

308 *Interior looking east, Church of
S. Martín de Frómista, 1066*
307 *Church of S. Martín de Frómista,
Spain, from the south-east, 1066*

interiors are easier to comprehend. *Perpignan Cathedral* (then in Spain) is a good example of these churches. Lombard influence shows chiefly in the bell towers. These have many storeys, are unbuttressed and have no batter. Pilaster strip decoration is usual and small windows, increasing in size towards the top. Many small churches of the period survive, but few important ones and these have been greatly altered, e.g. Gerona and Tarragona Cathedrals and Ripoll Abbey. The Benedictine *Abbey Church* at *Ripoll* was rebuilt in 1020 and was the Catalan equivalent of Santiago. It was drastically restored in the late nineteenth century from a ruined condition and with the aid of drawings. It was originally inspired by Old S. Peter's in Rome and is a cruciform church with double aisles and seven apses. It had magnificent vaults based on the conceptions of Imperial Rome and was one of the great abbeys of its age. The west portal and arcade with its twelfth century sculpture, representing scenes from the Old Testament, still remains, but the sculpture is now in a crumbling condition. There is still a fine, two-storeyed cloister dating from *c.* 1125 (**304**). *Tarragona Cathedral* was begun in 1171 and has mainly pointed arches, but is predominantly Romanesque in its heavy construction and masonry though some of it has been rebuilt later. The interesting cloister is of late twelfth century design and part of the west front is Romanesque. Some of the portal sculpture here is Gothic in date but Transitional Romanesque in its solid character.

Castile and Central Spain

The main *pilgrimage route* from the Pyrenees to Santiago extended across this area and, mounted by the Cluniac Order, the pilgrimage was

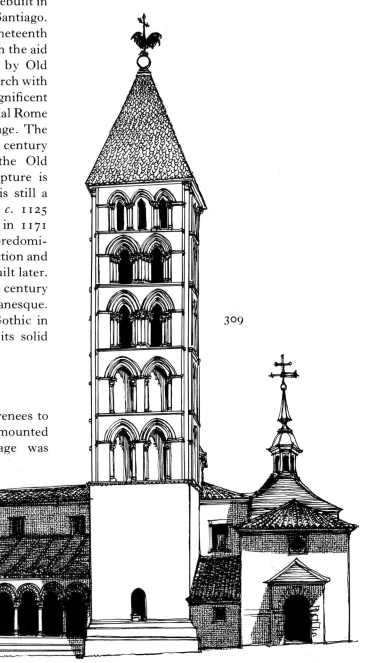

309 Church of S. Esteban, Segovia, Spain, eleventh to thirteenth century

309

ROMANESQUE IN SPAIN

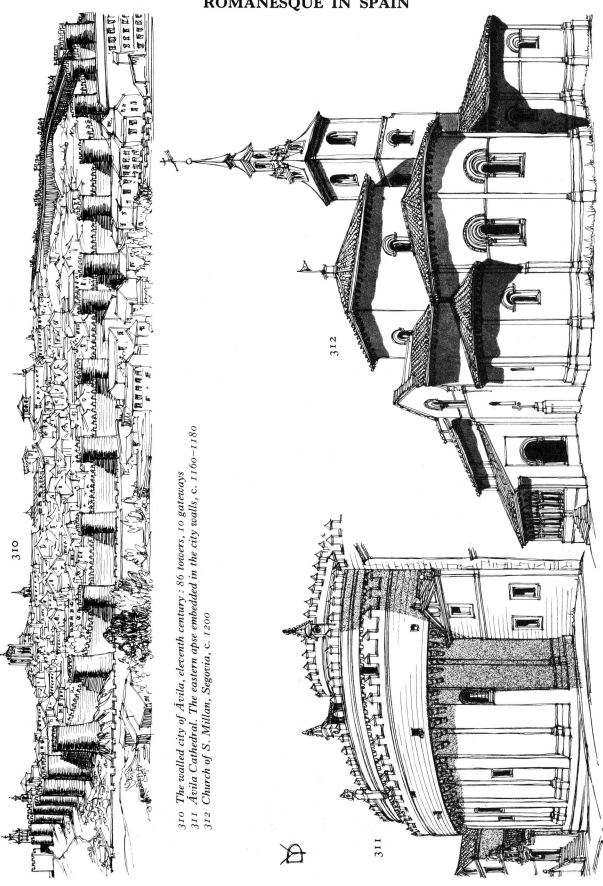

310   *The walled city of Ávila, eleventh century : 86 towers, 10 gateways*
311   *Ávila Cathedral. The eastern apse embedded in the city walls, c. 1160–1180*
312   *Church of S. Millan, Segovia, c. 1200*

established on a large, international scale and churches were built. The usual route was through Pamplona, Logroño, Santo Domingo de la Calzada, Burgos, Frómista, León and Astorga; bridges were constructed where necessary and information given to pilgrims to assist their journey, which generally took 14 days from Roncevaux in the Pyrenees. The Romanesque churches built along this route were, therefore, monastic and French in origin. Characteristically, they had a nave and aisles of similar height, and, as a result, no triforium or clerestory. The choir arm was short, ending in three parallel apses which abutted directly on to the transepts. The central, larger apse was used as a sanctuary and the choir was then moved westwards into the nave. The classic surviving example of this pattern is the *Church of S. Martín* at *Frómista*, which is roughly half-way between Burgos and León on the route. Fig. **307** shows the church from the south-east with its three apses, octagonal lantern over the crossing and twin, circular turrets at the west end. The aisled nave has four bays and the church is barrel vaulted throughout at almost the same height—there is neither triforium nor clerestory. The church, which was built in 1066, is as finely proportioned and designed as any in France of this period (**308** and **404**).

There are three interesting Romanesque churches in *Segovia*: S. Martín, S. Estéban and S. Millán, all of twelfth century origin. *S. Estéban* has a later tower (**309**) and *S. Millán* is the most unusual and striking. It has the normal tri-apsidal east end but the most interesting feature is the arcaded entrance (**312**). Nearby is the ancient town of *Ávila*, now comparatively small, but of great importance in the Middle Ages and, still surviving here, are the remarkable *city walls* and *gates*, the *cathedral* and the *Abbey Church* of *S. Vincent*. This last-named was begun in 1090 in the style of S. Martín of Frómista but was completed later under Burgundian auspices. It was a pilgrimage church and follows the classic Spanish pattern for such designs. The *city walls* are the best examples in Europe for their completeness and lack of alteration. Unlike Carcassonne in France they have not been extensively restored and compare more closely with Aigues Mortes (See pages 93, 94). At Ávila the walls are of granite and there are 86 towers and 10 gate-

ways (**310**) all dating from the eleventh century. There is a battlemented parapet walk-way round which is very extensive (like that at York in England). The *Cathedral* apse provides a bastion in the city walls and this part of it was built 1088–91. The apse contains an ambulatory in this vast semi-circular projection (**311**).

Galicia, West and North-West Spain

In the western area the most interesting examples are at Zamora, Salamanca, Toro and Ciudad Rodrigo. *Zamora Cathedral* was begun in 1152. Typical of late Romanesque in Spain, the pointed arch is used predominantly and vaults are quadripartite in pointed barrel design. One of the most interesting features here is the central lantern which has eastern fish-tail covering like the examples in France at Poitiers, Angoulême and Fontevrault (**316**). The *Collegiate Church* at *Toro* (**318**) was built in 1160–1240 and has much in common with Zamora Cathedral; its vaults are almost entirely of pointed barrel type. The *Cathedral* of *Ciudad Rodrigo* (1165–1230) has domical octopartite vaulting and shows French influence on the Poitiers pattern. *Salamanca Old Cathedral*, so-called because it forms one unit with the much larger New Cathedral, was built in 1120–78 (Vol. 1,**165**; **379**). It is particularly noted for its dome with high drum, supported on pendentives and pierced with two rows of windows and crowned by a stone ribbed cupola (**313**). On the exterior is an octagonal spire, called the *Torre de Gallo*, after its weathercock. The only access to the interior of the Old Cathedral now is through the New.

The great *Church* of *Santiago* (S. James) *de Compostela* is a fitting climax to the end of the pilgrimage road. This is the greatest Romanesque church in Spain. The town itself, not very large, has been preserved in the centre and the traffic diverted round the outside. Inside the walls it is still, today, a haven of pilgrimage and peace. The exterior of the church is now largely Baroque, rebuilt in the eighteenth century, but the interior remains Romanesque on pilgrimage church lines. It was largely based on the design for S. Sernin in Toulouse and was started after but completed earlier than the French church (**423**). The nave has single aisles and is very long; it has a barrel vault while the aisles are cross-vaulted

313 Cupola and pendentives. Old Cathedral, Salamanca,
Spain, 1120–1178

314 Barrel vault

315 Barrel intersecting vault

316 Central cupola, Zamora Cathedral, Spain, 1131–
1174

317 Canterbury Cathedral, England. Ernulf's crypt,
c. 1096–1107

318 Central cupola. Collegiate Church of S. Maria,
Toro, Spain, c. 1250

319

319 The nave looking east. The great pilgrimage church of S. James, Santiago de Compostela, Spain, begun 1077

(**319**). There are transepts and a French style chevet, with ambulatory and five radiating chapels. Apart from the interior, the south transept portico remains from the Romanesque period; the portico—*la Puerte de las Platerías*—was built in 1103; it has some fine sculpture of 1116 (**396**). The outstanding part of the building sculpturally, however, is the *Portico de la Gloria*, originally the façade but now approached via the classical stairway on the west front, from the square below. This Romanesque triple portico is sculptured by *Master Mateo* (who is buried in the church) and who worked on it from 1168–88. The statue of S. James the Apostle decorates the trumeau and on each side are statues of apostles, prophets and elders. The whole portico tells the story of Man's Trials and Salvation. It is one of the great examples of European Romanesque art (PLATES 42 and 52).

The Cistercian Abbeys

The important Benedictine Order had become wealthy and more worldly all over Europe and in Spain as in England, the Cistercian Order was founded and flourished with the aim of re-asserting the vows of poverty, austerity and dedication to a monastic life devoted to the original humble origins. The Cistercian Order in Spain, as in England, played an important part in establishing Gothic architecture. In England are abbeys such as Fountains and Rievaulx. Spain has many examples too. A number of them were largely built in the late Romanesque style and of these some survive in whole or in part. The churches are large, very simple and austere and have little of the richly carved doorways, capitals and mouldings of other Romanesque work. Among the more interesting examples are the *Abbeys* of *Moreruela*, 1169, near Zamora, which is ruined but retains a complete chevet, of *Veruela*, 1170, in Aragon and the famous *Abbey of Poblet*, 1151–96, in Catalonia. This has been altered greatly in later times and was neglected in the nineteenth century. Parts of the buildings, particularly the church interior and cloisters, are still very fine. The drawing in Fig. **306** shows the interior of the *Abbey Church* at *Meira* in Galicia. This church, c. 1190–1258, follows closely on its Burgundian pattern and is extremely austere. It is remotely situated in this small town high in the

mountains. The Romanesque is of Transitional type, with wide pointed arches and barrel vault, a clerestory but no triforium. On the façade, the portal still possesses the original and unusual doors and above is the typical circular window (**378**).

Portugal

The French influence here was even greater than in Spain and in the eleventh century the northern region had broken free to become a satellite of Burgundy, though later it became independent. There is, however, little Romanesque work existing. Surviving examples include the *Church of S. Salvador* at *Travanca*, the *Cathedral* at *Evora* and the *Church* of the *Convent of Christ* at *Tomar*, all twelfth century but with considerable alterations in later periods. The best and most typical Portugese example of Romanesque is the *Old Cathedral (Sé Velha)* in *Coimbra*, begun 1162. The east end (**305**) is tri-apsidal, there is a square tower with cupola, which has Byzantine type coloured ceramic tiling, and the west façade has a fine portico, approached up a flight of steps (**388**). The cathedral has a castellated, fortified appearance and obviously incorporates Moslem features. The façade, in particular, is severe and in sheer, block form; it is impressive in its austere simplicity. The interior is very Romanesque. There is a barrel vaulted nave with transverse arches and a triforium which has a wide ambulatory supported over the full width of the aisle vaults. The square tower is rib vaulted and its windows give good light to the cathedral.

Germany

Romanesque architecture developed early in Germany. It was clearly related to the Lombard style of Northern Italy owing to the political links between the two countries under the Holy Roman Empire. These ties were particularly strong during the Hohenstaufen dynasty in the twelfth and thirteenth century. The predominant characteristic adopted by the Germans from Italian patterns was the conception of arcading as an all-over pattern, especially on the apses. The Germans developed their own style later and this was eminently suited to the character of the people, producing buildings which were

GERMAN ROMANESQUE CATHEDRALS

320 Worms Cathedral from the south-west, c. 1110–1200
321 Speyer Cathedral from the north-east, c. 1110
322 Limburg Cathedral from the north-west. River Lahn in the foreground. c. 1215–35
323 Plan. Worms Cathedral

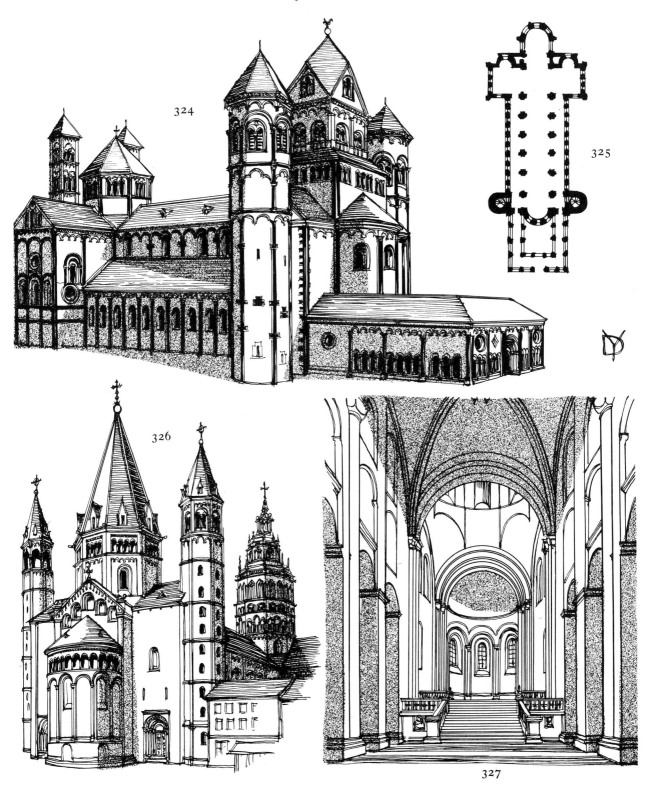

324 *Abbey Church of the Monastery of Maria Laach from the north-west, c. 1112 to thirteenth century*
325 *Plan. Maria Laach*

326 *Mainz Cathedral from the north-east, 1085–1239 (central tower completed 1361)*
327 *Interior, Mainz Cathedral looking east*

strong, dignified, austere, with limited decoration and fine masonry. A peculiarly German Romanesque feature is the church planned with an apse at each end of the building, west as well as east. Many important buildings have this characteristic, though the western apse was generally single and the eastern might be triple. This feature, which is thought to have developed from a desire for an apse and altar both for abbot and his monks at the east end, and for the bishop and laity at the west, gave no opportunity for masons and sculptors to decorate a deeply moulded western porch, as was usual in France or England. The entrance doorway on such churches as *Mainz, Worms* or *Speyer Cathedrals* are usually lateral transeptal ones. A second feature which characterises German Romanesque churches is the dramatic skyline pattern created by the multiplicity of towers, cupolas and turrets. It was common for larger churches to have one or two cupolas, often polygonal, over the crossing and nave (or choir) and four towers, two at each end. These towers were transeptal or set just behind the apses and were polygonal or circular in form. Circular towers are unusual in the Romanesque architecture of other European countries, except in northern Italy, but they are a common feature of German ones as at, for instance, *Worms Cathedral* (**320**). The German helm type of covering to the square or polygonal tower was especially typical of the Rhineland, of which the *Church of the Apostles* in *Cologne* is a notable example (**328**).

Romanesque architecture in Germany lasted very late, as it did in Lombardy. There are many examples which date from well into the thirteenth century in a style not much altered from 100 years earlier. Having established this effective, impressive mode of building, so suited to their race, the Germans seemed unwilling to abandon it. The majority of surviving buildings are in stone but there were originally a vast number of timber and half-timber (*Fachwerk*) constructions. All along the Baltic region brick building began early, owing to the lack of stone materials, but such work has mostly been altered later, in the Middle Ages, or was destroyed in the Second World War.

The external walls of the churches are decorated simply by pilaster strips and corbelled string courses with arcading, as in Lombardy.

Inside, the layout and execution are simple and austere. Stone vaulting developed fairly late and most of these vaults are replacements of the timber roofs. When vaults were used, the square bay pattern was adopted, with one nave bay being equal to two aisle ones as at *Worms Cathedral*. Some examples have a western atrium as at *Maria Laach Abbey Church* (**324**).

The Rhineland

Although most of the great churches and cathedrals of this area suffered greatly from damage inflicted in the Second World War, the region still possesses some impressive examples of German Romanesque architecture. The three famous cathedrals of Worms, Mainz and Speyer were all severely damaged, but are all now largely restored and rebuilt once more. Apart from wartime damage, *Worms Cathedral* is the least altered of the three in that it retains its Romanesque plan and general layout (**323**). It has east and west apses and there are two large, and four staircase, towers which break the skyline. It is a highly typical example of German work in its restrained, symmetrical severity. The entrances are in the aisles. Exterior decoration is by pilaster strips and arcading which continues round the church. The interior is completely vaulted on square bay pattern, one nave bay to two aisles (**320**).

Mainz Cathedral is immense and was altered in later periods when the crossing towers were rebuilt in different styles and houses were constructed abutting on to and becoming part of the cathedral flanks. Despite this, the vast red sandstone bulk of the cathedral towers above the severely damaged and consequently modern city, the impression it creates little affected by the trolley bus wires which cross the tourists' line of vision. The eastern end (**326**) illustrates the original German design, its apse surmounted by a gable end flanked by two towers. The interior (**327**) is plain and dignified.

Like Mainz, *Speyer Cathedral* is very large. Its west façade was rebuilt in the eighteenth and also in the nineteenth century. The remainder (except for parts devastated by war and now being renewed) retains its Romanesque characteristics and is accessible and attractively sited amongst the trees in a park (**321**). The crypt is the

ROMANESQUE IN GERMANY AND SWITZERLAND

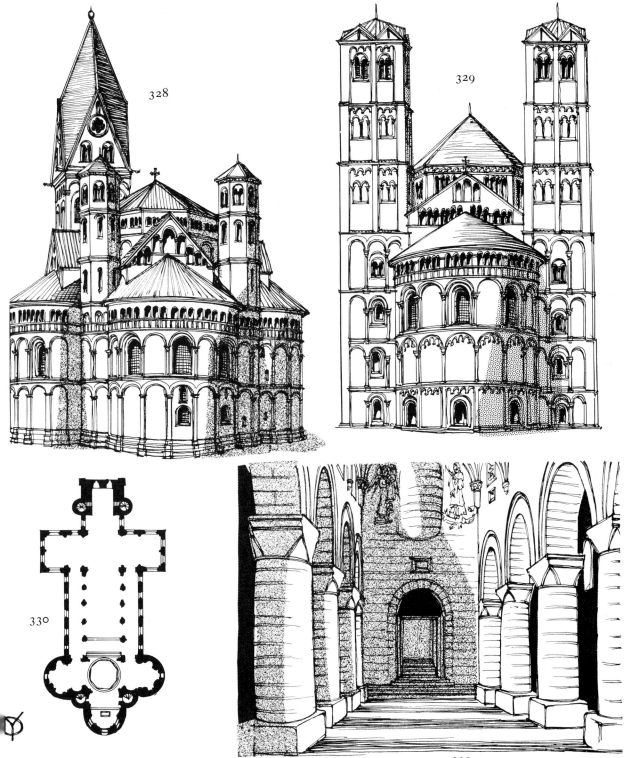

*328 Church of the Apostles, Cologne, Germany. East end
c. 1190–1200.` (N/W tower missing)*
*329 Church of S. Gereon, Cologne. East end c. 1160
(west end severely damaged in second World War)*

330 Plan. Church of the Apostles
*331 Interior. Church of Romainmôtier,
Switzerland, c. 1000*

earliest extant part of the cathedral, c. 1030, and is remarkable. It is large, with stout columns and cubiform capitals supporting a heavy groined vault. The nave is wide and long, with immense piers supporting a very high domical, groined vault. At the crossing, the vault is higher still (the loftiest Romanesque example in Europe) and has a great octagonal tower built on squinches. The nave arcade is high but there is no triforium between it and the round-headed clerestory windows.

Further north, but near the Rhine, is the magnificently preserved and untouched *Monastery* of *Maria Laach*. The *Abbey Church* was begun in 1093 and was built slowly over many years but all in one style. There are six towers, two large and four smaller, and three apses on the east side and one on the west, with an atrium in front of it. The narthex has 82 small columns and some beautifully carved capitals as well as a western doorway. Built of local stone, the church is simply and typically decorated by pilaster strips and corbel arches (**324, 325** and **410**). Inside, the church is austere and serene. The groined vault is carried on grouped piers.

Also on the Rhine are a number of interesting churches in and near *Cologne*. These all suffered damage, in the Second World War, varying from partial to almost total destruction. After nearly 40 years' work almost all are now fully and beautifully restored. The classic pattern for the region, based in a number of instances on Lombard design, is for a triapsidal east end, a cruciform ground plan and a tall tower, or more often, an octagonal lantern or cupola over the main crossing. In a number of designs there are double transepts and most churches in the city of Cologne have several towers, often roofed in Rhenish helm style (**328, 330**). This diamond-shaped form of roof is rare outside Germany, though that on the Saxon tower of *Sompting Church* in Sussex survives (page 14). The most important Romanesque churches of this type in the city of Cologne are that dedicated to the twelve apostles (*S. Aposteln* **328, 330**), *S. Maria im Capitol*, the earliest of the group, constructed on the foundation walls of the Roman Capitoline Trias, S. Martin (*Gross S. Martin*), S. Gereon (**329**) and *S. Pantaleon*.

Apart from the Rhineland, Romanesque examples are scattered throughout Germany. Not far from the Rhine are the churches in Soest

and Freckenhorst. In this area, the façades, like the Dutch churches of the period in Maastricht, are fortified castle wall exteriors. *S. Patroklus* in *Soest* has small corner towers and a tall gable with a vast western tower. *Freckenhorst Abbey Church* (**332**) is typical, with flanking, circular western towers and a cliff-like central mass with a tiny doorway at the bottom, tiny windows above and surmounted by a tall roof and turret. Behind this vast, *westwerk*, a long nave and aisles lead to a transept and two further, eastern towers. The masonry is good but rugged and the whole ensemble is imposing. Inside is a fine Romanesque font, c. 1130 (PLATE 49).

Also not far from the Rhine is *Limburg Cathedral* on the river Lahn. It is smaller than those of the Rhineland but is characteristic nevertheless. It is sited on top of a hill in an attractive old town overlooking (and reflected in) the river. Like Durham, it appears to grow out of the rocks above the river bank. It has seven towers, attractively grouped. The octagonal crossing tower rises high with its spire. The nave is short and the other towers make a compact composition. In date and style it is a Transitional or late Romanesque building and shows a French influence in its choir ambulatory (**322**).

The *Church* of *S. Quirin* at *Neuss* also has a cliff-face façade, arcaded and gabled, while above it rises the large, square tower; a typical, interesting example (**333**).

Further south, on the river Moselle, is *Trier* where the *Cathedral* and the *Liebfrauenkirche* form a group. The town was an important Roman centre and the cathedral incorporates a Roman building which occupied the site in 1019 when the cathedral was begun (**334**). The Liebfrauenkirche is of early Gothic date and makes a group side by side with the cathedral in a tree-lined square. In Bavaria the town of *Regensburg* on the Danube possesses the interesting *Church* of *S. Jakob* (the *Schottenkirche*) which has an elaborate portal, finely sculptured (**394** and **402**). The church is basilican with triapsidal sanctuary but has no transept.

In the north, on the borders of East Germany towards Berlin, is the *Abbey Church* of *Königslütter*. The carving and sculpture here is outstanding, particularly the apse corbelling and arcading and the cloister capitals and columns

GERMAN ROMANESQUE CHURCHES

332 Freckenhorst Abbey Church, Germany, c. 1130. Viewed from the south-west
333 Church of S. Quirin, Neuss, Germany. West front, begun c. 1209. Tower c. 1230

333

332

334

334 Trier Cathedral, Germany. From the west, 1016–47

335 Imperial Palace (Kaiserpfalz) Goslar, Germany, eleventh century (restored)

(**406** and **416**). Inside, the apse has painted decoration of a very high order. At *Hildesheim*, not far away, the town was badly damaged during World War II and the famous *Church* of *S. Michael* has had to be almost entirely rebuilt. Its magnificent sculptured bronze doors still exist but are now on view inside the church, hung on the inner side of the west portal. There are 16 panels depicting high relief figures on a low relief and incised background. The standard of craftmanship is remarkable for bronze work of this date, 1015. At *Goslar*, in the region of the Harz Mountains, the *Kaiserpfalz* here was restored in the nineteenth century on its original pattern, 1132. The main hall of the palace is built over a large undercroft and has twin naves with columns supporting a timber roof. A balcony opens from the hall on to the façade through a triple arched opening. The building includes a two-storeyed chapel and the imperial apartments (**335**). Nearby is the site of the cathedral which is now destroyed but whose narthex still remains, with its original entrance (**409**).

Austria

Remains are scarce as most of the work has been rebuilt at a later date. *S. Stephen's Cathedral* in *Vienna* still has a Romanesque wing though it was built in the mid-thirteenth century. The Giant's Door here is finely carved with notable multi-column jambs, foliated capitals and typically Romanesque sculpture (**336**). In the *Cathedral* at *Gurk* there is a vast crypt possessing 100 columns which support a groined vault dating from 1160.

The round columns have cubiform capitals and moulded bases.

Switzerland

A number of small country churches exist with remains of this period. *Romainmôtier Church* was originally part of a Cluniac Monastery, built in the early tenth century. The present building dates from about 1000 and is basically in Lombard style. The interior shows many original features such as the columns, capitals, nave arcade and apsidal end (**331**). In the *Church* of *S. Jean* at *Grandson* the nave capitals are of varied Romanesque design, depicting animals, birds and demons. The vault is in stone, in barrel form (**418**). The *Church* at *Zillis* has the most remarkable painted wooden ceiling, illustrating in panels, scenes from the New Testament in rich

336 Detail of the Reisetor (West Portal) S. Stephen's Cathedral, Vienna, 1258–67

Plate 49
Detail, font. Freckenhorst Abbey Church,
Germany, 1129
Plate 50
Cloister garth lavatory cistern. Much Wenlock
Priory, England, *c.* 1160
Plate 51
Column support, porch. Trogir Cathedral,
Yugoslavia, *c.* 1240. Master Radovan
Plate 52
S. James. Portico de la Gloria, Cathedral of
Santiago de Compostela, Spain. 1166–88, Mateo

Plate 53
South portal arch
mouldings. Lund
Cathedral, Sweden

Plate 54
Painted ceiling, Zillis
Church, Switzerland.
Scenes of the New
Testament. 12th
century. Restored
19th and 20th
centuries

ROMANESQUE CHURCHES IN THE LOW COUNTRIES

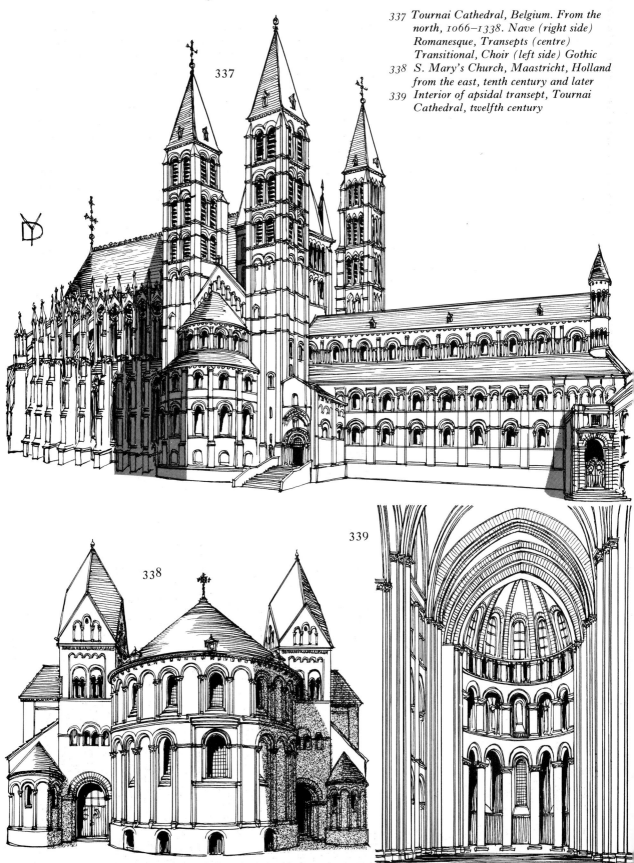

337 *Tournai Cathedral, Belgium. From the north, 1066–1338. Nave (right side) Romanesque, Transepts (centre) Transitional, Choir (left side) Gothic*

338 *S. Mary's Church, Maastricht, Holland from the east, tenth century and later*

339 *Interior of apsidal transept, Tournai Cathedral, twelfth century*

colours. The ceiling has been restored in the nineteenth and twentieth centuries (PLATE 54). *Basle Minster* was originally Romanesque but much of it is now Gothic. The east end retains its Romanesque characteristics and the *Galluspforte* (the portal named after S. Gall) is a twelfth century design with elaborate sculptured decoration. The Minister has a magnificent position on the top of the hill above the town and with a steep hillside descending on its east side towards the river Rhine (**385**).

Belgium

In comparison with Germany, France, England or Italy, little Romanesque architecture survives in the Low Countries, in Scandinavia or in Eastern Europe. In Belgium the outstanding example is *Tournai Cathedral* which, although added to and altered later, is certainly one of the finest Romanesque buildings in Europe. It is large and tall and difficult of access and to view due to its position in the centre of the town, closely hedged in by other buildings. The east end of the Cathedral is Gothic, but the long nave is still Romanesque and the transepts are in a Transitional form of the style; the two parts of the cathedral form a marked contrast, particularly inside the building, and a useful study. The cathedral exterior, largely built of black Tournai marble, has a large central tower and spire and four spired towers grouped around it and flanking the north and south apses (though it was originally designed for nine towers). The towers, like the semi-circular ended transepts, are Transitional. The nave dates from 1110; it is lower than the Gothic choir and still has its original fenestration (**337**). The interior of Tournai Cathedral is magnificent. The nave is simple Romanesque, the transepts in Transitional style (**339**) are higher, having a tall tower arcade, a shallower triforium arcade with a smaller sub-triforium above, before reaching the clerestory, giving lofty arms to the interior and suitably connecting without awkwardness the long, low nave and short high choir. The crossing has very tall piers and arches under the central tower.

There are a number of *castles* in Belgium with work dating from Romanesque times. In *Antwerp*, the castle in the port area, called the Steen, dates

340 Antwerp Castle (The Steen), Belgium, tenth century onwards

340

ROMANESQUE ARCHITECTURE IN YUGOSLAVIA

341 *Zadar Cathedral, west front, twelfth and thirteenth centuries*

342 *S. Grisogono, Zadar from the south-east, c.*

343 *Trogir Cathedral from the east, 1206–59*

344 *Trogir Cathedral plan*

from the tenth century onwards and still has Romanesque doorway and window openings inside (**340**), while in *Ghent* the *Gravensteen Castle*, which belonged to the Counts of Flanders, has interesting remains. The hall dates from the ninth century and is divided in the centre by a row of four circular columns with simple leaf capitals, like the design in S. John's Chapel in the Tower of London (**300**). The entrance barbican has a Romanesque doorway and window openings. In the exterior walls prison chambers still survive which are of Romanesque date, while the audience chamber possesses a fine wall-fireplace.

Holland

The chief Romanesque work here is in *Maastricht*, which was at the centre of a prosperous region in the twelfth century. The *Church* of *S. Servaas* has a Romanesque east end with apse and twin towers. *S. Mary's Church* is like Freckenhorst Abbey Church on the west front and has *westwerk* pattern in the form of a formidable fortified wall with small twin towers. At the east it has a large semi-circular apse and Rhenish capped towers (**338**). The interior is simple and also in German style.

Eastern and Central Europe

Most contemporary building here was in timber and has not survived. The tradition in this region was, as in pre-Romanesque times in Western Europe, to build in solid wood, not half-timber work as was the western European method during the Middle Ages. In the east the forest reserves were so vast that solid timber construction was possible in quantity.

In *Yugoslavia*, particularly on the Adriatic Coast, the Italian influences led to Italian-style stone churches and cathedrals of which a number survive. In *Zadar* the Cathedral and the *Church of S. Grisogono* are good examples, the latter especially showing strong Italian influence; both Lombard and Pisan (**342**). The *Cathedral* has much in common with contemporary Norman cathedrals on the Italian southern Adriatic coast opposite. Begun in 1105, the east end is Lombard but the west front has a tower like that at Trani (**374**) and Tuscan type arcading on the gable

façade and the three Romanesque doorways (**341**). *Trogir Cathedral*, despite its late date, 1240, is Romanesque in style and has a magnificent entrance portal by *Master Radovan*, the Slav sculptor who had been trained in Apulia (PLATE 51). The church is basilican and has three apses at the east end (**343** and **344**). It is stone vaulted throughout, with massive piers to support the vaults.

The Lombardic influence also extended to *Hungary* and the monastic orders. Benedictine and, later, Cistercian, built a number of abbeys and churches. Many of these have been rebuilt, like the *Cathedrals* of *Esztergom* and *Székesfehérvar*, although some original sculpture survives in both these examples. The chief monument in the country is the *Cathedral of Pécs* (Fünfkirchen), rebuilt about 1150 and restored mainly in the nineteenth century. This, the oldest cathedral in Hungary, is of a German pattern, like Bamberg, with four corner towers and arcading decorating the whole building. The east end is triapsidal and the choir is raised high above the superb crypt. The cathedral possesses some fine capitals and sculpture. A smaller Romanesque church survives at Lébeny, near Györ. This is a remarkable example in its purity of style; it was restored to the original design in the nineteenth century (**345, 346**) and inside the tall nave has a lofty, stone barrel vault. The clerestory windows are small and there is no triforium. The nave arcade has round arches behind which are lower aisles. The semi-circular chancel is covered by a semi-dome. The *Church* of the *Premonstratensian Abbey* at *Zsámbék*, near Budapest, is one of the oldest in Hungary. It was built in the later twelfth century and altered again about 1258. The architect, a Frenchman, is said to have based his church on the Cathedral of Notre Dame in Paris. This impressive stone building has a commanding sight on a hill above the surrounding plain. The interior is partly ruined but there is a fine Romanesque façade (**347**). Among other Romanesque churches are the decorative example at *Ják*, with its richly sculptured doorway and chevron ornament and the interesting churches of *Század*, *Ócsa* and *Karcsa*.

In *Rumania*, the *Cathedral of Alba Iulia* (Gyulafehérvar) was completed about 1239 but reconstruction was necessary after the Tartan invasion of 1242 (**348** and **349**). Some of it is now

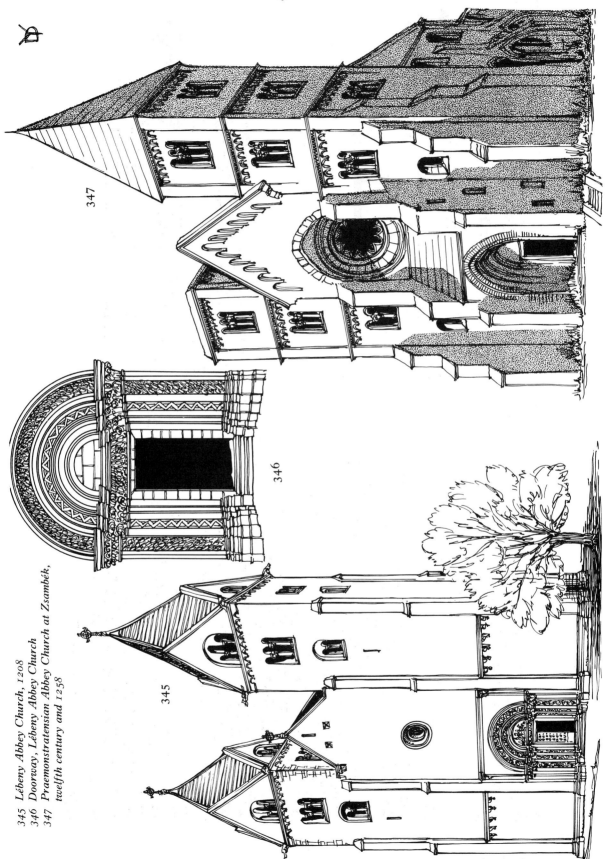

347

346

345

345 Lébeny Abbey Church, 1208
346 Doorway, Lébeny Abbey Church
347 Praemonstratensian Abbey Church at Zsambék,
      twelfth century and 1258

348 *Façade of the Cathedral at Alba Iulia, Rumania.*
Re-built in Romanesque style 1272–91. Gothic and
Renaissance additions
349 *Plan of cathedral*

Gothic and later, but the Lombard/German plan is still distinguishable, as are the nave supports of alternating columns and piers. There are two western towers with a high, open vaulted porch between (p. 188).

Further north, in *Poland*, extensive Romanesque work in stone and/or brick was carried out, but much of this has been altered through the centuries and the limited remains suffered damage in the Second World War.

The capital of the north-central area, and its cultural centre, was *Gniezno*, a not very large town about 30 miles south-east of Poznan. Pagan until the tenth century, Gniezno became the seat of the first Polish archbishopric in A.D. 1000, when the stone, rotunda building there became the Metropolitan *Cathedral*. This was replaced by a second Romanesque cathedral in 1097 which, in turn, was largely demolished when the present Gothic cathedral took its place (**558**). Remains of both the earlier cathedrals can be seen in the walls of the present building, while the magnificent bronze doors from the second cathedral, with their twelfth century Romanesque sculpture in 18 relief panels representing the life of S. Adalbert, are now displayed in one of the chapels of the choir. These are in low relief and are fine examples.

The *Cathedral church* of *S. Mary* at *Plock* (north-west of Warsaw), a twelfth century granite structure, which also had some fine bronze doors

(now in Novgorod Cathedral in the U.S.S.R.), is typical of such Romanesque structures in that it retains little of the original work. Better preserved are the *Collegiate church* of *SS. Peter and Paul* at *Kruszwica*, which has a Baroque interior, the circular *Church of S. Procopius* (*c.* 1160) and the *Church of the Holy Trinity*, both in *Strelzno*. These small towns are in the Gniezno region. The *Abbey Church* at *Trzebnica*, on the outskirts of Wroclaw (Breslau), still has some of its Romanesque (1219) exterior, but the interior is entirely Baroque (Volume 3, p. 162).

A number of Romanesque structures were built in *Cracow* on *Wawel Hill*, where a royal castle and church were erected, surrounded by a walled, fortified town. The city developed chiefly after 1040, when the residence of the kings was transferred from Gniezno to Cracow, and stone buildings began to replace the wooden ones. The earliest Romanesque structure was the Rotunda *Chapel* dedicated to the *Virgin*, built in the tenth century. In circular form, with a surmounting cupola, it had four adjacent apses, each with a semi-circular roofing. In its simple manner it is like other contemporary examples in Germany, Yugoslavia, Italy or Greece, and the building style resembles some Anglo-Saxon structures in England (**351**). Later called the Chapel of SS. Felix and Adauctus, its walls are incorporated in the later palace.

The first Romanesque *cathedral* was then begun (*c.* 1020) (**350**) and this was largely replaced in the early twelfth century by another, larger one. It was designed on German lines, with four large towers in the angles of the cruciform plan. Remains of this building exist in the present structure, of which the *crypt* of *S. Leonard* is the chief part. It is situated under the cathedral nave and has a typical vault supported on rows of columns (**352**).

Not far from the Wawel Hill in Cracow is the *Church* of *S. Andrew* (1086), which, despite a Baroque interior, is a fairly well preserved Romanesque building, especially in its fortified, massive walls.

In *Czechoslovakia* Romanesque structures were being erected from the early tenth century, in the form of castles and churches. Remains are, in many cases, little more than fragmentary, as in the *cathedral* on *Castle Hill* in *Prague*. The present, fine Gothic building (p. 130) replaced

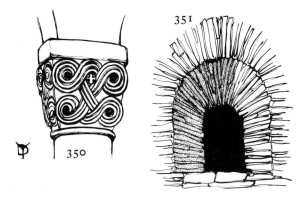

350 *Capital from the first Romanesque cathedral on Wawel Hill, Cracow, Poland, early eleventh century*

351 *Window opening from the Chapel of the Virgin (S.S. Felix and Adauctus)*

352 S. Leonard's Crypt from the Romanesque cathedral
     at Cracow, *1090–1115*. Situated under present
     cathedral
353 Basilica of S. George, Castle Hill, Prague,
     Czechoslovakia, from *1142*

two earlier Romanesque ones. These are now
only visible in the foundations excavated and
preserved under and near the cathedral. The
nearby *castle* retains Romanesque portions, like
the barrel vaulted Romanesque hall and parts of
the mural towers, but the chief surviving building
from this period on Castle Hill is the *Basilica of
S. George*, built originally in 920, but the
Romanesque church dates from its rebuilding in
1142 after a fire. The façade is now Baroque, but
inside it retains its simple Romanesque form,
though it was extensively restored in the late
nineteenth century (**353**).

Remains exist of one or two stone Romanesque
rotunda churches in *Prague*, but these are in poor
condition and are, in general, small and primitive.
A typical example is that of *S. Longinus*.

Scandinavia

For the majority of building, wood was the chief
material and little has survived, though rebuilding has often been in similar traditional
style. Masonry was used for important, ecclesiastical work, especially in the south and some of
this work is extant. In this material Scandinavia
was strongly influenced by foreign designs and
workers, in general, Denmark by Germany,

France and Holland, Norway by England, and
Sweden by all sources.

Denmark

In this flat country building materials available
were, apart from timber, limestone, brick and
flint. Masonry developed traditionally at the
same time as Norman England, but most of the
buildings have been altered. Amongst surviving
examples are the cathedral at Ribe in South
Jutland, begun *c.* 1130 and Viborg Cathedral in
North Jutland, of granite, from *c.* 1140. The large
cathedral at *Ribe* is situated in the centre of the
small, old market town. Like Lund Cathedral in
Sweden, it is a mixture of Rhineland and Italian
Lombard designs. The exterior is severely
Romanesque with a gabled façade, transeptal
towers and spires and an apsidal east end. The
interior, though restored, is based on the original
pattern, though with later vaults and enlarged
clerestory windows (**354**). *Viborg Cathedral*,
though still on original lines, is extensively
restored and so possesses that machine finished
appearance typical of Scandinavian nineteenth
century work. It has twin west towers and gables
with similar eastern towers flanking the apse.

Several large *abbey churches* survive, mainly
built in brick, and all carefully restored. The two

354

354 Ribe Cathedral, Denmark, begun c. 1130

ROMANESQUE IN DENMARK AND SWEDEN

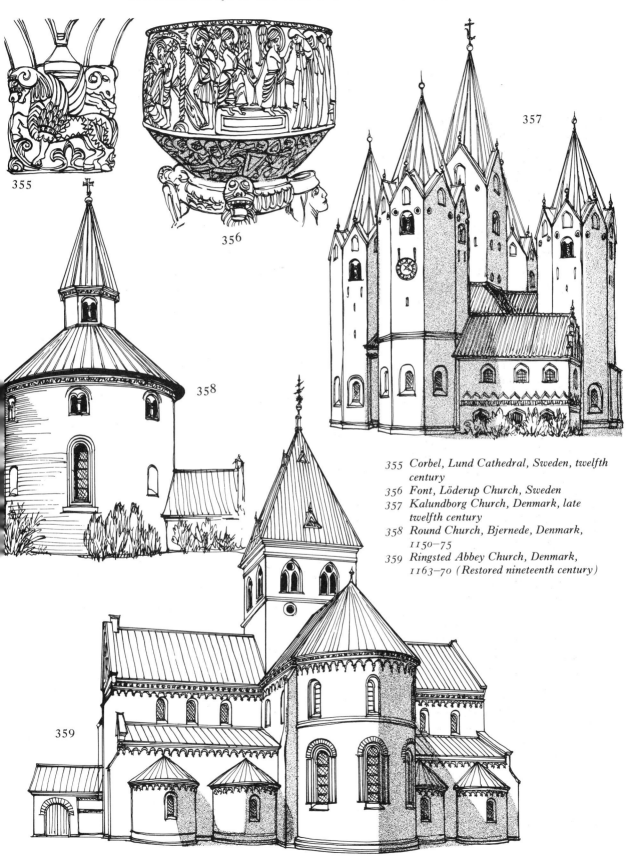

355 Corbel, Lund Cathedral, Sweden, twelfth
    century
356 Font, Löderup Church, Sweden
357 Kalundborg Church, Denmark, late
    twelfth century
358 Round Church, Bjernede, Denmark,
    1150–75
359 Ringsted Abbey Church, Denmark,
    1163–70 (Restored nineteenth century)

chief examples are close together on Zealand: Ringsted Abbey and Sorø Abbey, both of brick. The *Abbey Church* of *S. Benedict* at *Ringsted* is on Latin cross plan with apsidal east end and a later crossing tower (**359**). Inside, it is more Scandinavian than Ribe. It has no triforium and small, round-headed clerestory windows. *Sorø Abbey* has a very similar interior treatment but outside it is large, long and low.

The most original and interesting Romanesque building in Scandinavia is the *Church* at *Kalundborg*, north-west of Sorø on Zealand. Also of brick, it is large and imposing and, despite restoration, has a Medieval feeling still. On Greek cross plan, it has one square tower over the crossing and an octagonal one over each of the four arms (**357**). It is a centralised structure, a Scandinavian version of a Byzantine theme. There are four simple columns supporting the crossing; all arms are barrel vaulted.

There is a tradition in some parts of Denmark for *round churches*, probably based on Eastern European origins. This is particularly so on the *Island of Bornholm* where these distinctive buildings were used sometimes as fortresses. They have single, central piers supporting conical roofs. The best examples are at Østerlars, Ny, and Nylar. In *Zealand* the example at *Bjernede* survives (**358**). The lower part is of stone, the upper of brick. Inside, four large stone columns on torus moulding and square bases support a quadripartite ribbed vault on their cushion capitals, while groined vaults cover the encircling ambulatory.

Sweden

Timber was the chief material and the stave churches of the later Medieval period were influenced by this tradition. Christianity gained a hold here later than in Denmark but was established by the twelfth century and the Cistercians began to found monasteries soon after, as at *Varnhem* and *Alvastra*. The early Christian influence came from England from the tenth century onwards and its principal centre was at *Uppsala*. Architectural influences from outside were strong and, apart from England, included France, Russia and Byzantium. The work in Sweden was simple, sometimes crude but not unattractive. The outstanding *cathedral* of the

period to survive is at *Lund*, in Skåne, which was begun about 1080. Built in limestone, it was extensively restored in the nineteenth century when the Rheno-Lombardic west front took its final form. The apsidal east end, which resembles Speyer in Germany without the flanking towers (**355** and **360**), is largely in its original design, as is also the south portal (PLATE 53) and the crypt. This is very fine, groin vaulted throughout and supported on cushion capitalled columns with varied shafts (**368**). The interior, despite restoration, has a Romanesque effect (**362**). It is severe and built on monumental lines. There is no triforium and clerestory windows are tiny. The choir is on a higher level than the nave built, in Italian Romanesque fashion, over the crypt.

Most of the Swedish Romanesque stone churches are tall, with semi-circular eastern apses, lofty nave and choir and tall towers. The churches are wide and are generally vaulted. Typical examples include the late Romanesque *Church* at *Lärbro* on the Island of Gotland. Of German, fortified type, like Freckenhorst, is the *Church* at *Husaby* in Skaraborg. This was originally a stave church. In 1057 an immense stone tower was added. This square tower has circular turrets on each side, the whole making a fortified place of retreat. About 1090, the stave church was demolished and the stone church added to the tower (**361**).

While the fortified tower façade at Husaby shows German influence, the body of the church is more English in derivation. Also English in pattern are the remains of the three Romanesque churches at *Sigtuna*, near Lake Mälar. *S. Olav* is the most complete of these stone churches (**369**); *S. Per* shows a square tower and part of the nave but *S. Lars* is only fragmentary. They were all made of large, irregularly cut stone blocks and of simple cruciform structure.

Swedish Romanesque churches, like their English counterparts, are noted for their carved stone *fonts*. Outstanding examples are those at *Löderup Church* in Skåne (**356**) and *Varnhem Abbey Church* near Skara (**363**).

As in Norway, the first churches from the early days of Christianity in Sweden were of wood. These were generally of log structure, with corner joint method or timber framed with in-filling of boards. The commonest type, also as in Norway, was the stave church, but few examples

ROMANESQUE IN SWEDEN

360 Lund Cathedral from the east,
from c. 1140
361 Fortified Church at Husaby,
from 1057
362 Lund Cathedral nave
363 Font, Varnhem Abbey Church,
thirteenth century

survive in Sweden. One is the *stave church* at *Hedared* in Västergötland. It is small, consisting of nave and chancel. Restored, it is in good condition and retains its later, eighteenth century furniture and wall paintings. The staves rest on a wood sill.

The little wooden *church* of *Södra Råda*, remotely situated in rural surroundings near the vast inland sea of Lake Vänern, dates from about 1300. The exterior is shingled and very simple, but inside, the nave and chancel roof and walls are painted all over. It is reminiscent of the Swiss church of Zillis (p. 155), showing circles filled with figure compositions depicting biblical scenes. The style of work too is much like Zillis, though these are mainly fifteenth century paintings and less restored. The work is very fine.

Norway

Architectural influence here is not notable since timber has been for centuries the traditional building material. Most of the work is of later date, though building styles changed only slowly. It is a remote country with difficult communica-

tions, climate and geography. These factors created an original architectural form which was less closely related to the rest of European development than work in Denmark or southern Sweden.

Contacts and connections with the British Isles were close and the *stone churches* show this influence. From about 1100 such churches were built, very much in Norman style. *S. Magnus' Cathedral* at *Kirkwall* in Orkney (then under Norse control) shows a close relationship to English Norman cathedrals, as does also *Stavanger Cathedral*, which was begun *c.* 1130. It still has a Romanesque nave with large circular columns; these have varying types of cushion capitals, and chevron decoration remains on one or two of the nave arcade arches (**364** and **366**). There is a large, semi-circular headed chancel arch leading into the Gothic choir, which is at a higher level than the nave. The cathedral is all of stone, quite small, but despite restoration a good example of Anglicised Norwegian Romanesque building and the finest in Norway.

The smaller stone churches are generally very simple and most have been greatly altered. *S.*

364 The nave, Stavanger Cathedral, Norway, 1125–50. Modern roof and seventeenth century pulpit

364

365 Stave construction, Lom Church, Norway, thirteenth century

366 South doorway capital, Stavanger Cathedral, Norway, twelfth century

367 Doorway detail, Borgund Stave Church

368 Crypt column, Lund Cathedral, Sweden, twelfth century

369 Plan, S. Olav's Church, Sigtuna, Sweden, twelfth century

370 Dragon finial, Borgund Church

371 Borgund Stave Church, Norway, from the south-east, c. 1150

372 Nave capital, Urnes Stave Church, Norway, c. 1125–50

373 Dragon finial, Gol Stave Church, Norway

Mary's Church in *Bergen* is one example. It has a plain exterior with two western towers. The interior is mainly in plain, massive Romanesque style with nave arcade and triumphal arch to the chancel; there is a triforium but no clerestory. The homogeneity of this monumental Norman workmanship contrasts with the crude, over-decorated Baroque pulpit, altar and other, later decoration.

Wooden Churches

The *mast* or *stave* churches of Norway are now unique in Europe and were built during the whole of the Middle Ages from the eleventh century to the Reformation, after which timber churches based on the Eastern European pattern were more usual. There were, at one time, over 500 of these churches extant; now only a handful survive and these are largely restored. The method of construction is different from that of Romanesque stone building. Here, the roof is not supported on the walls, but each part of the church is separately supporting. The walls (the stave screens) are self-contained units and rest upon the ends of timber sleepers but do not take the weight or thrust. The whole church is based on a skeleton framework, the supporting roof poles are placed on top of the intersecting ground sills and there are cross beams on top of the poles. The design is based on the timber ship building pattern in which each section is a self-sufficient unit. The most advanced type of stave church has another row of poles or pillars inside the four which frame the external wall and this row supports its own part of the divided roof. The interiors of these churches are tall and dark and bear strong similarities to inverted ships.

The finest, least altered examples of these churches are at Borgund and Urnes. *S. Andrew's Church* at *Borgund* is inland from the end of the Sognfjord, near Laerdal (**371**). It dates from mid-twelfth century and is nearly 50 feet high, built in six stages. Its height is the striking feature and this is emphasised by the spire. The highest roofs terminate in dragon's heads (**370**) (the Viking art symbol). The construction is based on 12 'masts', or posts of wood, standing on four sleepers or sills under the floor which enclose the plan. The name 'mast' comes from these pillars and the alternative 'stave' derives from the name given to the wall screen sections. The masts extend upwards to support the central roof and are joined together with three stages of horseshoe timber arches and timber boarding. At the east end is a rectangular choir and later apse. The inside is plain; the interior of the steeple is not roofed over so the construction is visible. Outside is a richly carved doorway (**367**).

The *Church* at *Urnes* (Ornes) is at the top of a small village built on a hill overlooking the Lusterfjord, which branches northwards from the end of the Sognfjord. There is no road link with Laerdal, Kaupanger or Årdal and the only means of access for visitors is by hiring a small boat across the Lusterfjord from Solvorn. In this fine, lonely situation, the little church is in good condition. It is a combination of two old structures, one of about 1130—50 and the other rather older. Despite some later rebuilding it still possesses much work from the oldest stave church in Norway. Of especial interest are the exterior carvings on the north portal and the carved capitals inside (**372** and PLATE 40).

Other surviving (though much reconstructed) examples remain at Lom, Kaupanger, Fantoft and in the Oslo Museum. *Lom Church* has a fine mountain situation near Gudbrandsdal. It is a large stave church with later transepts and spire. Of especial interest is the interior stave construction (**365**). This type of S. Andrew's cross structure can also still be seen in the *stave church* in the Norsk Folkemuseum at Bydøy Park across the ferry from Oslo. The church comes from *Gol* in Hallingdal and dates from 1200; it was re-erected in the museum in 1885. The exterior is very picturesque, though reconstructed, and still has dragon finials and carvings (**373**). The examples at *Kaupanger* (Sognfjord), built *c.* 1200 but rebuilt in 1862, and at *Fantoft*, near Bergen are simpler but also of considerable interest.

ROMANESQUE TOWERS

374 *Zadar Cathedral, Yugoslavia, thirteenth century*
375 *Canterbury Cathedral, England, Norman tower, south side, c. 1100*
376 *Angoulême Cathedral, France, west tower, twelfth century*
377 *Amalfi Cathedral, Italy, campanile, twelfth century*

378 Meira Abbey Church, Spain
379 Salamanca Old Cathedral, Spain
380 Church of S. Miguel de la Escalada, Spain
381 Church of S. Miguel de Liño, Spain
382 Trani Cathedral, Italy

383 Modena Cathedral, Italy
384 Angoulême Cathedral, France
385 Basle Minster, Switzerland
386 Worth Church, England
387 Castle Rising Church, England

COMPARATIVE ROMANESQUE PORCHES AND PORTICOES

388 West porch, Church of S. Nicola, Bari, Italy, 1098
389 West porch, Church of S. Trophîme, Arles,
France, 1150–80

390 West porch, Modena Cathedral, Italy, twelfth century
391 West portico, Abbey Church, S. Gilles,
France, 1140–1195

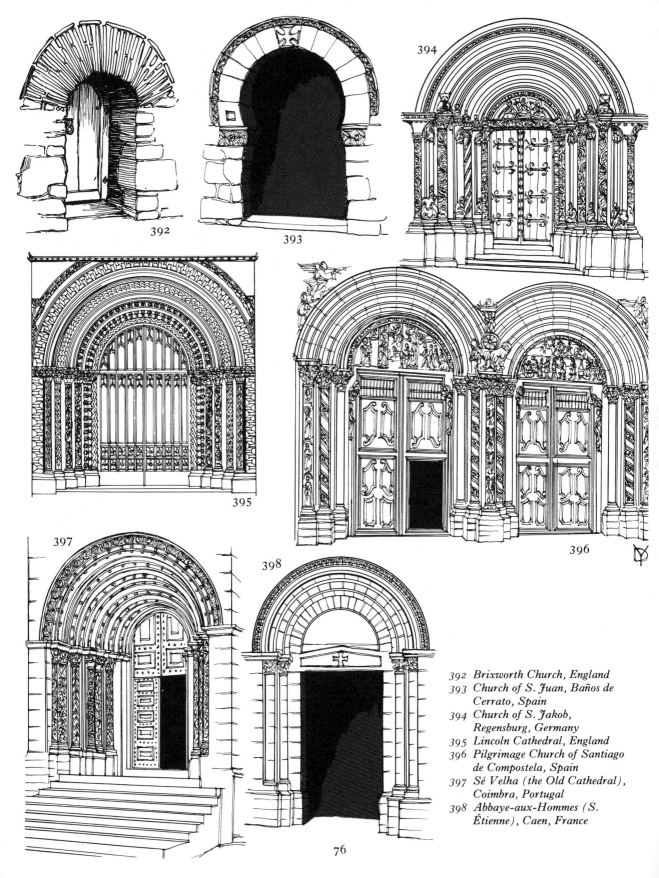

392 Brixworth Church, England
393 Church of S. Juan, Baños de Cerrato, Spain
394 Church of S. Jakob, Regensburg, Germany
395 Lincoln Cathedral, England
396 Pilgrimage Church of Santiago de Compostela, Spain
397 Sé Velha (the Old Cathedral), Coimbra, Portugal
398 Abbaye-aux-Hommes (S. Étienne), Caen, France

399 *Crypt, S. George, Oberzell, Reichenau, Germany,*
ninth century
400 *S. Salvador de Priesca, Villaviciosa, Spain,*
Visigothic, 921
401 *S.S. Peter and Paul, Niederzell, Reichenau,*
Germany, 1050
402 *S. Jakob, Schottenportal, Regensburg,*
Germany, c. 1180
403 *S. Miguel de la Escalada, Spain, Visigothic, 913*
404 *S. Martín, Frómista, Spain, 1066*
405 *Leominster Priory Church, Norman, England*

406 *Cloister, Königslütter Abbey Church,*
Germany, c. 1135
407 *Kilpeck Church, England, c. 1140*
408 *S. Michele, Pavia, Italy, 1188*
409 *Narthex, former cathedral at Goslar, Germany, c.*
1150. Built on to the 1050 cathedral. Cathedral demolished
1819, narthex remains
410 *Abbey Church of Maria Laach, Germany, c. 1220*
411 *and 412 Abbey Church of S. Madeleine, Vézelay,*
France, 1120–30

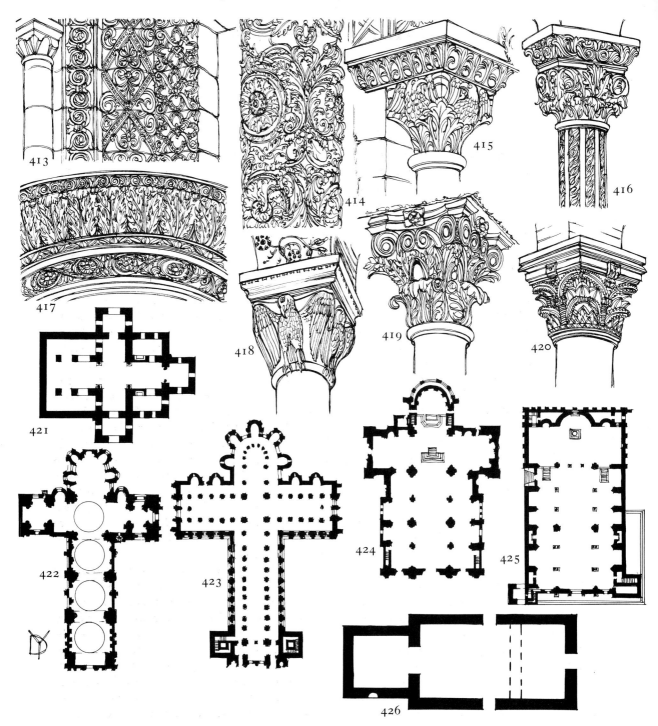

413 *Porch, Malmesbury Abbey, England*
414 *Column, baptistery, Pisa, Italy*
415 *Doorway capital, S. Michel d'Aiguilhe, Le Puy, France*
416 *Cloister capital, Königslütter Abbey, Germany*
417 *West doorway voussoirs, Bitonto Cathedral, Italy*
418 *Nave capital, S. Jean, Grandson, Switzerland*
419 *West portal, S. Trophime, Arles, France*

420 *Nave capital, S. Pietro, Tuscània, Italy*
421 *Plan, S. Pedro de la Nave, Spain, Visigothic*
422 *Plan, Angoulême Cathedral, France*
423 *Plan, Santiago de Compostela, Spain*
424 *Plan, S. Michele, Pavia, Italy*
425 *Plan, S. Nicola, Bari, Italy*
426 *Plan, Boarhunt Church, England*

2

Gothic: 1150–1600

It is a truism that artistic endeavour is influenced by current fashion. So the designs of one era are often rejected by another, usually in reaction and because of the human need for change. Such reaction gave birth to two at least of the names applied to architectural styles. These are Gothic and Baroque; both misnomers. They were coined in a later age as terms of disapprobation, even contempt. It was Giorgio Vasari who applied the word 'Gothic' to Medieval architecture. Vasari, a sixteenth century Mannerist architect and historian, was only expressing the thinking of his time in equating Medieval architecture with barbarism. To a post-Renaissance intellectual, the Middle Ages had advanced only a small way beyond the sixth century Goths; it was the Renaissance which brought greatness to architecture.

Similarly, the term 'Middle Ages' was applied to this period in the seventeenth century by a German scholar. He likened it to an intermediate era between the collapse of the Roman Empire in 476 A.D. and the re-birth of classicism in the Renaissance ideals of the fifteenth century. To him also it represented a period of barbarism and decline.

Seen from a more distant perspective, we can appreciate that Gothic architecture (for the term is now synonymous with Medieval building) was a great art form in its own right. It emerged from Romanesque into a specific style, different from but no less fine than the works of the Renaissance. Its conception and inspiration were totally dissimilar from the later classical form but, diverse and richly variable as it is throughout Europe, Gothic architecture is characteristically definable wherever it is to be found.

The all pervasive influence during the Middle Ages was Christianity. By 1200 its dominance extended over most of Europe when the Western church from Rome had met and joined the Greek centre from Constantinople. Churches and cathedrals, in stone, brick and timber were built in increasing numbers all over Europe from Scandinavia to Sicily and Portugal to Russia. The Church was the essence of being to Medieval peoples whether in town or village. Portal sculptures, wall paintings and mosaics created in each church a pictorial record of the Bible stories and teaching. To an illiterate population they gave tangible reality to their beliefs. Despite the happenings of the 400 years which have passed since the last of these buildings were being constructed, the quantity which exists in all European countries is testimony to the ability of the builders and the truly vast numbers of structures which were put up between 1150 and 1550.

Though the Church was the great patron of the Middle Ages, the rising wealth of the merchant classes, especially in the fourteenth and fifteenth centuries, led to the erection of many fine secular buildings: town halls, trade and guild halls, palaces, manor houses, town mansions and bridges. Castles and towns were still fortified but, in the later Middle Ages, as prosperity and a greater peacefulness spread to many parts of Europe, the fortification diminished and both towns and individual buildings were extended and elaborated.

It is difficult to pinpoint the exact beginning of a new movement. Gothic architecture evolved from the Romanesque style but its characteristics are different. The feature usually described as predominant in Gothic buildings is the use of the pointed arch in place of the semi-circular one which had been employed in both Roman and Romanesque structures. In the past it has been stated categorically that the originator of the Gothic style was France. Late nineteenth century historians, either French or French orientated scholars in England or Germany, asserted this clearly. It is undoubtedly true that the earliest buildings completed in the Gothic style come from the Île de France, a small area in the neighbourhood of Paris, and that the classic pattern of northern Gothic cathedral was established here, witness such famous examples as *Notre Dame, Paris, Reims, Amiens* and *Laon*. It cannot be argued so categorically that this was the sole source of the style in the twelfth century or that it would not soon have developed in a similar manner elsewhere if the Île de France had not then produced it.

Great movements in all subjects—arts, sciences, medicine—begin and establish themselves because the climate is ready to receive them. The need is there and so is the ability to create the new development. In the case of Gothic architecture, the pointed arch was evolved because it became the key to constructing buildings which were then desirable. The low pitched timber roof of the basilica type church had to be replaced by stone vaults for safety and durability, and extension of size of the vaulting system itself (see p. 81) depended on arched support of a specific type and adequate wall abutment. This led in turn to larger and higher buildings, extended window and door space and a complexity of design for exterior and interior undreamed of in Romanesque architecture. The pointed arch was not new. It had long been used in the Middle East and, in Europe, was employed in areas subject to Moorish influence like Spain, Sicily and even Provence. Its use was being developed in these areas in the twelfth century. Northern France, though, was more suited to the establishment of a new style, being an area less troubled by warfare and of more stable economic climate.

The stability of the region led to the creation of schools of artists and craftsmen which spread to other suitable places, southern England and Flanders, for example. These craftsmen then travelled widely to execute commissions. The transition from Romanesque to Gothic proceeded at a variable speed in differing countries. Some, like parts of Germany, Italy and Spain, felt an affinity with Romanesque building. The style expressed their mood and artistic ideas and they clung to it well into the thirteenth century. Others, like England, Flanders, Northern France and the Baltic region adapted quickly. Transitional work can be seen in all these countries, with parts of a building in one style and other parts in newer forms.

As in Romanesque work, climate was an important factor. Northern Europe eventually established a Gothic style which was different from that in the warmer countries south of the Alps and the Pyrenees. In the north, the emphasis was on height, of steeples, buttresses, roofs and on large windows with richly coloured glass and large doorways with equally rich sculptural adornment. Further south where the sun was stronger and the rain and snow less damaging, roofs were flatter, the horizontal line predominated, window and door openings were smaller, stained glass rarer and decoration was more by painting, mosaic and other coloured media than by three-dimensional sculpture.

Whereas certain countries, in particular, Spain, Portugal, Germany and Scandinavia, were slower to adapt to Gothic forms, these same countries were, in the main, also slow to abandon Gothic for the Renaissance and classicism. An exception was Italy which slowly and reluctantly adopted Gothic tenets but, in contrast, was the originator of the Renaissance, establishing its forms nearly two centuries before England, which was another exception. England had been one of the first countries to adopt Gothic designs but was one of the last to relinquish the style which passed into a Perpendicular phase unique to the British Isles.

As the Gothic period advanced, buildings became larger and higher, window and doorway openings increased in size so the churches were flooded with light. The knowledge of structure in masonry was extending quickly and with this advance in technique came the means to erect buildings which were mere shells of stone ribs and pillars. The area of solid wall became less and the design correspondingly more complex. Each individual member of the building became more attenuated. Heavy columns and solid piers were replaced by slender, lofty piers encircled with clustered column shafts, terminating in small moulded or foliated capitals. Some shafts rose the full height of the wall to support the vault springing, others ended at the nave arcade. Towers became slenderer and many had elegant spires set on them. These became taller and steeper as time passed. The exterior became a forest of vertical stone pinnacles, stretching up into the vaults of heaven; the interior a mystic chiaroscuro in stone, gently illuminated by shafts of sunlight gloriously coloured by their transition through the cathedral glass.

This miracle of immense stone buildings

pierced by great openings and carved into tracery was only made structurally possible by the engineering development of the stone vault and its consequent abutment. Both of these stem from the original adoption of the pointed arch. As mentioned earlier, this type of arch was not new but its replacement of the round one led to the variations and complexities of *Gothic vaulting*. The semi-circular arch presents great problems in vaulting a church. This is because the nave or choir and their aisles often have different widths and heights. Vaulting is made in bays and the semi-circular arch lends itself to a square bay. The bay is decided by the positioning of the supporting piers or columns. In Romanesque cathedrals the bay was transversed at roof level by two ribs which curved in diagonal line from nave pier to nave pier. As the diagonal ribs were longer than the four ribs connecting the four sides or faces of the bay, it was impossible for all these ribs to be semicircular in section unless the vault were domical (dome-shaped), thus creating an uneven ridge line, or the side arches were stilted. Alternatively two bays had to be treated as one. Further problems arose because the aisles were narrower and lower than nave or choir, and it was difficult to reconcile these variations with the use of a semicircular arch. The pointed arch provided a more flexible system since it could be varied in proportion of width to height in order to accommodate different spans and roof levels. The French aptly term this arch the *arc brisé*, the broken arch, which gives a clear picture of its function.

The basis of a structure with the pointed arch supported on piers led, over many years, to great variety in vault design. The Gothic vault is a framework of stone ribs which support thin stone panels filled in later over the centering. Early ribbed vaults are *quadripartite*, that is, each bay is divided into four compartments by diagonal ribs. The French then developed a *sexpartite* vault, wherein the intermediate pier is carried up as a vaulting shaft to carry a rib which transfers the vaulting compartment into six. The English introduced extra (*tierceron*) ribs into their quadripartite vaults. These spring from the same points as the diagonals and divide the four large compartments into smaller ones. The next stage was the *lierne* vault where many small lierne or tie ribs (so-called after the French word *lier* = to

bind) are used at different angles to connect the main ribs to form an intricate geometrical pattern. The *star* vault is a version of this. The final stage, a peculiarly English one, is the *fan* vault (p. 104). Decorative bosses are superimposed at the intersections of all rib vaults. They are to be seen in the late lierne examples as the boss covers the awkward junction of differing diameter ribs and creates a decorative design on the roof covering.

The Gothic *buttress* is the complement to the vault. As the latter progresses and becomes higher, wider and more complex, so does the abutment. The structure of a Gothic church, its arches, piers and vault, exerts an outward and downward thrust upon the walls. In order to avoid thickening the whole wall area, as the Romanesque builders had done, the Gothic mason provided extra reinforcement in the form of a stone buttress at the point on the wall where it was most needed. This point is just below the springing line of the vault. Early Gothic buttresses were simple designs. Slowly they became more complex. Pinnacles were added above the parapet level. These pinnacles are decorative but also functional in that the weight of the pinnacle above the arch springing exercises a vertical pressure which helps to counteract the vault's outward thrust. The buttresses themselves became larger, heavier and richly ornamented with carving and panelling. The final stage was the *flying buttress*, developed especially by the French, and to be seen in all its decorative glory on the chevet of many a French cathedral; *Le Mans* and *Reims* are two outstanding examples. A flying buttress transmits thrust rather then resisting it. Thus, starting high on the nave wall, between the clerestory windows, the buttresses progress downwards in arches and pinnacles, conducting the thrust, in stages, from the upper wall to the ground. Because of the flying buttress sytem, it became possible to construct thinner walls as time passed instead of increasing the thickness to offset the large windows and higher vaults.

Window design is also a characteristic feature of Gothic architecture. In general, window openings became wider and larger. At the same time, the window area was subdivided by more numerous stone ribs; the horizontal transoms and the vertical mullions. The window head was decoratively designed by stone ribs into varying

FRENCH GOTHIC CATHEDRALS

427 Notre Dame, Paris, from the
south-west, 1180–1330
428 S. Julien, Le Mans, from the
east showing the chevet, 1217–54

patterns; this was called tracery. The designs differed from country to country, but the general trend was from geometrical shapes—circles, triangles, quatrefoils—in the earlier period, to curved flamboyant forms in the later years. English designs of the fifteenth century were in Perpendicular tracery, which resembled panelling, and echoed the wall decoration. The circular window, the Gothic rose, evolved from the Romanesque wheel window. The rose designs were divided by tracery into geometrical and flowing shapes, instead of the radiating wheel spokes used before. Many windows were filled with magnificent coloured glass, ranging from those of the simple parish church to the wonders of *Chartres* or *León Cathedral*.

The affinity between the fellow craftsmen at work on great buildings grew closer during the Gothic period. The rapport among masons, glaziers, painters, mosaicists and metal workers was complete and satisfying. No craftsman was of more vital importance than the sculptor. It was the golden age for carvers and modellers, who enjoyed a freedom of expression and an architectural surface upon which to create and experiment never equalled before or since. The Gothic cathedral façade was here the supreme vehicle. The pattern was established in northern France in the early thirteenth century of a twin-towered façade with central rose window and a triple portico at base, spreading, like a Roman triumphal arch, across the full width of the elevation. The whole façade was decorated with symbolic sculpture, but these portals, encrusted all over, were the three-dimensional focal centre of the design. Jamb and trumeau figures, tympanum scenes, archivolt groups, gargoyles and cresting, all played a part in relating the Bible story from Old and New Testaments, in rich, full, glorious sculptures. French sculptors were supreme and they travelled all over Europe, showing other nations how to enrich their cathedral façades. As the Middle Ages advanced, sculpture changed from its Romanesque origins. The mysticism and incarnations of devilry gave way to realistic graceful expression, especially in treatment of the human figure and its drapery. By the fifteenth century portraiture in figure statuary was evolving and German sculptors began to challenge the French supremacy.

France

In the Middle Ages France was still not one nation. The country was large, by Medieval standards, the climate and peoples differed greatly from one region to another. Architecture reflected these differences. The contrast, architecturally, between north and south is especially marked. In the north, particularly in the area of Paris, Gothic developed early, before 1150, in buildings notable for their verticality, vigorous, bold plasticity, hand-in-hand with delicate, finely detailed ornament. In the south, Roman traditions made Romanesque architecture a natural style while, later, the climate made more suitable a greater affinity with Spanish and Italian Gothic forms than those of northern France.

In northern and central France a stupendous number of cathedrals and large churches were constructed in the thirteenth century. The majority of these, unlike their English counterparts, were not monastic foundations but new cathedrals purpose-built for the town they served. Paris was the focal centre of the Île de France region, which produced the early and most famous examples which set the pattern for the whole of northern Europe. One of the very first examples of Gothic architecture was the *Abbey Church* of *S. Denis*, built in the decade from 1135 by the Abbé Suger. Now in a Paris suburb, most of the church has been restored or rebuilt, but part of the original choir exists, while the reconstructed west front still shows the early mixture of round and pointed arch heads. *Sens Cathedral* of similar date has common features with S. Denis. Other examples followed. The establishment of the Gothic cathedral pattern began with the building of the Cathedral of Paris in 1163.

Cathedrals

The world famous cathedrals of the Île de France, all built between 1150 and 1300 (though parts were added to or altered later), are similar to one another. The Cathedrals of Paris, Laon, Reims, Amiens, Chartres have all been likened to the Parthenon in Athens in that they, collectively and individually, present the greatest contribution to the architecture of their time—Gothic—and became prototypes for churches all over Europe. They have a common form. The plan is cruci-

Reims Cathedral, France
Plate 55
Angel in the Annunciation, central portal, façade,
1250–60

Plate 56
Virgin on trumeau, central portal, façade, 13th centu
Plate 57
Jamb figure, central doorway, façade, *c.* 1240

Chartres Cathedral, France
Plate 58 Tympanum, central doorway, façade,
c. 1150–5

Plates 59 and *60*
Jamb figures, central doorway, façade, *c.* 1150–5

form, with an apsidal eastern arm, slightly projecting transepts and a longer nave. All are lofty with high vaults supported by flying buttress schemes. Numerous chapels are set in or added to the walls but the chief area for this is the *chevet*. This is a French innovation and refers to the apsidal east end which has an interior ambulatory behind the high altar, giving access all round the church usually at least at choir and triforium levels. Between the bays are set semi-circular chapels giving an exterior appearance of a gladiolus corm growing its smaller new corms around its base. Between the chapels radiate the forests of flying buttresses. The façade design is a classic one. *Notre Dame* in *Paris*, built 1163–1235 (**427**) is one of the early examples which set the character. There is a triple portal (**512**), sculpture filled across the width of the base of the elevation, above, a gallery of sculpture (here, the *galerie des rois*), then the central rose window.* Apart from the two flanking west towers, the architectural emphasis is horizontal.

All these cathedrals were intended to have many towers surmounted by spires. Few of the towers, apart from the western ones, were built and even fewer spires. Partly this was due to cost, but mainly it was because French cathedrals are so vast and so lofty, with high vaults of great span, that a steeple became too great an engineering hazard. As it was, some high vaults collapsed before towers were added, as at Beauvais. The lack of spires is one of the chief differences between French and English cathedrals.† The latter are smaller and lower and could bear the weight of a tall spire as at Salisbury (**450**). In France, a very tall but lightweight flèche was erected over the crossing.

French cathedrals are often difficult to view as few have any open space around them. They were built for and of the town and were surrounded, up to their walls, by houses and civic buildings. Only in the last 150 years have a number of these buildings been demolished, but even so it is only in Paris, Chartres and few other instances that an open space in front of the building offers a clear view. This is in contrast to the English monastic foundations which surround the cathedral with close and cloisters.

All these Île de France cathedrals are store-houses of magnificent craftmanship. *Notre Dame* in *Paris* suffered greatly in the Revolution of

1789 when much of its sculpture was badly damaged and had to be replaced by Viollet-le-Duc and others. It is chiefly famous for its architectural qualities of exterior and interior. *Laon*, built 1160–1225, is noted especially for its west façade, a masterpiece, which is less static than Notre Dame, and for its magnificent towers and rose window. High up the towers are sculptured bulls which commemorate the original animals which carried the building stones up to the top of the hill from the flat plain below.

Reims is the richest and most glorious, as befits the cathedral built as the Coronation Church for the Kings of France. The present structure was begun in 1211. Despite a long building period, both interior and exterior are remarkably homogeneous (**430, 600** and **610**). Its glory is its sculpture, especially that on the triple western portal (PLATES 55, 56 and 57). There are 500 statues here, as well as richly decorated gables. The cathedral suffered grieviously in the First World War, being bombarded mercilessly for four years, during which time it suffered 300 direct hits. Only its solidity and quality of construction saved it from total destruction. Today it is a tribute to the French architects and craftsmen who have been restoring it so faithfully ever since.

Amiens is the latest of the group and was built over a comparatively short period (1220–88). It has, therefore, a unity of design like its contemporary, Salisbury. Amiens is the classic cathedral on the Île de France pattern and typical of the French Gothic tradition. It has progressed beyond the Paris model and its façade (**431** and **464**) is more plastic with the horizontal emphasis more broken and sophisticated in handling. Its portal sculptures and great carved choir screen are Medieval masterpieces (PLATE 61).

Chartres Cathedral is of the same pattern as the others but is given a different appearance by the spires on the western towers (**433**). They are non-matching spires, the north, the *Clocher Neuf* being rebuilt in 1506–13 in contrast to the *Clocher Vieux* of 1145–70. The two superb features of Chartres are the remarkable coloured glass (**457**) and the exterior sculpture. There are 130 beautiful windows and 2200 sculptured figures. The latter, particularly those on the west front, are of especial interest on account of their transitional quality. They are unique in their

---

* At Notre Dame it is still of wheel design.

† *Norman cathedrals, like Coutances, are exceptions and set the pattern for English tradition.*

early period and are prototypes for later work. The drapery still has a formalised austerity of line, while the figures are serene and of a stylised, elongated proportion (PLATES 58, 59 and 60).

In northern and central France several outstanding cathedrals were built in the thirteenth century. These developed variations from the Île de France pattern. *Bourges*, in central France, built mainly 1190–1275, is of homogeneous design with an exterior and interior in simple Gothic. Sculptural decoration is restrained, as is the coloured glass and other ornamentation. It is an architectural cathedral, long and low on the exterior with geometrical traceried windows and simple flying buttresses. The interior is exceptionally fine, giving long vistas of ascetic Gothic forms (**434**). Further north is *Le Mans*, famous for having the finest chevet in France (**429**). The eastern arm was rebuilt in the thirteenth century on to a Romanesque nave. The chevet has 13 chapels radiating round the apse (**428**). The sophisticated scheme of abutment to this immense choir built on sloping ground is not only a remarkable engineering achievement for its day but a creation of great aesthetic beauty.

In *Normandy* are two interesting cathedrals at Bayeux and Coutances. Both are typical of Norman Gothic. They are severely simple with tall towers and spires and lancet or geometrical window design. At *Bayeux* the choir was rebuilt in the thirteenth century on to an earlier nave, presenting a fine composition from the east (**432**). *Coutances* is notable for its unity of design, internally and externally. The severe tall west front is finely proportioned (**469**), as is the contrasting eastern chevet showing the central tower above (**452** and **615**). The inside, like Bourges, is a masterpiece of superbly handled simplicity.

Of richer High Gothic phase are some widely separated examples, notably Rouen, Strasbourg and Beauvais. *Rouen Cathedral* suffered serious war-time damage in 1944, but is now largely restored. The building represents many construction periods from Romanesque to late Gothic. Of especial interest, apart from some fine sculpture on the north transept portal, is the *rayonnant* period work on the north and south transept façades, the magnificent west window and the early *flamboyant* gables above. The south-west tower is a wonderful instance of late Gothic

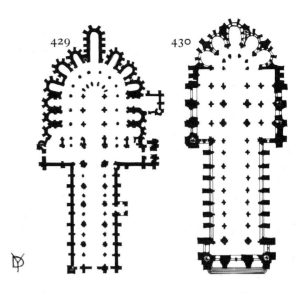

429 French Cathedral plans : Le Mans
430 Reims

work. It is 252 feet high in contrast to the older *Tour de Romaine* on the other side of the façade and is called the *Tour de Beurre* because money was provided for its erection from payments for dispensations given permitting consumption of butter during Lent (**471**). The 512 feet high flèche is a nineteenth century metal replacement.

Strasbourg Cathedral is a typical product of Alsace. It is a combination of German and French sources. It is basically a German cathedral as it was mainly built by Germans, but it clearly owes a great deal to the influence of French cathedral design. The western part of the cathedral was erected in the thirteenth century and culminated in one of the most beautiful façades anywhere in Europe. On traditional French pattern, it has a triple portal, a wonderful rose window and two towers. A lop-sided appearance is given by the fact that the north-west tower received its spire in 1399, but the south-west one was never built. The existing spire clearly shows the German origins of the building, with its openwork tracery designed by Urich d'Ensingen. The sculpture on the portals and the interior is magnificent, very French in treatment but German in expression; the wise and foolish virgins, for example. Damage to the sculptures during the Revolution was considerable, but the restoration has been excellently done (PLATE 62).

FRENCH GOTHIC CATHEDRALS

431 *West front, Amiens, 1220–88*
432 *Bayeux from the south-east, thirteenth century, central tower fifteenth century*
433 *West front Chartres, twelfth-sixteenth century*
434 *Interior, Bourges, early thirteenth century*

Beauvais Cathedral in northern France was an ambitious project of the High Gothic period. Begun in 1247, it was designed on a tremendous scale. The choir, completed 1272, has the highest Gothic vault in Europe (of 157 feet), with accordingly strong flying buttress reinforcement. The attempted creation of such an immense building led to problems. The roof collapsed in 1284 and the 500 feet high spire fell in 1573. The building has never been completed and, though the existing arm is of magnificent quality and proportions, with beautiful coloured glass and a fine chevet, it is still a truncated church, impossible to view as its builders intended. Even for the miraculous Gothic age its dimensions were excessive for the engineering accomplishment of that time.

In the *south* of France, and especially the south-east, the legacy of Ancient Rome represented the overwhelming influence on Gothic architecture just as it had on Romanesque here before this. As in Italy, pure Gothic never flourished. The tendency was for buildings with a horizontal rather than a vertical emphasis, with few piers or columns or any obvious constructive members. Nave and choir were wide and low, vaulting bays square and flying buttresses uncommon; indeed, the abutment was often internal and invisible.

There are a number of fine cathedrals in this region, at *Narbonne, Perpignan, Béziers, Carcassonne* and *Rodez*, for instance. The most unusual and interesting, as well as the one displaying the area characteristics most, is the *Cathedral* at *Albi*. It was begun in 1282, built of warm pinkish brick on massive lines, fortress-like and reminiscent of a Castilian castle. The only exception to the rounded, impregnable exterior is the richly carved stone porch, added in the fifteenth century to the south side. The cathedral shares no common denominator with those of the Île de France.

435 *Le Mont S. Michel, Normandy, France, tenth-thirteenth century*

435

FRENCH GOTHIC CATHEDRALS

436 *Vendôme Abbey Church, begun 1306*

437 *S. Pierre, Caen, from the south-east, 1308–1545*

438 *S. Ouen, Rouen, west front, 1318–1515*

439 *Church of the Jacobins, Toulouse, twin naves, 1230–92*

436

437

438

439

Its origins are closer to Catalan, and especially Barcelona, Gothic. There are no transepts and no western doorways; all the entrances are lateral. The building is a rectangular hall, nearly 60 feet wide and 100 feet high. The buttresses, also of brick, project outwards only slightly, but more into the interior, giving a thickness of 15 feet. Between them are the tall, narrow, round-headed windows. The interior is spacious and finely proportioned though the illumination level is low on account of the slit-like fenestration (**461**). The walls and wide, quadripartite vaults are in polychrome. All round the church are chapels at two levels, set between the buttresses and in the immense thickness of the walls. At the upper stage, windows are recessed into the quadripartite vault ceiling. At the west end is a 300 feet tower in the same architectural mode and crowned by a fine octagon.

French Gothic Churches

Among the monastic foundations in France, the *Abbey Church* of *Mont S. Michel* occupies one of the most picturesque sites. It is perched on top of a rock just off the Normandy coast and is connected to the mainland by a causeway (**435**). It is a fortified monastery, restored in the nineteenth century but still containing a beautiful Romanesque nave (see p. 11) and taller Gothic choir. Much plainer, but one of the best monastic examples in France is the *Church of La Chaise Dieu* in the Auvergne (*c.* 1344), while in *Toulouse*, the *Church of the Jacobins* is a quite different interpretation of Gothic from the north. Of brick and stone construction, it was built *c.* 1300 with twin naves of equal height divided by a central row of columns (**439**).

The fifteenth century saw the final phase of Gothic architecture in France, when many richly ornamented buildings were erected in the *flamboyant* style. These show the basic French Gothic characteristics of verticality, abutment and good proportion, but the flying buttresses are more slender and more decorated than before, the windows are larger with complex curvilinear tracery in the head, ogee arches and mouldings are found on all members. The *Abbey Church* at *Vendôme* is a good monastic example. Both west façade and eastern chevet are outstanding here, while the interior is simpler (**436**). In Normandy,

S. Pierre at *Caen* is a late example with an ornate eastern arm (**437**). In *Rouen* nearby are two particularly fine churches of this time, *S. Maclou* (1437) and *S. Ouen* (**438** and **470**). In *Abbeville* is the remarkable classic of *flamboyant*, *S. Wulfram*, largely built 1488–1534 but never finished (**516**).

A unique building, *La Sainte Chapelle* in *Paris* (the Chapel of the French Kings here), was built earlier, 1244–8. The design has gone beyond the style of the Île de France cathedrals. The fenestration is larger, breaking up the wall area into strips with buttresses, so that the impression is of coloured glass framed by masonry. The chapel has a high stone vault and is apsidal at one end.

Civic Building

Early Gothic work in this field was unpretentious and overshadowed by ecclesiastical architecture. By the fifteenth century the growing wealth of towns was reflected in the municipal buildings. These had all the Gothic characteristics of a vertical emphasis and elements of decoration and structure, but were more symmetrical and dignified. Some had tall towers and steeples like the *Town Hall* at *Arras* (restored in 1919). Many of these buildings which survive are in northern France and suffered bombardment in the First World War, but all are well restored to the original design. The *Town Hall* at *Compiègne* is shown in Fig. **440**. That at *Dreux* has a tall uncompromising donjon appearance, while the one at *Saumur* has a simple façade with rectangular windows bordering on Renaissance patterns. The famous *Palace de Justice* at *Rouen* is now largely rebuilt after its severe damage in the Second World War. It was erected originally in 1493, an important building reflecting the wealth of the city. The late Gothic façades are surmounted with steeply pitched roofs containing tall dormer windows.

Fortified Structures

Until nearly the end of the Middle Ages fortification was still necessary, for monasteries (Mont S. Michel, for example), for castles and palaces and even for bridges. The *Pont Valentré* at *Cahors* is an impressive instance (**444**). Towns were also fortified. These were often built on top of a hill like an acropolis in Ancient Greece. *Avignon* still has remains of such a town in buildings like the

FRENCH MEDIEVAL HÔTELS AND CHÂTEAUX

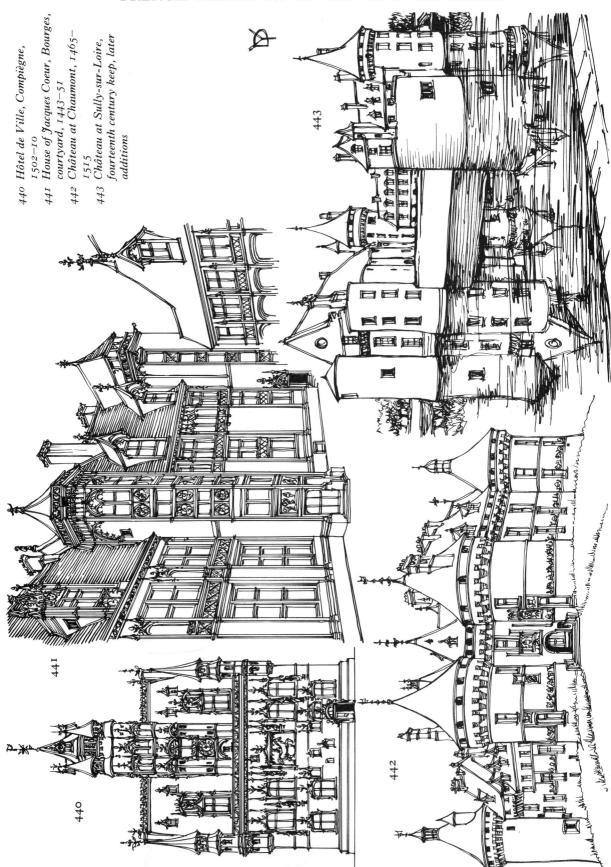

440 Hôtel de Ville, Compiègne,
1502–10
441 House of Jacques Coeur, Bourges,
courtyard, 1443–51
442 Château at Chaumont, 1465–
1515
443 Château at Sully-sur-Loire,
fourteenth century keep, later
additions

440

441

442

443

444 *Pont Valentré, Cahors, France, 1308–80*

fortress *Palace of the Popes* (1316–70), but the two most complete towns are Carcassonne and Aigues Mortes. The city of *Carcassonne* retains its picturesque setting. Built high above the river Aude, it constitutes a museum of military architecture extending from fifth century Visigoths to the sixteenth century. Much of the building is of the thirteenth century and comprises encircling outer and inner curtain walls incorporating over 50 towers. Inside the walls are narrow Medieval streets, shops, houses, the castle and the cathedral of S. Nazaire. Unhappily the city fell into partial ruin in the eighteenth and early nineteenth century, but restoration has been carefully continuing since it was begun by Viollet-le-Duc in 1844 (**445** and **447**). Though Carcassonne is more picturesque, *Aigues Mortes*, built in the thirteenth century at the mouth of the river Rhône near Montpellier, retains much more of its original work. The ramparts, with their mural towers, enclose a rectangular town which was built to house both maritime and fluvial ports. The characteristics of the landscape differ from Carcassonne. Here is a flat estuary region, but the town is as impressive in its individual manner (**446**).

Castles were built throughout the Middle Ages in all European countries. In France they were strongly fortified till after 1453, when the Hundred Years' War ended and the English retired from the soil of France. After this time existing castles were added to and adapted as palatial residences. The Loire valley region is especially noted for its châteaux as the fifteenth century court was not yet fixed in Paris and this hunting area was a favoured one for the royal house, who visited loyal subjects in their castle homes. The river was generally utilised to make water defences and it is these which give to the châteaux the picturesque quality which so many possess. Architecturally, the French castle has much in common with Scottish ones; the round towers with their pyramidal roofs, for instance. There was a close link between Scotland and France and the two countries tended to join forces against the English aggressor.

A late fifteenth century example is *Pierrefonds*, near Compiègne; a truly massive pile, fortified, its skyline broken by numerous towers and high pitched roofs. It was accurately but extensively restored in the mid-nineteenth century by Viollet-le-Duc. A beautiful castle of the same period is the *vieux château* at *Sully-sur-Loire* (**443**). The entrance (1304–8) of *Fort S. André* at *Villeneuve-les-Avignon* is another massive fortification. Even larger and more impregnable are the immense mural towers at *Angers*, while the fourteenth century keep of *Saumur* château rises above the river and the town, dominating the landscape.

Later fifteenth century châteaux show the beginnings of the transformation from fortress

FORTIFIED MEDIEVAL TOWNS IN FRANCE

445 *Entrance façade, the castle, Carcassonne, twelfth century*

446 *Town walls and gateway. Porte de la Reine, Aigues Mortes, thirteenth century*

447 *Outer walls and towers, Carcassonne, thirteenth century*

into palace. *Chaumont*, on the Loire is an impressive example. It has a commanding site and entrance (**442**) and the main courtyard is entirely domestic, containing a fine stone, Medieval staircase. A similar courtyard exists at *Montsoreau* nearby, while the Gothic Court at *Blois* is entirely palatial. Among other interesting châteaux are *Langeais* (Loire, 1465) and the beautiful façade of *Josselin* in Brittany.

Houses

Though the country house was still a semi-fortified château, the French town house, the *hôtel*, was evolving a specific late Medieval pattern suited to its smaller site. The *hôtels* which survive are not numerous and are the larger examples built by well-to-do merchants or church dignitaries. The finest of these is the house of *Jacques Cœur* in *Bourges* (**441**). It is in the classic pattern for the fifteenth century *hôtel*; built round a courtyard and with an entrance doorway leading up to the Medieval stairway in the centre of the court façade. High pitched roofs contain the typical ornamental dormers. Similar, though more simply decorated are two examples in Paris, the *Hôtel de Cluny* (**514**) and the *Hôtel de Sens* (**458**), both late fifteenth century and both retaining finialled dormers and *flamboyant* window tracery. A number of half-timber houses still exist. There are examples in *Chartres* and a few have survived the devastation in Normandy of the Second World War at *Lisieux, Caen* and *Rouen*.

England

The quality of Gothic work here is as fine and abundant as in France. England also developed the Gothic style early; in a transitional form at first, but, by 1200, all the characteristics of the Gothic form were fully evolved. The progress of the style was different from the French model, due largely to the island status of the country. During the Middle Ages, indeed for long after, the surrounding narrow strips of sea were sufficient to impede the easy spread of ideas. Thus Britain was isolated from Continental thought and evolved national characteristics in architecture as in other fields. Nevertheless, England was a maritime nation and had enough contact with the Continent, commercially, to acquire new techniques and influences.

The British climate was suited to the northern Gothic forms as established on the Île de France; more than adequate building materials were available, stone, granite, clay for bricks and timber so the development of the new style was rapid and complete. A much smaller country than France, English work in the Gothic mode varies much less from region to region. The climate differs less from north to south and distances are shorter. The only notable factor in determining regional differences was the availability of building materials. Transport of stone was difficult and costly so areas with available stone—mainly the north and south-west of the country—used this freely, while others like East Anglia and Cheshire, built in timber and brick. The types of building were much the same.

The Gothic style of architecture in England was employed from about 1170–1560; a long period, possibly longer than that in any other country. The style was adopted early and relinquished late; the former because it suited the country and its people, the latter because links with Renaissance ideas were slow to percolate due to the isolation from the Continent. Henry VIII, in the 1530s, had begun to encourage Renaissance work by importing Italian craftsmen, but his break with the Pope over his religious and marital problems postponed the arrival of the Renaissance in England for nearly a century. Gothic architecture in a pure form flourished into the reign of Elizabeth I. There were four distinct phases in this evolution. The first three, Transitional, Lancet and Decorated, ran parallel to French development but the last, Perpendicular, was uniquely English and lasted from about 1375 till 1560.

Ecclesiastical Architecture

Cathedrals, Churches, Chapels and Abbeys

As in France, Gothic buildings in England were at first *Transitional*, incorporating features of the new style into Romanesque work. The common expression of this phase was the appearance of pointed and round arches together in one structure, in windows and vaults especially. *New Shoreham Church*, Sussex is an example as is

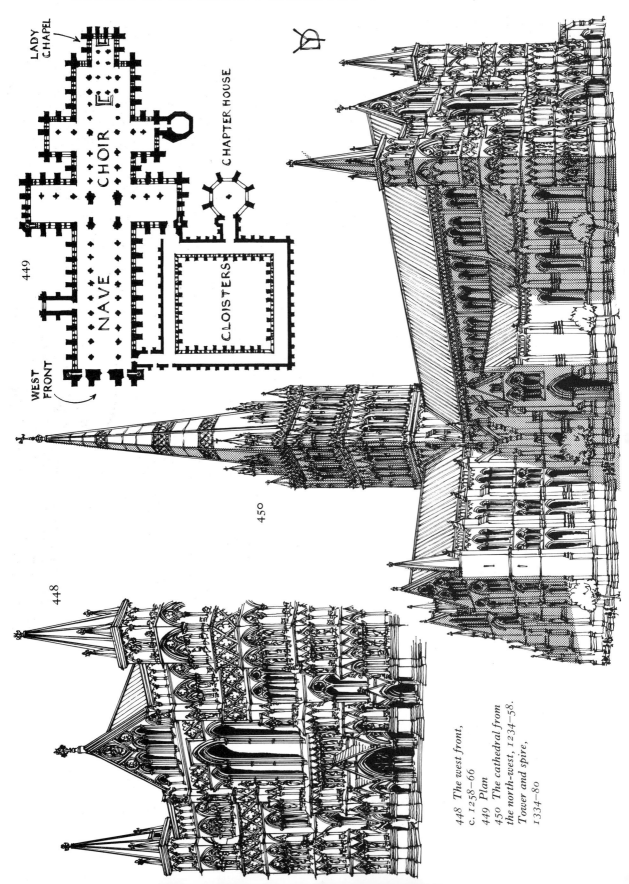

448 The west front,
c. 1258–66
449 Plan
450 The cathedral from
the north-west, 1234–58.
Tower and spire,
1334–80

GOTHIC VAULTS

451

452

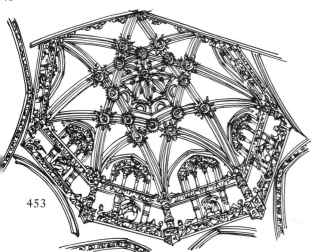

453

455

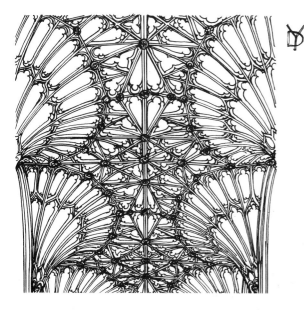

451 *Lantern and Octagon, Ely Cathedral, England, 1330*
452 *Lantern, Coutances Cathedral, France, early thirteenth century*
453 *La Seo Cathedral, Zaragoza, Spain 1498–1520*
454 *Nave fan vault, Sherborne Abbey, England, c. 1475–1500*
455 *Cloister, S. Juan de los Reyes, Toledo, Spain, c. 1470*

GOTHIC WINDOWS

456 *Carlisle Cathedral, England, fourteenth century*

457 *Chartres Cathedral, France, plate tracery, 1196–1216*

458 *Dormer, Hôtel de Sens, Paris, 1475–1507*

459 *Casa de la Conchas, Salamanca, Spain, (Palace of the Ambassadors), 1475*

460 *S. George's Chapel, Windsor, England, 1485–1509*

461 *Albi Cathedral, France, 1282–1390*

462 *Mechelen Cathedral, Belgium, begun 1341*

463 *Church of the Nativity of the Virgin in Putinki, Moscow, 1649–52*

464 *Amiens Cathedral, France, fifteenth century*

465 *Palacio del Infantado, Guadalajara, Spain, begun 1461*

ENGLISH GOTHIC CATHEDRALS

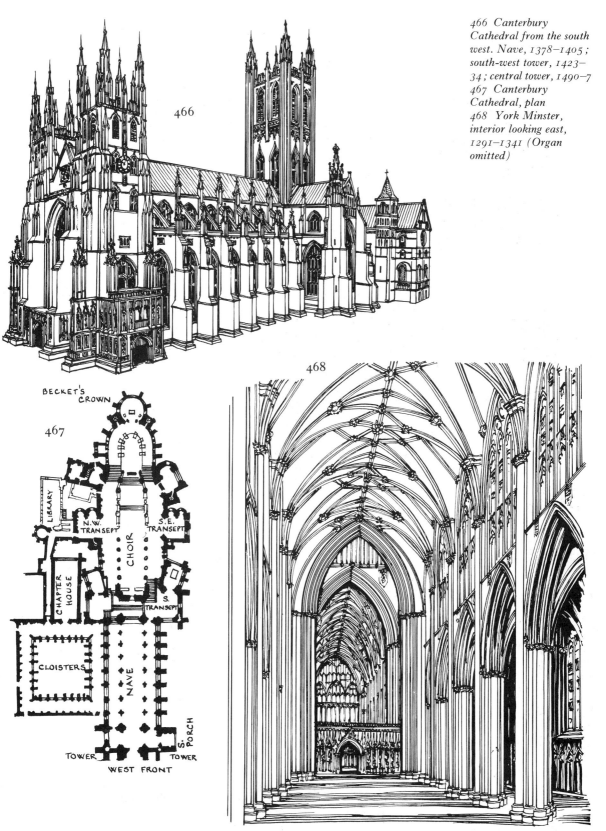

466 Canterbury
Cathedral from the south
west. Nave, 1378–1405;
south-west tower, 1423–
34; central tower, 1490–7
467 Canterbury
Cathedral, plan
468 York Minster,
interior looking east,
1291–1341 (Organ
omitted)

466

BECKET'S CROWN

467

LIBRARY

N.W. TRANSEPT

S.E. TRANSEPT

CHOIR

CHAPTER HOUSE

S. TRANSEPT

CLOISTERS

NAVE

S. PORCH

TOWER

TOWER

WEST FRONT

468

Buildwas Abbey, Shropshire. The outstanding instance is the choir of *Canterbury Cathedral*, rebuilt by William of Sens (so-called because of his work on that French Cathedral) in 1175–84.

From 1200–75 the *Lancet* or Early English style was fully developed. Ribbed quadripartite vaults are characteristic of this period, narrow, pointed arched windows arranged singly or in groups of three or five lancets, slenderer towers generally capped by spires, larger windows and stronger abutment. The vertical emphasis was strong, shown in a higher vault supported on taller nave and choir piers which, like the French ones, were slender and with clustered shafts encircling the central pier.

The supreme example of the style is *Salisbury Cathedral* (**448** and **450**). This is the only English Gothic cathedral to be built largely in a single operation and, therefore, single style. On a new site, the cathedral was begun in 1220 and by 1258 was virtually complete; the tower and spire were a little later. The cathedral is surrounded by a beautiful green-swarded close. Apart from its situation and its unity of style, Salisbury is also remarkable for its high standard of craftsmanship. Built on traditional cruciform plan, the tower and spire over the crossing is the tallest in England (404 feet). Inside appears the three-storeyed division of ground floor arcade, triforium and clerestory. The windows of the latter are of typical Early English design. The west façade is more richly decorated with sculpture than is usual in England (**448**). Other fine examples of Early English work are the nave of *Wells Cathedral*, the façades of *Peterborough Cathedral*, *Ripon Minster* and *Wells Cathedral*, much of *Lichfield Cathedral* and the *Abbeys* of *Glastonbury*, *Tintern*, *Fountains* and *Bolton*.

This first main stage of Gothic architecture in England is often likened to the springtime of the style. It was fresh and almost severe in its classic simplicity, comparable to Bourges and Coutances Cathedrals in France. The hundred years between 1275 and 1375 was the high summer or second stage. Windows are larger, stained glass richer, tracery more complex. There is a smaller area of wall, broken by more extensive abutment. Vaulting becomes more complex with rib and boss decoration. Exteriors and interiors have become more exciting, more three-dimensional. The ever expanding knowledge of the builders led to these forms. The comparative French work in the fourteenth century of *rayonnant* and *flamboyant* styles is similar. It is in this period that English and French work come closest together.

The designers experimented with new ideas in spatial forms and lighting. The work at *Ely Cathedral* (1323–30) is one instance. Here, the old central tower over the crossing was replaced by the unique octagon and lantern. From the interior, in particular, the effect is three-dimensional and remarkable; the tall piers at the crossing, with their alternating arch openings and windows, support the ribbed vault, which extends upwards on all eight sides of the panelled lantern. From directly underneath the view is of a star pattern in the centre of a radiating web of ribs, which culminate in the rich stained glass and curvilinear tracery of the windows (**451**).

In both window tracery and vaulting designs there are, despite many variations, two distinct types of pattern. The earlier style in window tracery is usually *Geometric*, based on the circle and its component parts and shapes, and the later style, *Curvilinear*, is composed of curved lines sweeping in all directions, based mainly on the ogee curve. This is a similar evolution to the contemporary French patterns (**456**). In *vaulting*, quadripartite designs spread to tierceron patterns, with intervening ribs as at *Exeter Cathedral*, and then to lierne vaults as in *York Minster* (**468**) or *Gloucester Cathedral* choir.

Two fine Decorated Gothic* west façades can be seen in *Exeter* and *York Cathedrals*. Exeter has a small but impressive sculptured screen. At York, the towers are later, but the façade fenestration is typical fourteenth century work. Other examples include the Angel Choir at *Lincoln Cathedral* (**608**) and several central towers as, for example, at *Hereford, Wells, Worcester* and *Lincoln* (**474**).

From about 1360 onwards, English development of Gothic architecture began to diverge from that on the Continent and the *Perpendicular* style was evolved. This, as its name suggests, was an exercise in vertical lines but there was also a new emphasis on the horizontal. The three principal features in this work are panelled decoration all over the building, in windows, wall and buttress alike, an increasing area of window space and consequently development of the flying buttress (much later than in France) and

* *This was the English name for this style of work.*

GOTHIC TOWERS AND SPIRES

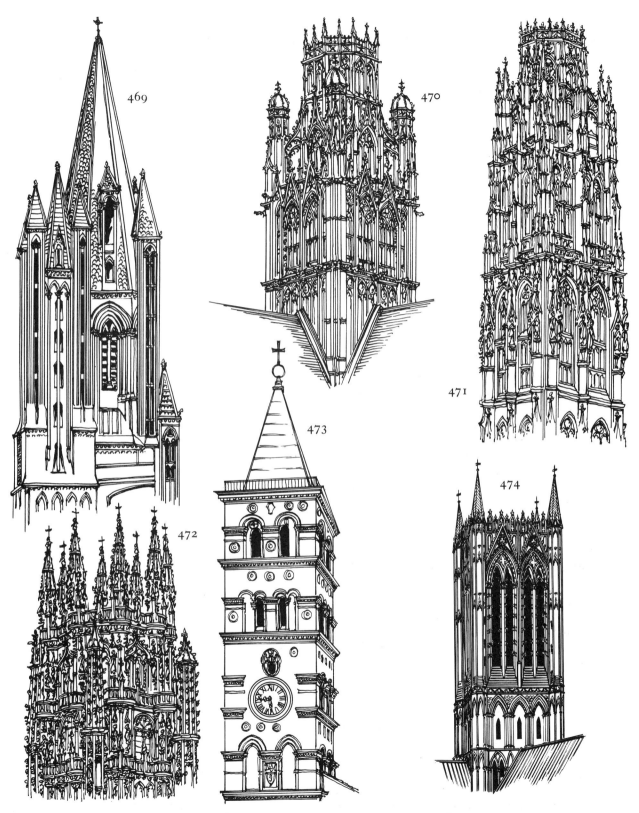

469 *Coutances Cathedral, France, thirteenth century*
470 *Church of S. Ouen, Rouen, France, 1318–1515*
471 *Tour de Beurre, Rouen Cathedral, France, late Gothic*

472 *Cimborio, Burgos Cathedral, Spain*
473 *Church of S. Maria Maggiore, Rome, Italy, 1377*
474 *Lincoln Cathedral, England, 1240–1311*

roofing by means of the fan vault. The finest Perpendicular examples are not confined to cathedrals and abbeys but are to be found in parish churches, chapels and houses. In the cathedrals, Perpendicular work is mainly limited to replacing towers, vaults or windows rather than large scale alterations. The best and most extensive work here is at *Canterbury Cathedral* where the nave, south-west and central towers, cloisters, transepts and Lady Chapel are in Perpendicular style (**466** and **467**).

Of buildings entirely in fifteenth century style, the chapels are supreme: outstandingly *Eton College Chapel* (1441), *King's College Chapel, Cambridge* (1446–1515), and *S. George's Chapel, Windsor* (1475–1509). In all these chapels the plan is rectangular and simple. There are many large windows, separated by finialled flying buttresses, leaving a small wall area. At the ends are gigantic multi-light windows (**460**). Both windows and walls are panelled alike, whether in traceried glass or in stone.

Similarly traceried are the *fan vaults* which roof these magnificent buildings. This peculiarly English design was evolved from the desire for a vault which would accommodate ribs of different curves as they sprang from the capital. The radiating ribs of a fan are of equal length and the bounding line is in the form of a semicircle. The whole group of ribs is made into an inverted concave cone. The radiating ribs are crossed by lierne ribs and the whole surface is then, like the windows, walls and buttresses, panelled and cusped (**454**).

The chapels mentioned are masterpieces of their period, entirely English and representing the climax of craftsmanship and design in the Gothic style, achieving a harmonious balance of mass and form. Also magnificent are many of the large parish churches, some of almost cathedral size, reflecting the wealth of the period in a number of centres. Many of these have tall towers, sometimes with spires, generally set at the west end. They were most common in flat landscape areas, on the eastern half of the country, where they are visible for many miles. Typical is *S. Botolph's Church, Boston*, in Lincolnshire, called colloquially the 'Boston Stump' because its top storey was added so much later than the rest of the church and for many years the tower had a decapitated appearance (**476**). Other

examples include *Louth Church*, Lincolnshire (**477**), *S. Mary Redcliffe, Bristol* and *Thaxted Church*, Essex. Among the less lofty towers are those of many remarkable churches like the richly decorated *Lavenham Church*, Suffolk, *S. Mary's, Taunton*, *S. John, Glastonbury* (**475**) and *S. John, Cirencester* (**478**).

Contemporary with the fan vault was the equally English development of the *timber roof*, used to cover church naves, guild and domestic halls. These evolved from the simple, massive tie and collar beam designs of the thirteenth and fourteenth centuries to the more complex, beautifully carved versions of the fifteenth and sixteenth. The outstanding example here is that covering *Westminster Hall* in *London*, designed by Hugh Herland and built *c.* 1395. There are many others, like those of the great hall of *Hampton Court Palace*, 1535, the great hall of *Eltham Palace*, and the more domestic type of *Rufford Old Hall*, Lancashire, 1505.

Until the death of Henry VIII, architecture in England held tenaciously to the Perpendicular Gothic style. Henry VIII himself, having heard and seen something of Renaissance art in France, tried to attract French and Italian craftsmen to England. Among those who came was *Pietro Torrigiano*, who designed the tomb of Henry VII and his queen in the new *chapel* at at *Westminster Abbey*. The chapel itself (1503–19) is a masterpiece of panelled, fan vaulted Perpendicular Gothic art, but the tomb, finished in 1518, is classical. After Henry VIII's break with Rome, England's tenuous links with Renaissance Italy were broken and the English Renaissance was postponed. Its form was also altered; Torrigiano's monument is Italian classical, the Elizabethan Renaissance forms are 'Mannerist', from Flanders and Germany (Volume 3).

Bath Abbey is the outstanding ecclesiastical example of Tudor Gothic. Designed all in one style, it displays an exceptional unity (**480**). *Hampton Court Palace* is its domestic equivalent. It is built in brick and has some fine Tudor gateways in this material which have the flattened, four-centred arch, typical of the later Perpendicular period. Though parts were altered in the seventeenth century, the Tudor Great Hall, entrance court and river façade remain as a tribute to Cardinal Wolsey's foresight and taste.

ENGLISH GOTHIC CHURCHES

475 *S. John's Church, Glastonbury, c. 1485*
476 *S. Botolph's Church, Boston, Lincolnshire,*
1350–1509
477 *S. James's Church, Louth, Lincolnshire, 1465–1514*

478 *Church of S. John the Baptist, Cirencester.*
Tower c. 1400 ; porch, 1500
479 *S. Patrick's Church, Patrington, Yorkshire,*
fourteenth century

480 Nave and choir, Bath Abbey, Somerset, 1501–39, Designed Robert and William Vertue

481

*481 Monnow Bridge with military gateway, Monmouth,
late thirteenth century*

Fortified Building

Fortification was necessary also in England,
particularly in the twelfth and thirteenth centuries. The years 1275–1350 are noted for the
building of the Edwardian castles, mostly in
Wales and Scotland, so-called because King
Edward I erected many of them to establish his
rule. These castles differ from Norman ones in
that they are built in concentric rings of walling,
studded with mural defence towers, with an open
space in the centre. Here was constructed the
domestic accommodation, while the space between the mural defences housed stabling,
garrison buildings, cattle and villagers. The

pattern was like a miniature Carcassonne. A
number of these castles exist in Wales, such as
Caernarvon, Caerphilly, Conway, Harlech and
Beaumaris. Bridges were also fortified at this time
and the *Monnow Bridge* in the Welsh border
region is a survivor (**481**).

As in France, fifteenth-century castles were
part defensive and part palace. The fortifications
were slowly curtailed, and the living accommodation became more spacious and comfortable.
Herstmonceux Castle in Sussex survives from this
period (**482**), as does the later moated house of
Oxburgh Hall in Norfolk (1482).

Domestic and University Building

Most numerous surviving examples come from
the fifteenth and sixteenth centuries. There are
stone manor houses from the twelfth century
onwards, like that at *Boothby Pagnell*, Lincolnshire (*c.* 1180) and the early brick house, *Little
Wenham Hall*, Suffolk (*c.* 1270). Fourteenth-
century houses were larger and less strongly
fortified. They comprised a great hall of two
storeys open to the roof timbers, solar, storage
accommodation and bedchambers. *Penshurst
Place*, Kent is a fine example, as is also *Ightham
Mote*, Kent and *Markenfield Hall*, Yorkshire.

England possesses many such houses from the
fifteenth and early sixteenth centuries, built in
different materials; stone, brick or half-timber.
Some are large and spacious like *Compton
Wynyates Manor House*, Warwickshire, *Hen-
grave Hall*, Suffolk and *Horham Hall*, Essex, all

482 Herstmonceux Castle, Sussex, c. 1440

482

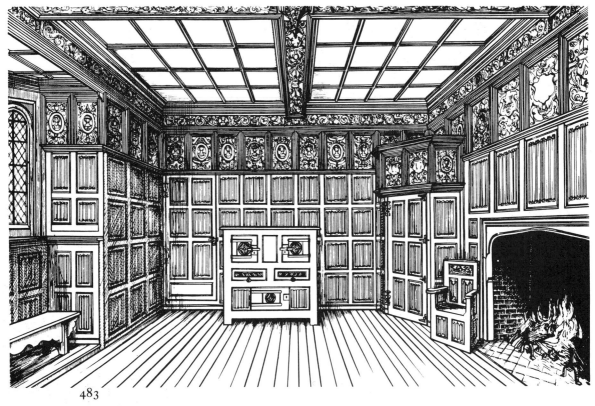

483

483 *Thame Park, Oxon, 1529. Parlour with wood and plaster ceiling and linenfold panelling*

484 *The Feathers Inn, Ludlow, Shropshire, c. 1520–30; timber-framed*

484

early sixteenth century. Others are less grandiose, such as *Paycocke's House* at *Coggeshall*, Essex and *Great Chalfield* and *South Wraxall Manor Houses* in Wiltshire (also see **483**).

Though she suffered from aerial bombardment England was spared the devastation caused by military engagement and occupation in the Second World War. Consequently, unlike Germany, France and Italy, who lost such a wealth of their Medieval *timber framed buildings*, England still possesses a fair number. One of the several inns of this type still in use is illustrated in Fig. **484**. Civic building in this medium also exists, as at the Guildhall in Lavenham and there are many houses like the Priest's House at Prestbury and Rufford Old Hall in Lancashire. All these date from the fifteenth century.

Both *Oxford* and *Cambridge Universities* contain fine work from the fifteenth and sixteenth centuries. There is Magdalen College, Oxford, begun in the mid-fifteenth century, whose tower, seen to advantage from the river, is of particular beauty. The front quad of New College, Oxford illustrates clearly the usual quadrangle method of

GOTHIC PORCHES AND PORTALS

485 *S. John's College, Cambridge, England, early Tudor*
486 *Coronation Church of S. Matthias, Budapest,*
Hungary, fourteenth century

487 *Central façade portal, Orvieto Cathedral, Italy, from 1482*
488 *Central porch, Regensburg Cathedral, Germany,*
fourteenth century

Medieval layout which was retained for so long by those universities. In Cambridge are a number of typical gateways, as at Jesus College and S. John's (**485**). Both show the four-centred arch with carved decoration above.

Belgium

The Low Countries, or Flanders as they were termed in the Middle Ages, were subject to varied artistic influences from different sources. Sandwiched between the Latin peoples of France and the Germanic peoples to the east, the architecture reflects both sources as well as some Spanish influence due to conquest. But in general the architecture of the area divides itself clearly in the period 1200–1600 into two main types. The country which is now Belgium was primarily French orientated and present day Holland was Germanic. The work in the Netherlands is therefore considered here with that of the Germanic Baltic group with which it has much in common.

Belgium was a wealthy area in the Middle Ages, particularly during the later years. In the fourteenth century, while France was being drained by constant warfare, the artistic centre of this part of Europe moved from Paris to Belgium, where Brussels and Antwerp were able to attract artists of fame and quality. The architectural style was mainly French. Important buildings were constructed in stone and have lofty towers and spires and great richness of sculptural and carved decoration. The fifteenth century saw an emancipation of Belgian architecture from the French. Bruges became the northern centre of the Hanseatic League and other important commercial centres grew up in Ghent, Antwerp, Louvain and Ypres. The rich merchants contributed to the magnificent civic building which arose in those years; the town and guild halls, exchanges, municipal belfries, warehouses and city houses. No other country in such a small area possesses as rich a heritage of this type of work from such an early date.

Ecclesiastical Building

The strongest influence on the design of these buildings was northern French. This is seen in the eastern chevet and the width of the churches, with double or triple aisles. A number of façades,

like those of Brussels and Antwerp Cathedrals, have twin western towers and portico below. German influence is evidenced by the churches with a single western tower and spire, like the Cathedral of S. Bavon in Ghent. These and other sources of style were welded by the Belgians into a characteristic mode of their own and many of the cathedrals and larger churches have the same features repeated again and again. Particular examples which show these features are *Mechelen (Malines)* and *Brussels Cathedrals* and the *churches of S. Jean, Louvain* and *S. Jean and Notre Dame in Mechelen* (**462**). These characteristics are the use of large columns to divide nave and choir from the aisles; piers are used only at the crossing and then have slender clustered shafts. The nave arcade is high and its columns are topped by foliated capitals and, below, are life-size sculptured figures attached to the column. There is no proper triforium, only a continuation of the clerestory window mullions downwards in blind form. Vaults are quadripartite. Interiors are light owing to the large clerestory and aisle windows. The east end is apsidal and has an ambulatory vaulted over pointed arches narrowed to accommodate the curve. The interior of Mechelen Cathedral shown in Fig. **491** is typical of this style. On the exterior, Mechelen has a flèche over the crossing, but a single tall western tower, one of the most beautiful in Belgium of this type.

Similar interiors can be seen at the *Church of S. Pierre, Louvain* (**489**) and the *Cathedral of S. Bavon in Ghent*. But in these cases, the cylindrical columns are replaced by slender vaulting shafts with tiny or no capitals and arcade piers with no break of any kind before the arch. *Ghent Cathedral* has brick vaults and walls. Stone is used only for ribs, piers and windows. The vault is most effective in its brick and stone colouring. Designs vary in the cathedral; the choir and nave are quadripartite with intermediate ribs, on the English pattern, and the aisles and crossing have lierne vaults which are not common in Belgium.

Brussels Cathedral (**490**) was built over a long period. The choir, begun 1226, is the earliest Gothic work in Belgium. It has an apsidal termination but no complete ambulatory; there are large flanking side chapels ending before the apse, and the ambulatory encircles only the end

GOTHIC CHURCHES IN BELGIUM

489 *Church of S. Pierre, Louvain,*
from the east, 1425–97

490 *West front, Cathedral of S.S.*
Michael and Gudule, Brussels,
1226–80. Towers 1518

491 *Interior, Cathedral of S.*
Rombaut, Mechelen (Malines)
begun 1341

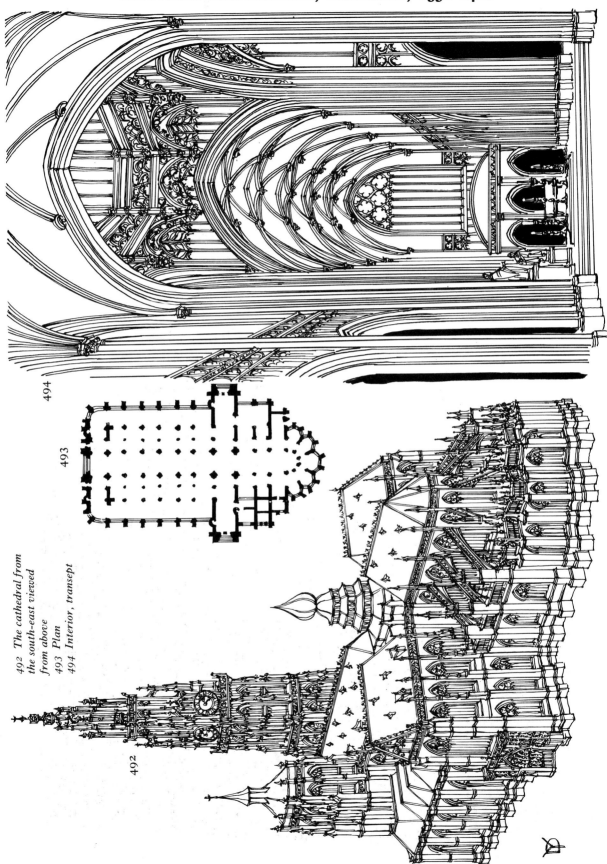

492 The cathedral from
the south-east viewed
from above
493 Plan
494 Interior, transept

492

493

494

495 Town Hall, Brussels, 1402–50 (Restored)

495

GOTHIC CIVIC BUILDING IN BELGIUM

496 *Town Hall, Oudenaarde, 1525–9*
497 *Town Hall, Louvain, 1448–63*
498 *Trade Hall 'La Vieille Boucherie,'*
   Antwerp, 1501
499 *Maison des Franc-Bateliers, façade, 1531.*
   (Caravelle relief over front-door). Quai-
   aux-Herbes, Ghent

part. The nave was built 1425–75 and is of the classic Belgian pattern as illustrated in Fig. **491**. The cylindrical columns support statues of the apostles (**612** and PLATE 63). The façade of 1518 is on Île de France pattern.

Antwerp Cathedral, a rich example of late Gothic, is the most impressive in Belgium. It was begun in 1352 at the east end, the choir being completed in 1411 and the nave by 1474 (**493**). The façade is richly decorated with a central sculptured portal and large window above. The twin towers are on French pattern, but one spire was built, the north one. This is graceful and finely proportioned, rising to 400 feet in height. The whole cathedral shows a greater French influence than elsewhere in Belgium. Apart from the façade, this can be seen in the chevet, transept portals and the triple aisles (**494**). The strange lantern over the crossing is an unfortunate relic of Spanish occupation. Apart from the west end, Antwerp cathedral is exceptionally difficult to view. It is surrounded by buildings, the houses being built on to it at the eastern apse. The best viewpoint is from above, from the tall modern buildings nearby some of which have suitable access. This view is shown in Fig. **492**.

Civic Building

In the fifteenth and sixteenth centuries in particular, the wealthy merchants were independent and organised members of society and had greater freedom than in many countries. They used some of their wealth to build the magnificent trade and town halls of the Belgian cities. These are unique in Europe for their quality of craftsmanship and richness of decoration and design.

Three typical *town halls* are illustrated; the somewhat restored *Brussels* example (**495**), the most richly ornate at *Louvain* (**497**) and a more provincial but very typical one at *Oudenaarde* (**496**). The *town hall* at *Bruges*, built 1377, is one of high quality, as befitted the town's importance as centre for the Hanseatic League. There is a fine hall inside on the first floor which has a pendant timber roof and modern frescoes round the walls. *Ghent* illustrates the metamorphosis from Gothic to Renaissance forms since the right-hand part of the building is in an exception-

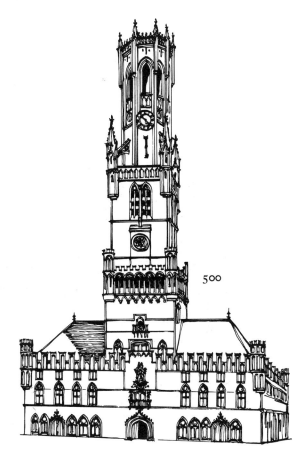

500

500 *Halles and 279 ft. belfry, Bruges, Belgium, 1280*

ally ornamented Gothic with a quantity of figure sculpture and the left portion is fully classical in a façade using three superimposed orders. The Medieval section dates from 1518–33 and the Renaissance 1595–1622.

The *guild halls* are equally fine and probably more varied in design. The most impressive and the greatest example of secular Medieval architecture in Europe was the *Cloth Hall* at *Ypres*, built 1200–1304. It was destroyed in 1915 during action in the First World War, then was rebuilt after 1918 to the original design. The exterior front elevation is in a low, unbroken façade, 440 feet long, simple in design but richly detailed. There is an immense square tower in the centre and a high pitched roof on either side of it. The later town hall, next door, is completely eclipsed in scale and dignity.

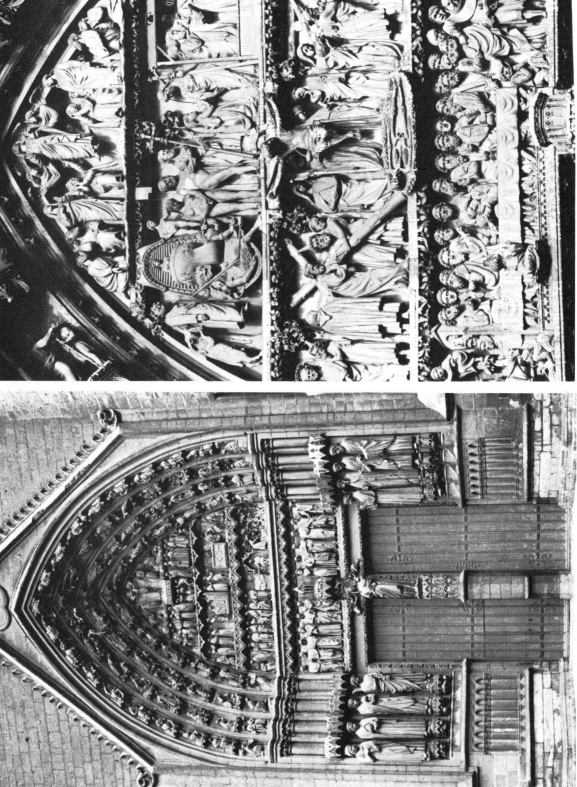

Plate 62
Tympanum, central portal, façade, Strasbourg Cathedral, France, 1276–1318

Plate 61
Madonna Portal, south transept, Amiens Cathedral, France, *c.* 1280

Plate 63
Nave columns. Cathedral of S. Gudule, Brussels, Belgium, 1425–75

Plate 64
Façade doorway detail. Plateresque. Salamanca New Cathedral, Spain, 15th and 16th century

Of different design, simple but also of classic proportions, are the *Grande Boucherie* in *Ghent* (1408) and the *Vieille Boucherie* in *Antwerp* (**498**). Both of these have stepped gabling, but the Antwerp example is tall and the Ghent one long and low. More ornate and late Gothic in treatment are the *Ghent Maison des Francs-Bateliers* (**499**) and the *Cloth Hall* in *Mechelen*. There are two outstanding municipal *belfries* in Belgium. The one at *Ghent* (1300–39) is 400 feet high and stands uncompromisingly four square, surmounted by an elegant spire. The building known as the *Halles and Belfry* at *Bruges* is unique. It has the same monumental simplicity as well as the fine proportions of the Ypres Cloth Hall (**500**).

Large *squares* were laid out in many city centres. Several still exist with some Medieval, some Renaissance and part later building. Among those which retain their unity of treatment are the Grandes Places in Brussels and in Antwerp. Here are narrow buildings with ornate, stepped and curving gables, topped by sculptured finials standing side by side, each one different but creating a homogeneous whole. Even where restoration and modernisation has taken place, it is discreet, as in the Grande Place in Antwerp.

The Germanic Influence

Germany, Switzerland, Austria, Hungary, Czechoslovakia

Germany

Medieval Germany was not a nation but a collection of states of differing sizes which covered much of central Europe. Architecturally the German influence extended from the Baltic coast to the Alps and from Alsace to modern Hungary. The building pattern of the northern part was dominated by the Hanseatic League and this work, together with areas to the west (Holland) and the east (Poland) along the Baltic are considered on p. 136.

In the remainder of the region now comprising East and West Germany Gothic development took a different form from that encountered in France, England and Belgium. In these countries the Gothic style evolved steadily and naturally from the Romanesque. In Germany Romanesque architecture had been so successfully adopted,

and suited the needs and character of the peoples so well, there was reluctance to change it. German builders tended to adopt the Gothic vault and the pointed arch to go with it, but little else. Till virtually the end of the thirteenth century building was on Romanesque style, as at *Bamberg* and *Naumburg Cathedrals*. Bamberg (**501**), in particular, is typical. It was rebuilt on the foundations of an earlier Romanesque cathedral in the early thirteenth century and largely completed by 1237. But it is still basically Romanesque, with its four terminal towers, polygonal ends, lateral entrance and round-headed window and doorway openings. Only the interior ribbed vaults are Gothic, and the abundance of fine sculpture both on the exterior and inside. This largely dates from the late thirteenth century (PLATES 66 and 70).

The House of Hapsburg came to power in 1273, and soon afterwards Gothic architecture made its appearance. But it did not develop from German Romanesque. The need for change was felt strongly, so builders cast their eyes at the ready-made style in neighbouring France and based their ideas of Gothic upon French schemes, especially Amiens Cathedral which, at that time, was the exemplar in western European architecture.

A number of important cathedrals, minsters and churches were begun in the late thirteenth century in emulation of the French prototype. The cruciform plan was adopted, a high vaulted nave and choir, with one or more flanking aisles, an eastern chevet and richly ornamented west façade. Some of these façades have twin western towers, but many retain a German preference for a single one. A particular German characteristic was the treatment of the towers and spires. Finials and crockets were profusely employed and the spire itself was a fretwork of stone with light shining through from all sides. These spires were masterpieces of craftsmanship and engineering. *Strasbourg Cathedral* is an example already discussed (p. 87).

Typical of the twin-towered façade type are *Cologne* and *Regensburg Cathedrals*. The building history of Cologne is probably the longest of any great Medieval Cathedral (**504**). It was begun early, in 1248, on the eastern arm, which is almost a replica of that at Amiens. Both exterior and interior are imposing in scale and detail.

GERMAN GOTHIC CHURCHES

501 *Bamberg Cathedral from the north-east, 1205–37*
502 *Church of S. Elisabeth, Marburg, from the south-east, 1235–83*
503 *The Frauenkirche, Nürnberg (Nuremberg), hall church, 1354–61*

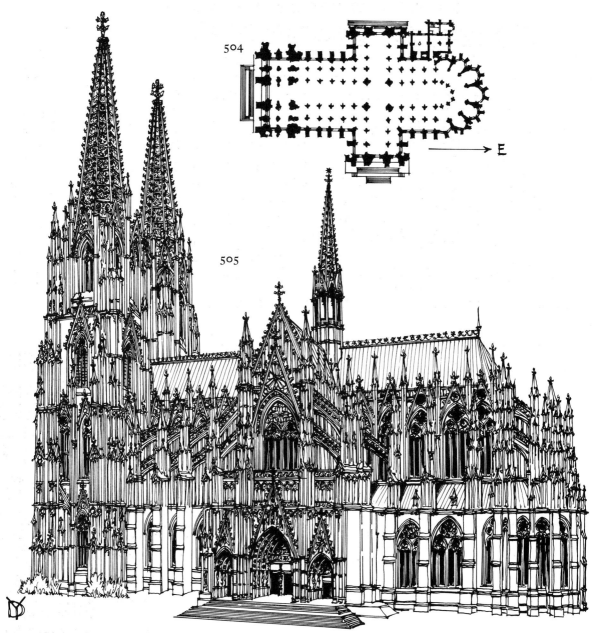

504 *Plan and*

505 *View from the south-east of Cologne Cathedral, Germany. Choir, 1248–1322; transepts begun 1325; west front completed to fourteenth century designs but work not finished until 1880*

The chevet has an ambulatory and seven radiating chapels, which are polysided; they are separated by great double arched flying buttresses. The choir was consecrated in 1322, transepts and nave were begun but the money ran out and the fabric slowly began to decay. Today, only the eastern arm is Medieval. The rest of the cathedral was completed in 1824–80, to the original designs, but nineteenth century stonework and craftsmanship was more mechanical than its Medieval prototype. The west front, with its two vast steeples, is harder in treatment than the east end. Cologne Cathedral is of immense size, the largest in northern Europe. It is 468 feet long and 275 feet wide; the nave vault of 150 feet is nearly the height of Beauvais and this is a complete building. It is French in inspiration, the essence of High Gothic yet still characteristically German, lacking the elegance of French prototypes (505).

Regensburg Cathedral (506) occupies a pictur-

GOTHIC CATHEDRALS IN GERMANY

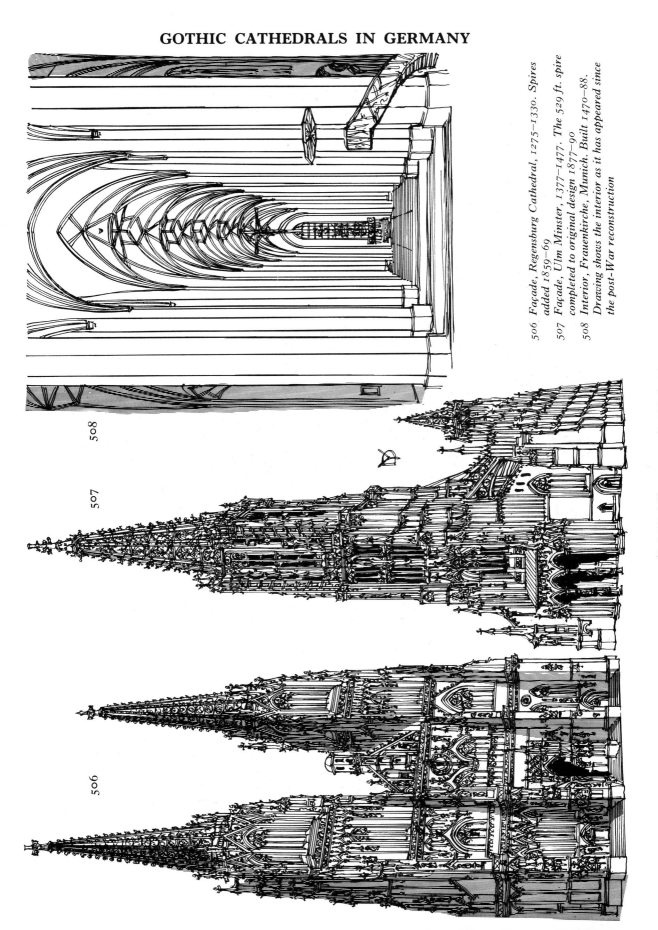

506 Façade, Regensburg Cathedral, 1275–1330. Spires added 1859–69

507 Façade, Ulm Minster, 1377–1477. The 529 ft. spire completed to original design 1877–90

508 Interior, Frauenkirche, Munich. Built 1470–88. Drawing shows the interior as it has appeared since the post-War reconstruction

506

507

508

GOTHIC IN GERMANY

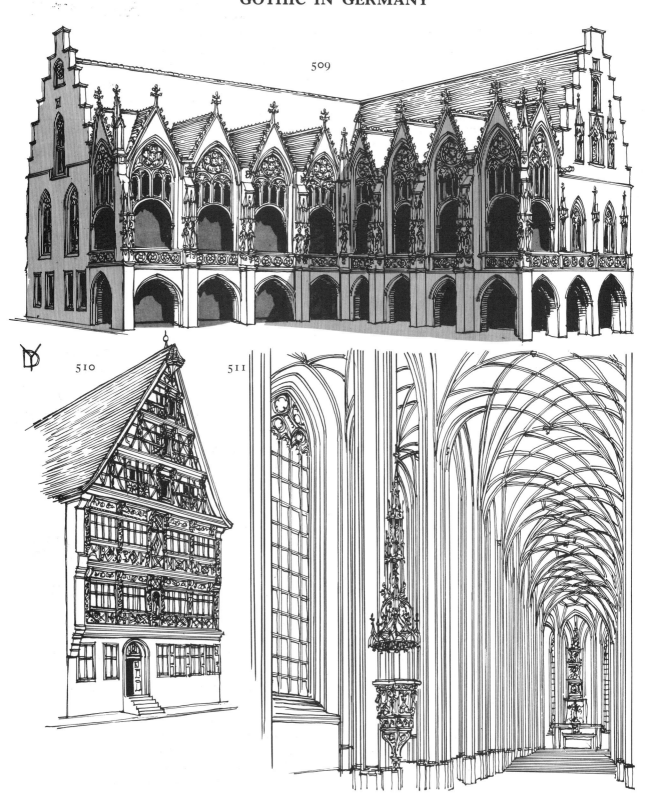

509 Town Hall (Altes Rathaus), Brunswick, 1393–1468
510 Half-timber house, Dinkelsbühl, c. 1440
511 S. George's Church, Dinkelsbühl, hall church design, 1448–92

esque position on the Danube in Bavaria. It replaced a Romanesque cathedral on the site and was begun in 1275. The façade has twin towers of which the spires were added in the 1860s. The elevation is slenderer, less weighty than Cologne and, being Medieval, has greater quality of craftsmanship in its stonework and glass. An attractive and unusual feature is the central porch, which is triangular (**488**). The eastern arm is polygonal-ended. It is simple and less obviously buttressed than French counterparts. On the exterior, but more particularly inside, is some fine figure sculpture (PLATE 67).

Beautiful examples of the single-towered west façade are the *Minsters* at *Ulm* and *Freiburg*. Ulm was begun in 1377; it is like a parish church on an immense scale, particularly at the west end. The lofty tower was completed in the sixteenth century, its spire was added, to the original design, in the nineteenth. It reaches 529 feet above ground. It almost overwhelms the building (**507**). The exterior is richly carved, with ornamented buttresses, fenestration and spire. The triple porch is especially noteworthy. The church interior is less successful; its proportions make it too high and dark. The glory of the interior are the carved wood choir stalls. German woodcarving was of a very high standard in the fourteenth to the sixteenth century, and these examples, together with those at Munich, are among the finest.

Freiburg Minster is somewhat smaller, but also on parish church pattern. Begun as a Romanesque basilica in 1200, it was completed at the west end in Gothic style about 1350. The façade has a 380 foot tower and spire; an early example of the open traceried type. In front of the main doorway, which has a fine sculptured tympanum, is the 'Golden Gate'. A Gothic choir was begun in the fourteenth century to a design similar to the contemporary one at Augsburg Cathedral, but was not completed till 1513 for lack of funds.

The cathedrals and churches just described are mainly in the French tradition of Gothic architecture. Much of the work in Germany was not like this: these buildings were an import of a foreign pattern. The Germans naturally excelled at a style developed by themselves; most commonly this was a simplification of Gothic features. Abutment was reduced to a minimum, transepts were often not built and the plan became a simple rectangle. From these ideas evolved the most usual form of German Gothic, the Hallenkirche or *hall church*. Apart from the features just mentioned, the important characteristic of a hall church is that the vaults of nave, choir and aisles are of the same height. This means that the building is, however richly ornamented, a simple hall. The nave and choir can have no triforium or clerestory so must be lit by exceptionally large aisle windows. Hall churches often have beautiful interiors. The tall slender piers support a high vault and there is no triforium or clerestory wall to obstruct the vista from end to end and from side to side of the church, only a forest of delicate piers. The vaults show a variety of quadripartite and lierne designs. The interiors are well illuminated, simple and finely proportioned. The hall church is only rarely found outside the realms of Germanic influence. There are two or three in Italy, as at Perugia and Todi.

The best instance of a hall church in Germany is the *Marienkirche-zur-Wiese* at *Soest*, dating from *c*. 1340. The exterior has a twin-spired façade on a large scale, like Regensburg Cathedral. Inside, immensely high piers ascend to the vault without any break for capitals. Both nave and aisles continue the same quadripartite vault, though the former is in square bays and the latter rectangular. There is no crossing or separation of nave and choir; tall windows continue all round the building including the apsidal east end. They are three- and four-light, with decorated traceried heads and very fine coloured glass, especially in the apse. The whole simple interior is of great beauty.

Two other excellent hall churches are *S. Elisabeth, Marburg* and *S. George, Dinkelsbühl* (**502, 511** and **613**). S. Elisabeth has a plain quadripartite vault; the one at Dinkelsbühl is more complex and resembles lattice work. Two other famous examples suffered in the Second World War. The *Frauenkirche* in *Munich*, now the cathedral, was rebuilt 1468–88, replacing a Romanesque basilica. It is a large, brick, hall church, 358 feet long, and has a nave over 100 feet in height (**508**). The onion-domed towers are believed to have been inspired by a visit to Jerusalem by the designer Jörg von Halspach, but were not added until 1525.* The interior received unsuitable eighteenth century classical additions, then nineteenth century Gothic Revival alte-

* The Church of S. Ulrich at Augsburg, built 1467, has one similar tower.

Plate 65
S. George and the
Dragon. Wood
sculpture by Bernt
Notke from Lübeck.
Storkyrka, Stock-
holm, Sweden, 1489
Plate 66
The Prophets.
S. George's Choir.
Bamberg Cathedral,
Germany, 1220–30
Plate 67
Pier figure,
Annunciation.
Regensburg
Cathedral, Germany,
1280

Plate 68
Pulpit. Siena Cathedral. Nicola Pisano, 1265–9
Plate 69
Chapter House window. Convent of Christ, Tomar, Portugal.
Manoeline, early 16th century. Diogo de Arruda

GOTHIC DOORWAYS

512 *Central façade portal, Cathedral of Notre Dame,
Paris, 1200*

513 *North transept, Barcelona Cathedral, Spain, 1300*

514 *Courtyard, Hôtel de Cluny, Paris, 1483*

515 *Frauenkirche, Nuremberg, Germany, 1354–61*

516 *Façade, S. Wulfram, Abbeville, France, 1483–1534*

517 *Cathedral of the Saviour, Andronikhov Monastery,
Moscow, 1425*

rations. It was severely damaged in 1945, but today has been well restored, though much of the carved stonework and decorative medieval painting was not replaced. The famous carved choir stalls, completed in 1502 by Erasmus Grasser, were tragically not stored with the other interior decoration during the war. Fortunately some of the half length figures have been preserved and are displayed in two museums. The *Frauenkirche* at *Nuremberg* was also damaged. The exterior is now fully restored (**503**) but the interior is partly modernised. The unpretentious but ornamental façade faces the market place. It has an elegant, carved, square porch, richly ornamented and, above, a finialled stepped gable (**515**).

Until 1939 Germany possessed many good examples of *civic architecture* from the fourteenth and fifteenth centuries. Like Belgium, there were ornately carved stone town and guild halls as well as brick and half-timber versions. Sadly, the Second World War took a heavy toll, especially in cities like Cologne, Ulm, Hildesheim and Lübeck. Many of these halls have been restored but, though the craftsmanship is good and great care has been taken, the task was too extensive to permit the finance necessary to restore the buildings to the standard of richness that they had originally. Several notable examples remain. The *Altes Rathaus* at *Brunswick*, built in stone and now restored, survives (**509**). This is a particularly outstanding town hall. Of simpler, provincial type is the stone *Rathaus* at *Goslar*, in the Harz mountains region. This is much smaller and less pretentious, but it has good geometrical window tracery above a ground floor arcade. There is a finialled, gable roof, and inside a decorative chamber.

Castles and *houses* have also suffered greatly from war-time damage in Germany. Before 1939, the country probably possessed more half-timber Medieval structures than any other. Now there are few. There is one at *Dinkelsbühl* (**510**) and there is the *Kaiserworth* (now a hotel) at *Goslar*. Probably the finest surviving instance of a fortified town is at *Rothenburg-ob-der-Tauber*, which still retains its picturesque walls and towers. Heidelberg possesses some of these, but most of the work here is of a later date or has been replaced. The timber and stone houses which made towns like Brunswick, Nuremberg, Frankfurt and Hildesheim so attractive have nearly all disappeared.

Switzerland

Swiss Medieval architecture is much like that in Germany though, in general, rather plainer, especially on the exteriors. The finest of the *cathedrals* is that at *Basle*, which has a picturesque situation on the Rhine. The west façade is fifteenth century and typical of Swiss Gothic work (**519**). *Berne Cathedral* is mainly of late fifteenth century construction. The architecture of *Lausanne Cathedral* is mainly thirteenth century Gothic, very simple, with plate tracery in the rose windows and lancet aisle windows all round the building. The west doorway, richly decorated with sculptured figures, is in late Gothic style, but was not constructed till the seventeenth century. The interior is simple and austere and has much in common with English cathedrals of this date. Pointed arches are used throughout. There is a tall nave arcade, a short arcaded triforium and a clerestory of one lancet window to a three arcade group. The glass is of good quality.

Fribourg is a small town built on a picturesque hilly site on a bend of the river Sarine. It retains many of its late Medieval buildings and much of the atmosphere of a town of this period. The *cathedral* is the largest monument. It has a fine Gothic tower (**520**) which was completed in 1490. The western porch below, surmounted by its rose window, is sculptured. There are apostles flanking the doorway also angels and prophets (**520**) and a Last Judgment tympanum. Nearby is the sixteenth century wooden *Pont de Berne* and the *Town Hall* of 1500–22.

Austria and Hungary

Austria also closely reflects the German Gothic style. Its supreme monument is *S. Stephen's Cathedral* in *Vienna* (**521**). It has two late Gothic towers, separated by the width of the church but, like Strasbourg, only one was surmounted by its spire, which is a graceful, ornate one. S. Stephen's is a hall church, thus having no triforium or clerestory. The interior is dark and full of Medieval atmosphere. It has an exceptionally lofty nave arcade whose pointed arches reach almost into the vault. The roof is vaulted in square bays in stellar pattern, as are also the aisles, but the chancel is quadripartite. Some of the original coloured glass is still in the windows.

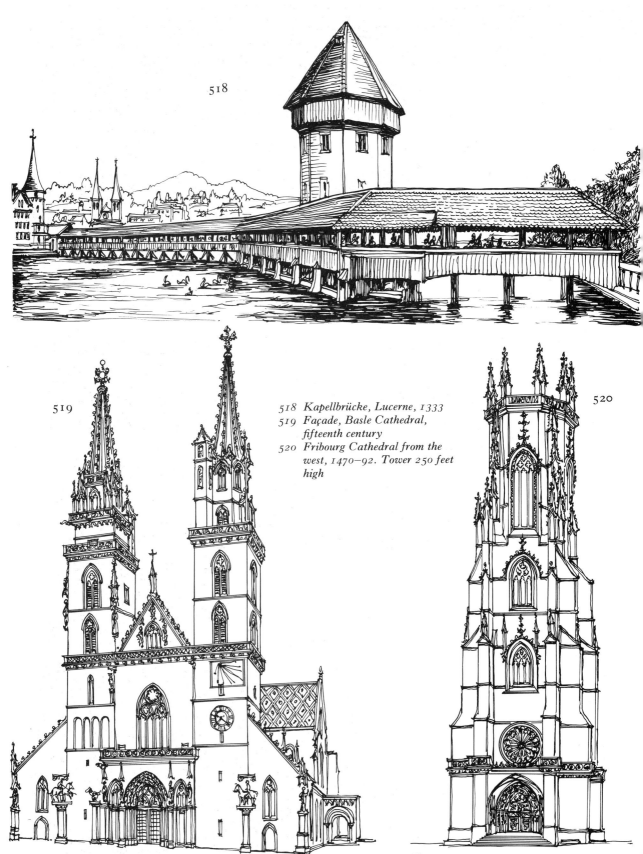

518

519

520

518 *Kapellbrücke, Lucerne, 1333*
519 *Façade, Basle Cathedral,
       fifteenth century*
520 *Fribourg Cathedral from the
       west, 1470—92. Tower 250 feet
       high*

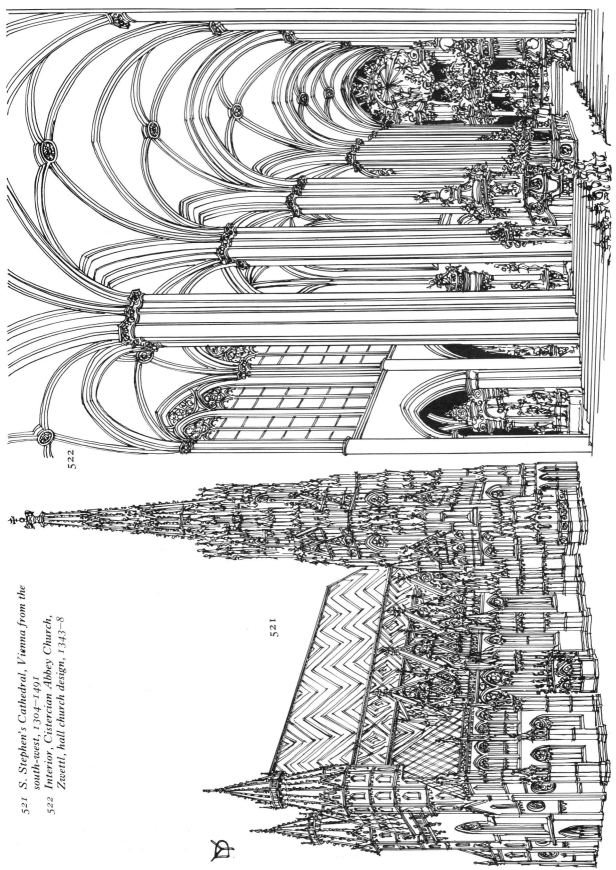

521 S. Stephen's Cathedral, Vienna from the
south-west, 1304–1491
522 Interior, Cistercian Abbey Church,
Zwettl, hall church design, 1343–8

522

521

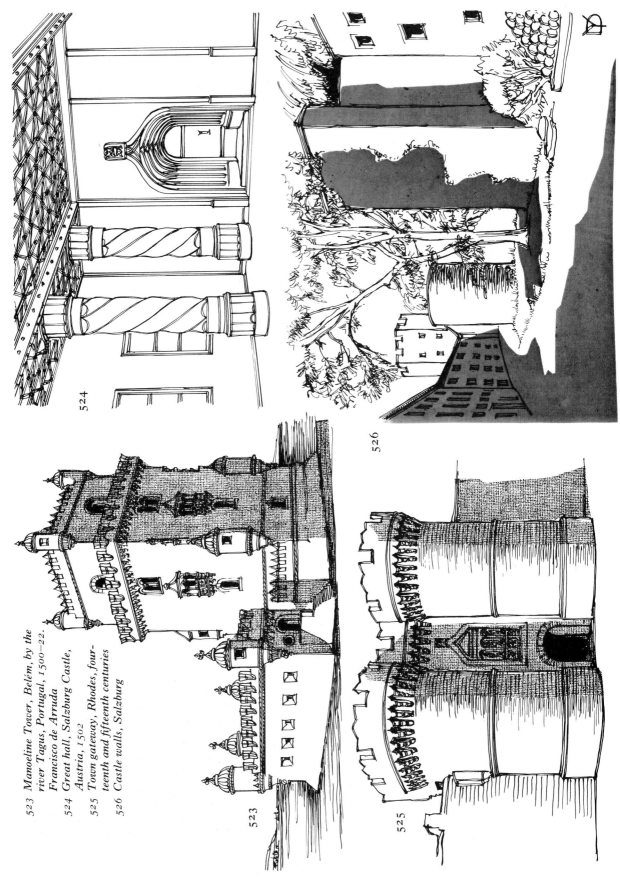

523 Manoeline Tower, Belém, by the
river Tagus, Portugal, 1500–22.
Francisco de Arruda

524 Great hall, Salzburg Castle,
Austria, 1502

525 Town gateway, Rhodes, fourteenth and fifteenth centuries

526 Castle walls, Salzburg

It is beautiful, but both the light and view are partly obscured by a later altar. The rest of the glass is mostly modern. There is some good sculpture and an especially interesting Medieval pulpit, traceried and carved with heads.

527 Church of S. Matthias, Budapest, Hungary. Reconstructed 1255. Tower 1470

The *Cistercian Abbey Church* at *Zwettl* is a superb fourteenth century work. The façade and steeple are rebuilt in Baroque style, but the interior is a classic hall church. The tall, grouped piers ascend to tiny, foliated capitals. The vaults of nave and aisles are of the same height and both are quadripartite. The windows are in simple Gothic style. Baroque altars and pulpits of great ornateness provide a foil to the severe grey and white Medieval interior (**522**).

The *castle* at *Salzburg*, impregnably and romantically situated on top of the hill Hohensalzburg, is a Medieval one. It is now partly a museum and partly a private residence. It has been restored but not altered a great deal in modern times. The central keep dates from the early twelfth century but concentric walling with mural towers was added during the Middle Ages, bringing its fortification up to date (**526**). The state apartments are interesting. The best of them, the great hall and the golden room (**524**) date from the early years of the sixteenth century. There are brightly coloured and gilded, patterned wood ceilings, curved columns, richly carved doorways under ogee arches and fantastic metal and ceramic stoves.

527

Medieval remains in *Hungary* are few. The best were in the city of *Budapest* which is divided by the river Danube into the hilly right bank where Buda is situated and the flatter lands opposite of Pest. The main population of the city has always lived in Pest but after the Mongol invasion of 1241, a citadel was built on the hills opposite, since known as castle hill. A whole Medieval fortified town was established in Buda, as it came to be called, named after Attila's brother. Here, before the destruction of the Second World War, were narrow streets and houses, mural towers and walling. There was also a seventeenth century Town Hall and the immense Royal Palace, with S. Stephen's Chapel.

The only great Medieval building to survive here is the *Coronation Church* of *S. Matthias* (**527** and **486**). This was originally a Romanesque building but was gradually turned into a Gothic one in the fourteenth and fifteenth centuries. During the Turkish occupation the church was used as a mosque and later became a Jesuit monastery. It was restored in Gothic manner under the Emperor Franz Josef in the nineteenth century and once more used as a coronation church. The damage caused in the Second World War has been repaired on the exterior, which now looks well. Inside, much remains to be done, especially to restore the frescoes which cover all surfaces of walls, vaults, piers and capitals, as at Chauvigny in France. It is a three-aisled church with triforium and small round clerestory windows.

Sopron, near the Austrian border, has several Medieval churches but they are mainly in a poor state of preservation. There is the *Church of the Holy Ghost* (1421), *S. Michael* (1484) and the *Cathedral, S. George*, a larger fourteenth century building.

Czechoslovakia

In contrast with Germany, there was no strong Romanesque tradition here and Gothic architecture, spread by the monastic orders, was soon accepted and established. Unfortunately, due to the troubled times in this area of central Europe, little survives of early Gothic building; the great Czech monuments of the Middle Ages are of the fourteenth and fifteenth century, and even later, and are, in consequence, in the richer, more decorative Gothic style.

The Cistercian and Praemonstratensian Orders were especially active in the building of *abbeys*. Many were designed by French builders but carried out by the local craftsmen. Few such churches remain in anything like their former state. A thirteenth century Cistercian doorway survives from the *Klôšter Hradiště* (near Mnichovo Hradiště), now part of the walls of a modern building, while at the Benedictine Monastery at *Sázava*, which stands above the river of the same name, a tributary of the Vltava, the Gothic church was never completed and only part of the nave exists. The best preserved Cistercian Abbey Church is that on the river Vltava south of České Budejovice at *Zlatá Koruna*. Founded in 1269, most of the building was of the fourteenth century, though it has been extensively restored after damage in the late Middle Ages.

From the fourteenth century onwards considerable building was carried out in the Gothic style. The chief city was *Prague* which, despite energetic later construction in the Baroque form, still possesses much of its Gothic heritage. Most of Czechoslovakia, and Prague in particular, was spared the devastation of the Second World War suffered by neighbouring countries. The great buildings of the country have, unfortunately, partially succumbed to a slower, more insidious destructive process; that of time and the decay wrought by lack of restoration when needed. Prague before 1939 was a beautiful city. Now, the signs of that beauty are still discernible but tend to be offset by the layers of crumbling stucco, stone or woodwork resulting from too many years of neglect. Specific buildings, notably those on Castle Hill, including the cathedral and palaces, are restored and in good repair. Elsewhere, the condition of many of the great monuments ranges from shabby to ruinous.

The *city of Prague* is built on both sides of the beautiful river Vltava. It is of ancient foundation though few Romanesque monuments survive (p. 65). Much of the great Gothic work is on the narrow hill ridge (**530**) on the north-west side of the river. Here on *Castle Hill*, the Hradčany, grouped around the courtyards, are the buildings of the castle-palace, the cathedral and S. George's Basilica (p. 65 and PLATE 72).

Outstanding, and the finest Gothic building in Czechoslovakia, is *S. Vitus' Cathedral*. It was designed and begun by *Matthias of Arras*, who

GOTHIC ARCHITECTURE IN CZECHOSLOVAKIA

528 Town Hall and houses in the Market Place, Tábor, fifteenth and sixteenth centuries
529 Convent Church, Market Place, Tábor, fifteenth century
530 View of Prague showing river Vltava, Charles Bridge, Castle Hill (Hradčany), with cathedral, castle, Church of All Saints and S. George's Basilica

529

528

530

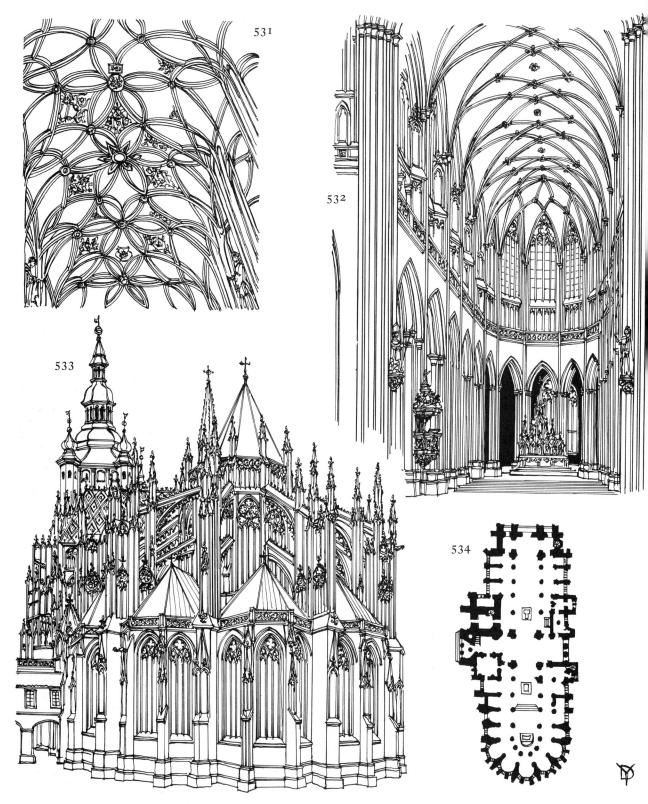

531

532

533

534

531 Vault, Church of S. Barbara, Kutnà Hora, fifteenth and sixteenth centuries
532 and 533 Interior and exterior of the choir, S. Vitus'

Cathedral, Prague, 1344–85. Lower part Matthias of Arras, upper part Peter Parler
534 Plan

GOTHIC IN CZECHOSLOVAKIA

535 *Façade, Church of S. Barbara, Kutná Hora, early sixteenth century*
536 *Façade, Tyn Church, Prague, 1365–1511*
537 *Vladislav Hall, Prague Castle, 1487–1500, Benedikt Rejt*

came to Prague in the 1340s from the court of the Popes in Avignon. As would be expected it is, therefore, on French Gothic pattern (**534**). The architect died in 1352 and his place was taken by *Peter Parler* from Cologne, who was invited to come from Schwäbisch-Gmünd to work on the cathedral. Parler brought with him the influence of the Cologne school and, though only the choir and chapels with part of the south façade were completed at this time, it is interesting to compare, both on exterior and interior, the work of Matthias on the lower part and Parler on the upper (**532** and **533**). Parler's influence can especially be seen in the vaulting, most particularly in the stellar designs of the Sacristy and Wenceslaus Chapel. The choir vault was completed in 1385 (**532**).

S. Vitus' Cathedral is cruciform and much in one style in the interior though the nave (the west end) is of nineteenth and twentieth century construction. There is a lofty crossing and short transepts. The interior vista is very fine, the vault throughout at one level with flanking, lower aisles. The vaulting shafts run up to the full height of the building. Both clerestory and triforium openings have glass. The east end is apsidal with ambulatory and chapels (**532** and **533**).

Peter Parler's work in Prague extended beyond the cathedral. From its commencement in 1357, he was in charge of the building of the *Charles Bridge*, which spans the Vltava and leads to Castle Hill (**530**); also of the entrance tower on the bridge (1376–8). It is a fine, Medieval bridge, guarded at each end and fortified as befitted its position as the sole river crossing and approach to the castle. It was of great length for its period, nearly 2000 feet from tower to tower. It was decorated by 30 sculptured figures on the parapet, created over the years from the fifteenth century onwards, but mainly of the eighteenth and nineteenth century date. Most of these are now being replaced as the soft sandstone from which they are carved has become seriously eroded.

Peter Parler was also responsible for the choir of *S. Bartholomew's Cathedral* at *Kolín* (1360–78), which is a fine example of his work. The Parler family was an architectural one, the members of which had a great deal of influence on Gothic architecture both in Czechoslovakia

and further afield to Vienna and Milan. The family architects included Peter's brother Michael and his sons Wenzel and Johann; indeed, work on Prague Cathedral was a family affair.

The *castle-palace* near the cathedral on the Hradčany in Prague has several Medieval interiors. Of these, the *Vladislav Hall* (**537**) begun in 1487, is of particular interest. The interiors here are of a later date and were designed or influenced by *Benedikt Rejt* and *Matthias Rejsek*. The vaulted ceilings of the palace interiors are unusual, as can be seen in the plaited swirls in the Vladislav Hall and in the Old Diet Chamber. Other interesting late Gothic buildings in Prague are the *Powder Tower* completed by Rejsek, the *Old Town Hall*, the restored *New Town Hall* in Charles Square, which is only a little later, and the *Týn Church*. This was built over a long period—both Peter Parler and Rejsek worked on it. Standing in Town Hall Square in the Old Town, it is fronted at the base by seventeenth and eighteenth century gabled houses, while behind is the Renaissance Týn Court with Doric loggia. The stone church is well proportioned and has a fine exterior which can be clearly viewed from the Old Town Hall tower opposite (**536**). Inside, it is a tall, aisled church without transepts, Medieval in structure but with Baroque decoration and furniture.

Outside Prague there are a number of outstanding later Gothic churches. One of these is *S. Jakob* (S. James in English) in *Brno*. The exterior is plain and undistinguished but with a tall, elegant tower. Inside, the hall church is very fine and in good condition. The stone nave piers are grouped columns which soar up to tiny capitals and then to the beautiful vault which springs from them (**538**).

In *Kutná Hora* there are several interesting churches of which the most notable is that of *S. Barbara*, which is large and imposing and in a fine state of repair. The west façade, which is the later part of the building, shows the complex flying buttress system on either side (**535**) which extends all round. Inside, the five-aisled church is immensely tall, its piers extending up to the complicated stellar and geometric ribbed vaults of nave and choir. The nave arcade has tall pointed arches above which is a gallery whose columns support aisle and nave vault (**531**). The choir has an ambulatory behind the lancet-

538 *Church of S. Jakob (James), Brno, Czechoslovakia, 1480–1500*

pointed arches of the arcade. The church is very light because of the large, decoratively traceried windows. It is a stone building, constructed over a long period and one of the richest Czech Gothic ecclesiastical structres. Also in Kutná Hora is the Medieval *Church of S. James*, which has a tall western tower and apsidal eastern termination. It is a hall church, simple and a good stone example. There are no capitals to the nave arcade which supports the quadripartite vault over naves and aisles. The eastern windows are obscured by a vast Baroque alterpiece.

At *Košice* (Kassa) the *Cathedral of S. Elizabeth* is a magnificent Gothic building of the fourteenth and fifteenth centuries. It was begun in 1380 but the tall tower was not built until after 1500. Some of the fine craftmanship was carried out by Viennese artists. Other notable examples include the *Church* at *Znojmo* and *S. Maurice* at *Olomouc*, though the latter has been much altered on the exterior; it has a hall church interior.

Secular remains of Gothic architecture in Czechoslovakia are fewer. The *town hall* at *Olomouc* dates from the late fourteenth century. Though it has been altered in later periods, it retains some Gothic features. *Znojmo*, which is a town listed as an ancient monument, needs a good deal of restoration but its *town hall* of 1445 still possesses its tall, elegant steeple. The *town hall* at *Brno*, on the other hand, which had a fine late Gothic pinnacled portico, is now rebuilt, showing only the decoration above the doorway.

Tábor retains its late Medieval aspect best in the market square and castle. The *market square* is attractive and homogeneous. There is a late Gothic *church* (**529**), which has a wide, short, dark interior on hall church pattern. The octagonal nave piers have no capitals and ascend to carry the reticulated nave vault above. The choir vault is of radiating, lierne design. Nearby are some gabled *houses* and the *town hall* (**528**). The latter is now much restored in nineteenth century Gothic style as a museum. The whole group of buildings in the square present a charming provincial ensemble. The town is still largely encircled by its fortified walls, at one point of which stands the *castle*, overlooking the river gorge.

The Baltic Region

Holland, Northern Germany, Poland and Northern U.S.S.R.

It is convenient to discuss the architecture of this area separately, although it cuts across the geographical frontiers of a number of present day countries. This immense stretch of Europe, extending over 1200 miles along the North Sea and Baltic coasts from Bruges in Belgium to Novgorod in the Soviet Union, displays a close unity of architectural style. There are two chief reasons for this: first, the control and wealth of the Hanseatic League, and second, the paucity of building materials which caused brick to be most commonly used for Gothic buildings. This is a limiting material for design purposes, so it was inevitable that a strong similarity of form should prevail.

The Hanseatic League* was originally a German federation, primarily concerned in trade, protection from piracy then rife in the northern seas and promoting successful commercial interchange as a result of close co-operation between towns and guilds. There was sometimes a political element in the League's activities, but this was subordinate to the commercial projects. Exact beginnings are not clearly known but by the mid-thirteenth century Lübeck and Hamburg in Germany were co-operating together and soon other German towns were joining: Lüneburg, Wismar, Stralsund, Soest and Dortmund. Utrecht in Holland became a centre, Bruges in Belgium, and even London was drawn in. Scandinavia co-operated, as did Danzig (Gdansk) and Novgorod. The corridor of land administered by the League extended as far south as Cracow, Göttingen and Cologne. Its power continued till the fifteenth century, after which it declined in face of competition from new trade routes opening up.

This wide coastal belt is a generally flat plain, only partially wooded, containing little building stone. Brick was the material developed and used almost universally for permanent buildings, timber for some other structures. This forced on builders a simple form of Gothic architecture. Brick is unsuitable for spires, finials, flying buttresses and carved ornament is impossible. Thus, walls, vaults, piers were all plain. Buildings were large and barn-like.

* *From* hansa, *an old high German word for company or guild.*

GOTHIC IN HOLLAND

539 *Church of S. Jan, Maastricht, c. 1450*
540 *Tower of Utrecht Cathedral, 1321–82*

541 *Steeple, Nieuwe Kerk, Delft, 1383–96*
542 *S. Peter's Church, Leyden, 1339–1426*

By the thirteenth century a need for decorative additions was felt. This was provided by polychrome or coloured brick surfacing. Black, yellow and white bricks were introduced to give a pattern, as were also small quantities of other materials. Ceramic polychrome was introduced and coloured tiling for roofs. Builders became expert in providing plastic forms in brick. Panelling was achieved on walls, giving blind recesses of differing shapes. Windows in the later period were very large and had ornate geometric or curvilinear tracery. Sometimes brick tracery was used, sometimes the small quantity of stone needed was found for important buildings.

Holland

Dutch Medieval work is very typical of the Baltic area, though it is generally plainer than that of neighbouring Germany. *Cathedrals* and *churches* tend to be large, with lofty nave, choir and transepts, but with few projections such as porches, portals or buttresses. *Utrecht* and *Haarlem Cathedrals* are of this type. Utrecht is in warm coloured brick, barn-like in general form but having very fine large traceried windows. Now the nave has gone, only choir and transepts with cloisters are left, separated, by a space where the nave stood, from the great fourteenth century tower. The latter was a prototype design for many other Dutch towns (**540**). Haarlem is a fifteenth century cathedral and very similar. It has a lantern tower over the crossing. The *Cathedral* of *S. Jan* at *'sHertogenbosch* is an exception to the usual plainness of Dutch Gothic design. Perhaps because it is situated not far from the Belgian border where stone is more readily available, it is a richly decorated late Gothic cathedral, definably Dutch in treatment but Belgian or French in design. It is a fifteenth century building with some sculpture dating from early in the sixteenth century. It has transepts and an enormous ornately decorated south porch, a central and western tower and forests of flying buttresses (**543**).

543 Cathedral of S. Jan, 's Hertogensbosch, Holland, 1419–1529

543

The *Oude Kerk* in *Amsterdam* and the *Nieuwe Kerk* in *Delft* (**541**) are typical of some of the fine Dutch steeples as is *S. Jan* in *Maastricht* (**539**). The steeples are often in a later style, partly Renaissance and reminding the onlooker of Wren's designs of the city churches of London. The Oude Kerk in the centre of Amsterdam was begun *c.* 1300 and is a large, many-gabled church with simple fenestration. Building continued till the later sixteenth century and the steeple is typical of this period. One of the greatest and most typical churches in Holland is that of *S. Peter* in *Leyden* (**542**). This has no tower. It is a large, spreading, brick church of the fourteenth and fifteenth centuries. Inside, the crossing piers are cut back and a wooden barrel vault extends across all four arms of the cross. The interior walls are also of plain brick with stone arches and columns and particularly fine late Gothic traceried windows. Large columns with foliated octagonal

capitals are used throughout the church, supporting an arcade of pointed arches which narrow round the choir ambulatory. This eastern termination is polygonal. There is a blind triforium and large clerestory windows above which brightly illuminate the whole church.

Equally typical is the simple and remote *Grote Kerk* at *Brouwershaven* in south-west Holland on the north coast of the Island of Schouwen-Duiveland. The fourteenth century choir is very fine, with its columns, capitals and pointed arches in similar style to S. Peter's in Leyden. Here also is the lancet-arched, blind triforium with geometric clerestory windows above, the whole roofed in wood (**544**).

Remains of a number of fortified buildings exist in Holland, also constructed in brick. The *Amsterdamsche Poort* at *Haarlem* is a fine town gateway (**546**) and the thirteenth century moated castle at *Muiden* is a picturesque solid structure (**547**).

544 Choir and ambulatory, Grotekerk, Brouwershaven, Island of Schouwen—Duiveland, Holland, early fourteenth century

544

MEDIEVAL CASTLES

545 *Bran Castle, near Braşov, Rumania, fourteenth*
century
546 *Amsterdamsche Poort. Town Cateway, Haarlem,*
Holland, 1488
547 *Muiden Castle, Holland, thirteenth century*
548 *Hunedoara Castle, Rumania, fifteenth century.*
Later restorations

Northern Germany

All along the coastal plain bordering the North Sea and the Baltic, stretching from the Dutch frontier to that of the U.S.S.R., the towns suffered years of bombardment from sea and air during the Second World War. The devastation of these Hanseatic towns, where the best of this type of Gothic architecture had survived remarkably well until 1939, extended up to 150 miles inland. Such towns, which had magnificent brick cathedrals, churches and civic structures, included Hanover, Hamburg and Lübeck in West Germany, Wismar, Prenzlau and Stralsund in East Germany and Szczecin (Stettin) and Gdansk (Danzig) in Poland.

Four great Gothic monuments survive in

Lübeck, though considerably restored and rebuilt: the Marienkirche, the Petrikirche, the Cathedral and the Holstentor. The *Marienkirche* (S. Mary's Church) is the finest of these and forms an architectural group with the *Town Hall*, round the market place. Built mainly in the thirteenth and fourteenth centuries, it is a typically German, brick, Hanseatic church. It is large, with tall, twin western towers and spires, nearly 400 feet high. The east end is polysided, with ambulatory, radiating chapels and flying buttresses. There are no transepts (**549**). Severely damaged, the church is now largely restored and in the interior, which is virtually complete, the work has been beautifully done. The building is lofty and light in its tall nave and choir, with the shafts of the ribbed vaults ascending unbroken between the high clerestory windows. The aisle vaults are lower, but are also ribbed and painted (**550**). The neighbouring town hall is also now rebuilt; it is part Gothic, part Renaissance (**549**).

The *Petrikirche* (S. Peter's Church) is restored on the exterior but inside the work is only partly advanced. It is a five-aisled hall church, entirely of brick and with a single, very tall western tower and spire. Inside, the vaulting is quadripartite throughout and all of one height. It is supported on octagonal ribbed piers with tiny foliated capitals. All round the church are tall, geometri-

549 *S. Mary's Church and part of the Town Hall in the Market Place, Lübeck, Germany. Viewed from the bell tower of S. Peter's Church*

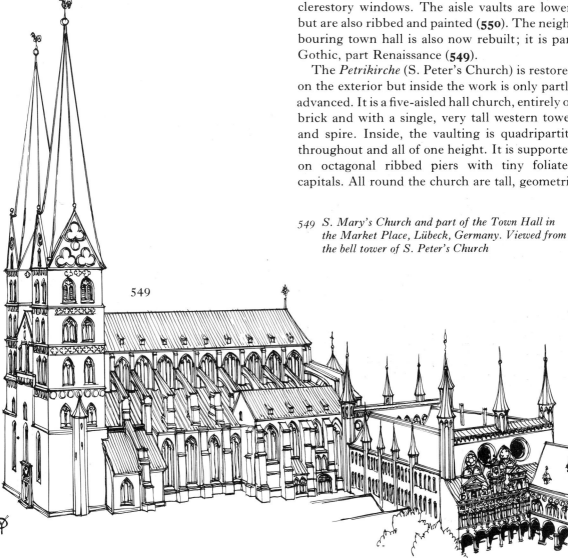

549

550

550 Interior, S. Mary's Church, Lübeck, Germany, 1251–1302

cally traceried windows. The *Holstentor*, which is still the town gateway though the walls have partly disappeared, is now fully restored. It is a fine example of Baltic patterned brickwork (**552**).

Lübeck Cathedral is an immense building which is still under restoration at the time of writing. Originally built in Romanesque style, a Gothic choir and aisles were added in the fourteenth century, making it into a hall church. It has tall, twin western towers and spires and a long

142

GOTHIC ARCHITECTURE IN NORTHERN GERMANY

551 *Hanover Town Hall, thirteenth century (left), Marktkirche, fourteenth century (right)*

552 *Holstentor, Lübeck, fifteenth century*

553 *Town Hall, Stralsund, late fourteenth century*

GOTHIC IN POLAND AND NORTHERN GERMANY

554 *Torun Town Hall, Poland, 1259. Enlarged 1343*
and 1602. Spire lost 1703
555 *S. Mary's Church, Stralsund, East Germany, late*
fourteenth century
556 *Church of Our Lady of the Sands, Wroclaw,*
Poland, fourteenth century

nave and choir. Inside, the west end, nave and crossing are now restored though the woodwork is all modern. The Romanesque nave is domical barrel-vaulted, in square compartments supported on great square piers, all in whitewashed brick. The aisles of the same height are in Gothic design. The east end, still partly unrestored, is apsidal, with ambulatory encircling the great, round, Romanesque brick piers.

In *East Germany*, the great churches such as S. Mary's Church in *Wismar*, S. Mary's Church at *Prenzlau* and the *Szczecin* churches were, by 1971, still roofless shells. *S. Mary's Church* in *Stralsund* was in fair condition but needed considerable repair. It is an immense brick church, dominating the town, with its octagonal tower and steeple and tall west façade, nave and choir (**555**). The beautiful, richly decorated brick façade of the *Town Hall*, adjoining the great Church of S. Nicholas, survived (**533**), though badly damaged. The gables are a façade in a literal sense, only sky being visible through the tracery.

The great West German city of *Hanover* was the target for countless raids in the Second World War. Not surprisingly little of its pre-war architecture survives, but the fine monumental group of the *Marktkirche* and the *Town Hall* (**551**) survived in shell form and both are now fully restored. The thirteenth century Town Hall is a great gabled rectangular building, panelled and decorated entirely in typical Hanseatic style brickwork. The Marktkirche was built in the fourteenth century, adjacent to the Town Hall. Also in brick, it has a tall, German-roofed western tower, a lofty nave and apsidal choir, but no transepts. The hall church interior is very fine. It is simple and monumental, its tall, round, brick columns, without capitals, supporting a simple quadripartite vault.

Poland

Over much of the country a fine Gothic heritage, largely in brick building, survived until 1939, but after 1945, all the major Polish towns, except Cracow, had been severely damaged or totally devastated. Progress towards rebuilding has been slow. The great Medieval buildings are now, one by one, being rehabilitated and these, where the work is completed, illustrate (as in Germany) a very high standard of workmanship, faithful to the Gothic traditions, spirit and design. Two of the cities which had the finest heritage, Gdansk (Danzig) and Wroclaw (Breslau), suffered the greatest destruction.

Gothic architecture was brought to Poland by the monastic orders, firstly the Cistercian, then the Dominicans and Franciscans. In general, Romanesque style work continued late and Gothic design was slow to develop. The majority of new churches and cathedrals were monastic settlements. Over much of the country brick was still the building material. Typical examples of the monastic churches include the *Dominican Monastery* of *S. Adalbert* in *Wroclaw* and the *Dominican Church* and *Franciscan Church* in *Cracow*. All these have suffered from rebuilding. The Wroclaw example was largely destroyed in the Second World War. The monastery has gone, but the church is now rebuilt. A large, brick building, it has a tall nave, choir and transepts and apsidal choir termination. Inside, it is simple and lofty, with a fine vault and traceried windows in the choir. The Dominican Church in Cracow has a Medieval Baltic, brick façade with decorative gable. Much of the church was rebuilt in the nineteenth century and both Cracow churches have lost some of their Medieval character.

The German pattern of *hall church* spread widely in Poland and there are still a number of large brick examples. One is the *Church of the Assumption* at *Chelmno*, entirely Gothic on the exterior but, inside, the Baroque features overpower the simplicity of the brick vaults and columns. Others include the *Church of S. John* in *Torun* and the *Collegiate Church of Our Lady* in *Poznan*. There are two fine examples in *Wroclaw*: the *Church of the Holy Cross* and the *Church of Our Lady of the Sands*. Both of these were badly damaged in the War. The former is of unusual design as it was built in two storeys (largely in the fourteenth century), one church above the other. It is therefore a tall but also slender building, all in brick, with a high, elegant south tower and spire. The interior is still in ruinous condition though the exterior is fairly intact. Both this church and the Church of Our Lady of the Sands (na Piasky) have *Piast vaults*.* These are unusual in design, being tripartite but divided into nine, panelled compartments. The Church

---

* *As do also a number of famous Polish Medieval churches, particularly in Wroclaw, Szczecin and Torun.*

557

558

559

557 *Castle of the Teutonic Knights, Malbork (Marienburg), c. 1400. From the river bridge*
558 *Gniezno Cathedral, mid-fourteenth century*

559 *S. Mary's Church, Cracow, fourteenth and fifteenth centuries, Baroque porch*

of Our Lady of the Sands was badly damaged but has been beautifully restored (**556**). It is a hall church, with soaring, ribbed nave piers. The nave and choir have the usual Gothic ribbed vault but in the aisles the Piast vaulting can be clearly studied. The choir is apsidal with very fine modern glass in the windows. The whole interior is in red brick, partly whitewashed.

Among the most outstanding Medieval ecclesiastical building in Poland are the Cathedrals of Wroclaw, Cracow and Gniezno and the two churches dedicated to S. Mary, one in Cracow and one in Gdansk. The *Cathedral* at *Wroclaw* was heavily damaged in 1945 but is now reconstructed, apart from the western spires. It is a brick building with a long nave which has simple, rectangular plan piers, without capitals, supporting a pointed arched arcade. There is a short, square-ended choir and almost no transepts. *Cracow Cathedral* was based on a similar design but, being later, is of more advanced Gothic form. Built on the site of two earlier Romanesque cathedrals, it is situated on the crown of Wawel Hill (p. 64). The dramatic, fourteenth century exterior shows to advantage on this site and, despite its Renaissance and Baroque towers and chapels, presents a homogeneous whole. The interior is less satisfactory; it is muddled and confused by a multiplicity of bric-à-brac in a variety of periods. The choir, with its carved wood stalls and Gothic vault is the most impressive part. *Gniezno Cathedral* is also built on the site of two earlier Romanesque ones (p. 64). It is mainly a fourteenth century building though its western towers are Baroque. A simple, monumental structure, it has no transepts, but an apsidal-ended choir with ambulatory and chapels round it; an unusually French design for Poland. The interior is plain. The large nave piers have simple capitals and above is a pointed arched arcade. There is no triforium. Both nave arcade and clerestory windows continue uninterrupted, but in narrowing form, round the choir apse.

The *Church of S. Mary* in *Gdansk* (Danzig) is the largest Gothic church in Poland. It was built in the later fifteenth century and was seriously damaged in 1944, but is now excellently restored. It has one large, tall tower and a number of turrets. Inside, it is a hall church, all of whitewashed brick. Octagonal piers divide the nave from aisles; these piers have no bases or capitals.

The nave arcade has tall, stilted arches. The rectangular vaulting bays are mostly star vaulted in many different designs. The tall aisle windows illuminate this beautiful stellar vaulting. The *Church of S. Mary* in *Cracow* is the town church, built in the market place in the fourteenth and fifteenth centuries but with the addition of a Renaissance cupola and a Baroque western porch. The church has lofty western towers, also a tall nave and choir. It is on basilican plan (**559**). The interior is dark due to the coloured glass in the narrow windows, the wealth of Baroque ornamentation and the deep colours of blues, reds, brown and gold with which vaults, walls and arcade are painted. Like most buildings in Cracow, the church escaped war damage, but badly needs cleaning and repair.

Many fortresses and *castles* were built in the Middle Ages in Poland. Struggles for power within the country and attacks from outside were violent and sustained. Earlier structures had central keeps surrounded by walls and moat. After the thirteenth century larger schemes were built of stone but, more often in the north, in brick. There are examples of large castles at Niedzica, Czersk and Mir (now in the U.S.S.R.), but one of the greatest was the vast complex built as the headquarters for the Teutonic Knights, on the river Norgat, an arm of the Vistula, 35 miles south of Gdansk. It was called Marienburg (now *Malbork*). One of the most powerful fortresses in Europe, it has many parts, built at different times. Still extant, and now repaired after war damage, are some impressive Gothic rooms like the *Grand Refectory* and *Capitular Chamber*, which have rows of columns supporting fine vaulted ceilings, and two immense *courtyards*, that of the Middle Castle and that of the High Castle. The latter has an upper gallery which goes round the whole court, providing impressive vistas through the traceried openings. The large church is still under repair. Especially notable is the approach view from the road bridge, where the vast pile can be seen rising from the banks of the great river. Even to twentieth century eyes it is a symbol of power (**557**).

In *Cracow*, sections of the city walls survive from Medieval building. The city had been walled and moated since the thirteenth century. It had a number of fortified gates, of which the barbican and *S. Florian's Gate* exist.

MEDIEVAL BUILDING IN THE U.S.S.R.

560 *Church of the Ascension at Kolomonskoe,*
near Moscow, stone, 1532
561 *Wooden Tower fortification from the*
White Sea, 1690. Now at Kolomonskoe
562 *The Kremlin, Rostov, seventeenth century*
563 *The Kremlin, Pskov. Showing buildings*
inside the fortified walls, sixteenth and
seventeenth centuries

There are a number of examples of civic Medieval building still in Poland. *Torun Town Hall* has retained most of its Gothic character. It was begun in 1259, though Renaissance gables and turrets were added in 1602. The tall spire was unfortunately lost in 1703 but the building remains a good example of a Medieval town hall (**554**). In *Cracow*, the tower of the fourteenth century *town hall* survives in the Market Place, while the richly decorated example at *Wroclaw* in the Rynek, the central square of the town, though altered later, is still in Gothic style; it has a tall tower and ornamental gables. The *Town Hall at Gdansk* has an exceptionally lofty tower and elegant lantern. The building is brick and dates from the fourteenth century, though with later fenestration and entrance doorway.

The *University of Cracow* was founded in 1364. The buildings were rebuilt from about 1500 in stone and brick and survived until 1837, when the architect K. Kremer was commissioned to enlarge and adapt the university, called the Cracow Academy. In recent years, further restoration has been carried out and, though the work is obviously of the nineteenth and twentieth century, a Medieval spirit has been retained. The courtyard behind S. Anne's Street and Jallegonska Street gives a good impression of how the small Medieval court would have looked.

Northern U.S.S.R.

There is very little Gothic architecture in the Soviet Union. The Byzantine style dominated important building, particularly in the ecclesiastical field, until the seventeenth century (see Volume 1, p. 140). There are some Byzantine buildings with Gothic fenestration and detail (**463** and **517**) and later, there are similar buildings with Renaissance features (Volume 3). But in the Baltic area, in *Lithuania, Latvia, Estonia* and right round to the coastal strip of the White Sea, there are brick and timber buildings which have much in common with those found in the Baltic region of eastern Germany and Poland. The example illustrated in Fig. **561** is a purely timber log structure of the type built all over eastern Europe till long after the Middle Ages. Whole logs are used in such heavily wooded areas, not just timber planks as in western Europe where wood was less plentiful.

This structure, from the White Sea area, is similar to some churches in the Carpathian mountains in Rumania (**643**). Fig. **563** illustrates a brick and timber construction. It is a Kremlin, that is, the fortified citadel of the town. Here shown are the defensive walls and towers and, inside, the Byzantine style churches.

Two towns on the Baltic coast where some good Medieval buildings survive are Riga in Latvia and, further east, Tallinn in Estonia.

564 City Hall, Tallin, Estonia, U.S.S.R., fourteenth century, brick with tiled roof

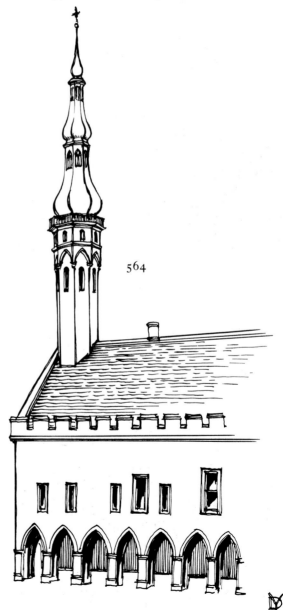

564

In *Riga* are some stepped gable façades in brick with pointed and round arched windows together and a deeply recessed pointed arched doorway below. In *Tallinn* there is a fourteenth century town hall of brick with battlemented parapet and steeply pitched roof above. Although typical of the Hanseatic area, the pointed arch ground arcade and the tall, elegant tower are reminiscent of Italian Medieval town halls (**564**). Here also are some fine Medieval façades with tall pointed gables, decoratively recessed in brick and with two rows of windows above the street arcade. These date from the fifteenth century. Nearby is a solid, fortified fourteenth century Knight's Castle, built on a mound. It is similar to Castilian examples in the strength and solidity of its exterior brick walls and towers.

There are some churches in the area; some are of hall church pattern, others have an English influence from commercial contacts with seafaring traders.

Scandinavia

In the Middle Ages architectural development was not in accordance with the existing geographical boundaries of the four countries; it was determined by climate, distance from the main European influence, terrain and available materials. In the south, that is Denmark and southern Sweden, the influence was from the Baltic: Holland, northern Germany and Poland. This was the most prosperous area with the best climate, richest land and closest proximity to European influence. The style was, therefore, chiefly in brick building with decorative brickwork on gables, fenestration and doorways, though a limited French and Belgian influence existed. In Norway, in the west, the land was poorer, the terrain mountainous and difficult of access, the climate inhospitable. Here the building was chiefly of wood, retaining the national craft styles already established. The few stone buildings showed English and Scottish influence above all. In the east, in northern Sweden and in Finland, building was in brick, stone or timber; the two former in larger centres, the latter in the villages.

There is, however, apart from these regional differences, a similarity about most Scandinavian Medieval architecture. It never reaches the heights of drama, of aesthetic beauty, of religious experience that is felt and seen in the contemporary cathedrals and churches of France, Germany and England. There is a poverty of architectural splendour which reflects the poorer regions in which these churches were built. But the question is not only one of poverty but of social and natural development. In the chief centres of Europe in the Middle Ages the cities, the universities and the monasteries were being established. Christianity was the moving, living force of life. From vitality of faith sprang the great cathedrals of France and England. In Scandinavia, at this time, development was slower, the cities poorer and smaller, universities late to appear and the prime force in life was commercial, seen chiefly in dependence on the Hanseatic League.

The great cathedrals and churches are therefore only copies from those in the main centres of civilisation. Technically the buildings are as good as some of those in central and western Europe, but the Medieval spirit is missing. In architectural terms this is evidenced in the smaller, narrower windows, lack of intricate tracery or coloured glass, the almost total lack of development of the flying buttress system, the poverty of decoration in sculpture and carving. There are exceptions but these are few. Because of the inadequate fenestration later Gothic buildings, in particular, are dark inside compared to their equivalents elsewhere. In view of the northern latitudes, the windows should, logically, have been larger, not smaller.

Denmark

Here, as elsewhere in Scandinavia, the chief buildings to survive are ecclesiastical; some are based on the French or English pattern but most are of Baltic design, in brick, with decorative gables and on hall church pattern. Denmark has three important *cathedrals*: Roskilde, Odense, Aarhus. *Roskilde* was an important town in the Middle Ages, a royal residence, and the cathedral was used as the burial place for the Danish kings. The present structure was built from 1190 in brick, though its slender, western spires were seventeenth century additions. This is the least Hanseatic of Danish cathedrals. It clearly shows a French influence in its triple-aisled plan, while

GOTHIC BUILDINGS IN BRICK IN DENMARK

565 *Aarhus Cathedral from the south west, mainly thirteenth and fourteenth centuries*
566 *Løgumkloster Abbey Church, west front, c. 1300–50*
567 *S. Mary's Church, Helsingør, fifteenth century*
568 *Odense Cathedral, c. 1290– fifteenth century*

the choir resembles that of Tournai Cathedral in Belgium.

The *Cathedral of S. Knud* (Canute) at *Odense* is one of Denmark's finest Medieval buildings. Re-built in Gothic style from 1247 in brick, it is large, simple and spacious. The exterior, with its tall, single, western tower and spire is dignified and solemn (**568**). *Aarhus Cathedral* is even larger, also with a lofty western steeple. This brick building replaces a stone Romanesque cathedral and dates from the thirteenth century onwards (**565**). Inside, the nave and choir are also lofty, the brick walls and ribbed vaults whitewashed with painted decoration on the vaulting. Though sometimes described as a hall church, it is not one. The choir is of hall pattern, with aisles of the same height as the central area, but the tall transepts are aisleless and the nave aisles are barely half the height of the nave itself.

Decorative brickwork is seen more on smaller churches and abbeys. Developed from the Romanesque craft, it has much in common with Dutch, northern German and Polish examples. Blind openings, window surrounds and especially gables are decorated with arcading, saw-tooth courses and herring-bone brickwork. The mullions of traceried windows are also in brick.

After the Reformation the *monasteries* were largely destroyed or fell into ruin. As in England, a number of abbey churches have survived and remained in use, while the abbey buildings have disappeared. A fine example of this type of *abbey church* is that at *Løgumkloster*, founded in 1173 by the Cistercian Order. The eastern part of the church was rebuilt from *c.* 1200, in Romanesque style, but the later western end is in early Gothic with tall lancet windows and stepped gabling (**566**). The fine brickwork has simple mouldings and decoration. The church is cruciform, in three stages, nave arcade, blind triforium and clerestory, showing an English influence. Inside, the lofty crossing is on square plan, a wide pointed arch on each side supported on ribbed brick piers. The night stairs to the cloister remain in the transept. *S. Mary's Church* at *Helsingør* survives from the Carmelite Convent. This has a Baltic style decorated brick, stepped gable façade (**567**).

The simple *Church* at *Bogense* is a typical example of gable decorative brickwork on a less ambitious level. It has two projecting gables with stepped and panelled decoration. The church dates from 1406; it has an unpretentious, whitewashed interior.

Norway

The mountain barrier between Norway and Sweden was so impassable in the Middle Ages that the easier exit from the country to the outside world was by sea, and the nearest important neighbour was the British Isles. This influence is shown especially in the larger stone churches in Norway. The square rather than apsidal eastern arm is usual and the style of vaulting and proportions of vault, tower and spire are English. *Stavanger Cathedral* (p. 70) was built in Romanesque design, but its fine choir is late Gothic.

The chief monument to the Gothic style in Norway is *Trondheim Cathedral* (a town which, in the Middle Ages, was called Nidaros). The cathedral was built between 1130 and 1290 but, due to several fires and other hazards, suffered damage and was extensively restored and rebuilt in the nineteenth and twentieth centuries. It is still an imposing structure and Medieval in concept (**571**). The central and western towers are heavy and solemn and the façade, though finely sculptured, is of recent restoration. It is a large cathedral and its interior retains a Medieval sense of spirituality. The choir is encircled by a stone screen with an ambulatory behind. The choir arcade piers are grouped with large carved foliated capitals. Over the crossing is a lantern, supported on lofty grouped piers with small, foliated capitals. The transepts are Romanesque and contain fine, round-arched arcading on the walls of triforium and clerestory. The arches are decorated with chevron ornament. The nave is of later style, loftier, and with grouped, shafted piers and moulded capitals. The triforium reminds one of the Angel Choir at Lincoln Cathedral in England. The clerestory has a passage also, in front of the Decorated Gothic windows. The façade rose window is very fine, in flamboyant style like that at Reims Cathedral in France (**570**). In general, the cathedral is dark but impressive inside. It is much the most imposing in Scandinavia. It is of typically northern design and finish, very much after the manner of buildings in northern England and Scotland.

Among the other Medieval, stone buildings

GOTHIC ARCHITECTURE IN NORWAY

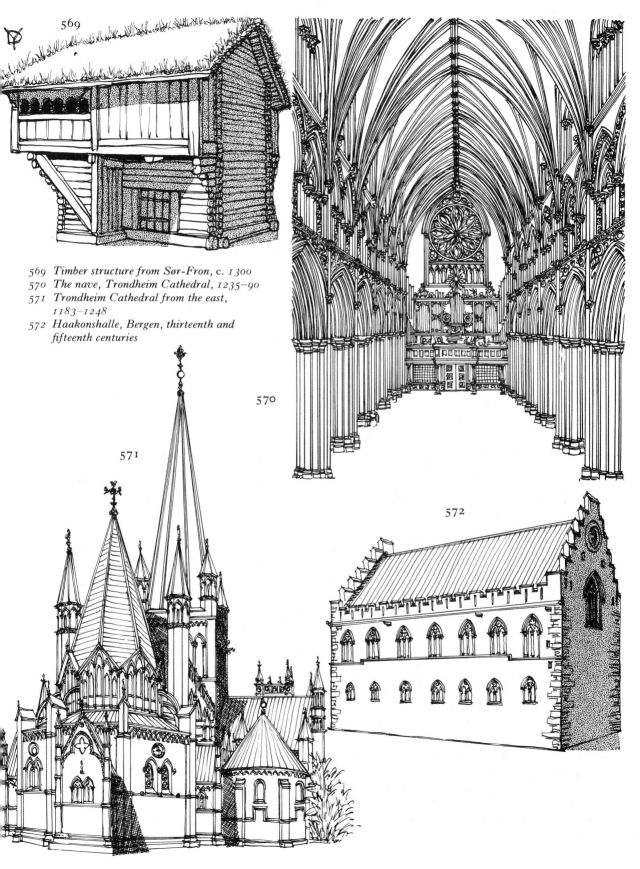

569 Timber structure from Sør-Fron, c. 1300
570 The nave, Trondheim Cathedral, 1235–90
571 Trondheim Cathedral from the east,
    1183–1248
572 Haakonshalle, Bergen, thirteenth and
    fifteenth centuries

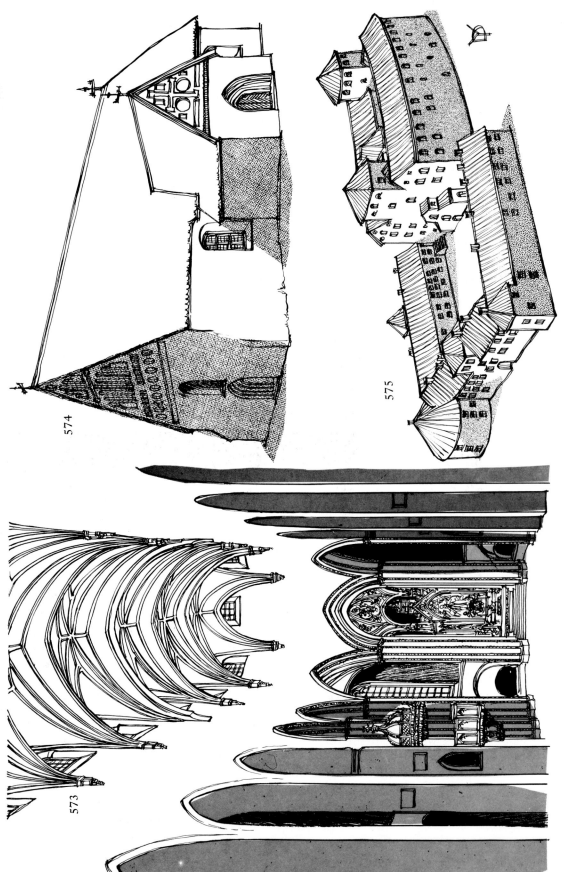

573 Turku Cathedral. The choir, thirteenth and fourteenth centuries
574 Pernå Church (Pernaja), late fourteenth century
575 Turku Castle, late thirteenth century (restored)

in Norway are the Archbishop's Palace at Trondheim and the Haakonshalle at Bergen. The *Trondheim episcopal palace* adjoins the cathedral and dates from the twelfth century. Like the Kaiserpfalz in Goslar, it is a Medieval palace in two storeys, with nearby gatehouse. The *Haakonshalle* in *Bergen* is part of the Bergenhus fortress group of buildings (**572**). The lower floor is early Gothic in style, with deep set windows and a groined vaulted roof. Above is the larger, later Medieval hall with plate traceried, deep-set windows along one side and larger windows at each end. At one end is the minstrels' gallery and, at the other, the daïs with high table and sedilia. The whole interior has been extensively restored.

Most of the building in Norway was still in *timber*. Structures were built of logs, the ends cut and dovetailed. Moss and cloth were laid between the logs to make the walls air and watertight. The standard of craftsmanship was good and many such structures have now been reerected in the Oslo Folk Museum at Bygdøy Park on an island near the city (**569**).

Finland

In the Middle Ages, Finland was a land on the north-eastern fringe of Europe to which architectural styles percolated slowly, and had then to be adjusted to suit national and climatic needs. Only the south-western, chiefly coastal part of what is now modern Finland was inhabited. Despite the distance from the centres of European culture, the inhospitable climate and the small population of barely a quarter of a million, Finland possesses, apart from one Medieval cathedral, a number of large churches. Those which survive are of stone and brick. The majority had been of wood and most of these were lost through fire.

Christianity was introduced to Finland via Sweden and the Åland Islands. The capital was Turku (in Swedish Åbo), on the coast in the south-west corner of the country. *Turku Cathedral* survives, though greatly restored and rebuilt, having been damaged and battered in its long history. It is of red brick and simple in style, with a massive western tower on square plan, now surmounted by a nineteenth century lantern. The cathedral was begun in the early thirteenth century and building continued till after 1300, while a later choir and chapels were added as late as 1520. Inside, there is a tall nave and choir on classic three-aisled pattern, with lofty vault, many times restored. Despite so much rebuilding, Turku Cathedral, like that at Trondheim, retains its Medieval character as well as a national one. It has a fine site, near the river and surrounded by trees. The interior is very simple, in brick, with square piers and no capitals in the nave and octagonal piers with small capitals in the choir. The vault stretches uninterruptedly along the whole length of the cathedral (**573**).

There are a number of surviving *churches* around Turku and along the coastal area eastwards towards the Soviet border. These mainly have an easily recognisable national character. They are fairly large hall churches on three-aisled plan. Vaults have generally replaced the original timber roofs in the later Middle Ages and most churches have a detached, later campanile. The buildings are generally of stone, with brick used for the decoration of the gables, window and doorway surrounds and interior piers and vaults. Many examples still have paintings over much of the vault and wall surface area and attractive, though rural, carved wood church furniture, especially pulpits.

Among the best examples with elaborate brick gable ornamentation and fine interior paintings and carvings are *Hollola Church, Porvoo Cathedral* and *Pernå* (Pernaja) *Church*. Hollola is a fine country church with decorative gables and detached, classical bell tower added in 1848. Inside, it is a hall church on a two-aisled, rectangular plan with a central row of square, brick pillars supporting the deep, pointed arched, ribbed and star vault. There is some good woodcarving and ironwork also (**576**).

Porvoo Cathedral was built c. 1415 and stands on high ground on the outskirts of the town. The exterior is like a larger version of Hollola Church and it also has a separate campanile and richly decorative brick gabling. The interior is more elaborate, but has also been more altered in later ages. *Pernå Church*, nearby, is much like Hollola on the exterior (**574**); this simple pattern of three-aisled, rectangular, hall church is more attractive and appropriate in the smaller country buildings than on the cathedral scale of Porvoo.

There are some beautiful vault and wall paintings inside Pernå Church and some outstanding instances of this work in the two small churches of Lohja and Hattula. The *Church of S. Lawrence* at *Lohja* (between Helsinki and Turku) has a large, simple, stone exterior with brick gable ornamentation. Inside, it is decorated all over walls and vault with biblical scenes, the figure groups and panels separated by arabesque banding. It was built in the fifteenth century and the paintings date from *c.* 1520; it is a very fine

example indeed. *Hattula Church* is very small. Standing in fields on the outskirts of the hamlet of Hattula, near Hämeenlinna, the exterior is unpretentious and rural. Inside, it is on three-aisled, rectangular plan with Medieval vaulting and walls painted all over in figure compositions. There is also a carved and painted wood pulpit with high relief figure decoration. The whole interior is of primitive, peasant standard and style, its colour and drawing charmingly handled;

576 Hollola Church, Finland, c. 1480

a superb example of the period. Another remote country *church*, near the sea and not far from Turku is that of *Inkoo*. It has a separate, wooden bell tower standing on a stone base, and decorative brick gabling. Inside, the two-aisled, hall church is vaulted and covered by paintings, but these are not so fine as those at Lohja and Hattula.

Many *castles* were built in Finland in the Middle Ages, for defensive purposes. Most of these have largely disappeared and the two chief examples surviving are those at Turku and Savonlinna. *Turku Castle* was built in the thirteenth century in a strategic position on the harbour. It was enlarged in the later Middle Ages and, in the sixteenth century, state rooms were incorporated. It is a large castle, strongly fortified and with small window openings high up on the massive walls. The interior has been excellently restored after damage caused in the Second World War, though it has been done in a modern, simplified manner. The exterior still retains its Medieval appearance. The drawing in Fig. **575** incorporates its existing state with that of the original structure as shown in the model in the castle.

The most complete Finnish castle is the *fortress* of *Olavinlinna*. It was built as a defence against the Russians, on whose border it still stands. It occupies a small rocky island in the Kyrönsalmi Strait, which is swept by rapid currents; the town of Savonlinna grew up around it between the two lakes. The castle is named after S. Olav and was built in 1475 by Erik Axelsson Tott. It has a strategic and romantic site and was, in its day, a modern fortress built on mural, concentric plan rather than the old central keep system. It was extensively restored in the nineteenth century; the courtyards are now used for staging dramatic spectacles.

Sweden

From the fourteenth century onwards the Church grew richer and more influential. The great cultural influence came from the monastic settlements, where the Cistercian Order was most active. After the Reformation these buildings fell into decay but, as in England, some of the churches were retained and enlarged as parish or cathedral churches. They were nearly all altered in the seventeenth and eighteenth centuries, then restored to their Medieval appearance in the nineteenth or twentieth.

Among such examples are the abbey churches at Varnhem and Vadstena, S. Mary's Church at Sigtuna and the Riddarholm Church in Stockholm. *Varnhem Abbey Church* in Västergötland was of the Cistercian Order. It was rebuilt after a fire in the thirteenth century, altered and restored in contemporary style in the seventeenth, but returned to its former state in the 1920s. It is a simple, cruciform stone church with tall western, fortified towers. The interior is monumental and most interesting. It is broad and low with wide, pointed, quadripartite stone vaulting, the vaults being supported on columned corbels with foliated capitals. The nave piers are plain and square, without capitals. The nave arcade is round-arched, simple and unmoulded. There is no triforium, but above are round-headed clerestory windows. The apsidal east end with ambulatory is the best preserved part of the original church.

The Cistercian *Abbey Church* at *Vadstena* on Lake Vättern was founded by S. Bridget and the church begun about 1368. The building has been carefully restored and in the process has lost its Medieval atmosphere, but it still retains a remarkable vault, supported on rows of octagonal piers, which covers the whole hall church interior. The seated statue of S. Bridget (c. 1440) survives and is displayed in the church with other sculptural fragments.

S. Mary's Church at *Sigtuna* is typical of the Scandinavian brick church design, based on Baltic influences from northern Germany and Holland. Such buildings are often large; they are wide and low, rarely having towers, except when of cathedral status. S. Mary's Church was part of the Dominican monastery. It is a hall church with typical Baltic decorated gabled façade in ornamental brickwork. Inside, the church has three aisles separated by brick piers without capitals. Above is a wide, pointed arched, quadripartite vault. It is a simple church, well built and very Nordic. Similar are the *Convent Church* at *Ystad* on the southern coast of Sweden and the *Church of the Holy Trinity* at *Uppsala*. The Ystad church has a particularly fine Baltic brick, gabled façade (**577**), while Holy Trinity Church is more interesting inside. The simple nave arcade is of moulded brick in wide pointed arches. The quadripartite vault is higher than usual (this is not a hall church) and both nave and aisle vaults are painted.

There are one or two *cathedrals* on a similar but slightly larger, more ambitious scale; *Västerås* and Strängnäs, both on Lake Mälar, are two of these. *Strängnäs Cathedral* has a large square western tower, though its apsidal east end presents the finest exterior view of the building. It is a simple structure, a larger version of the churches just described, but it is impressive and well proportioned. Inside all is brick, piers, columns and quadripartite vaults. It is a five-aisled church, not of hall type, with a wide, lofty nave and ribbed vault. The aisle vaults diminish in height towards the outer walls. Because of this and the consequently small aisle windows which provide the limited nave lighting, the interior is darker than is usual in churches of the kind. The tall apse windows give better illumination to the east end.

In *Stockholm*, the *Riddarholm Church* survives from the Franciscan Abbey, founded in the thirteenth century. Originally it had no towers and was aisleless, but extensive additions in the fifteenth and sixteenth centuries made it into a three-aisled church with a tall tower. It became an important building as the burial place for the

kings of Sweden. Despite later additions of classical chapels and high altar, the Riddarholm Church retains a strong Medieval atmosphere with its wide, low, quadripartite vault and fine, arched nave arcade. Also in the city is the *Storkyrkan*, the church of S. Nicholas, founded in the early thirteenth century and rebuilt about 1306. It has been substantially altered in later periods and has a largely classical, dull exterior. Inside, though, remains a fine lierne vault over the main nave and choir while, in one of the aisles, is a magnificent example of Medieval sculpture, S. George and the Dragon (1489), carved in wood. Painted and over life-size, this is a vivid composition by the Lübeck sculptor, *Bernt Notke* (PLATE 65).

An important centre in the Middle Ages was the *Island of Gotland*, regained by Sweden at this time from control by the Hanseatic League. Its strategic value lay in its situation, ideal for commercial use of the trade routes to England and France in the west and Russia and Europe to the east. Its capital was Visby and both here and in other centres, architectural proof of its Medieval importance lies in the richness and quality of its Gothic buildings, constructed in local stone. After the Middle Ages, trade routes changed and the island lost is importance. Many of the churches are, unfortunately, largely ruined.

577 Convent Church, Ystad, Sweden, façade, fourteenth century

577

GOTHIC IN SWEDEN

578 *Uppsala Cathedral, interior looking east, 1270–1315*
579 *Skara Cathedral from the south-west, c. 1300*
580 *Kalmar Castle, late Gothic*

578

579

580

As in Finland, in country areas, Sweden retains some small but beautifully *painted churches*. That at Södra Rådå has already been referred to (p. 70). There is also an example in good condition at *Härkeberga*, a tiny village southwest of Uppsala. The exterior is very simple and unpretentious, but the interior is painted all over: piers, vaults and walls. The colours are soft, mainly browns and greens, on a gold and white ground. The subject is the Bible story.

In a purely Gothic and less Scandinavian manner, are the important *cathedrals* of Sweden: Uppsala, Skara and Linköping. Here is seen less of the Baltic brick approach and more a derivation of French and English design. *Uppsala* is the finest, despite a hard and heavy restorative hand by the nineteenth century

contemporary of Viollet-le-Duc, Helgo Zettervall. Though begun in *c.* 1270 on an English plan, the cathedral soon developed on French lines under the Frenchman Étienne de Bonneuil. It is very much a cathedral of one building operation and retains a Medieval impression despite the mechanical quality of its restoration. On the exterior it is tall, its two western towers and spires reaching high into the sky. The apsidal east end, with attendant chapels, is very French, as is the flèche over the crossing. Inside, it is impressive and lofty. Its height, its vault and fine proportions remind one of Bourges Cathedral as does the detail of the clustered columns and dainty capitals (**578**).

Skara Cathedral in Västergötland (**579**) is more English than French. Here is a stone, tall,

581 Interior looking east of Linköping Cathedral, Sweden, 1260–1412

581

well-proportioned cathedral, with western towers and spires, built on classic Latin cross plan. Inside, the tall nave is divided by piers with clustered shafts and foliated capitals. The shafts extend to the vault springing. There is an arcaded triforium below small clerestory windows. The vaulting is ribbed throughout, lofty and well-proportioned. The east end is rich in its coloured glass. The exterior of *Linköping Cathedral* is unimpressive. Inside, the hall church pattern is paramount and magnificent in its proportions and in the elegance and chiaroscuro of its vault (**581**). It is the least restored Gothic cathedral in Sweden, especially in its east end where the choir ambulatory, its star and lierne vaults on supporting pillars and the traceried windows are of great quality and beauty.

The majority of Medieval remains in Sweden are ecclesiastical. Most domestic building was in wood and has perished, but some of the great mural fortresses survive. Of these *Kalmar Castle* (**580**) presents a dramatic, fortified silhouette, picturesquely situated on a promontory on the eastern sea coast. It has a moat, drawbridge and surrounding ramparts with four corner towers. Originally it had gates and walls further out to sea. *Gripsholm Castle* is built on the edge of Lake Mälar, not far from Strängnäs. It is large and also picturesquely sited in a park. Built in 1537 of brick, it has immense circular mural towers and massive, impregnable walls. It is now used as a school.

Europe South of the Alps, Pyrenees and Carpathians:

Italy, Yugoslavia, Rhodes, Spain, Portugal

Climatic influence has produced specific features common to all Gothic architecture in the southern part of Europe. Unlike the Baltic zone, however, the similarities are far outweighed by the differences. The Gothic style in Italy developed hesitantly and was short-lived because of the country's overwhelming classical tradition. In Spain, on the other hand, development was late but, having arrived, became deep-seated, and slow to be altered in favour of Renaissance forms which were as alien to Spain as Gothic was to Italy. The other countries under discussion in this section were influenced by either Italy or Spain.

The sunny, warm climate of the Mediterranean countries made certain features desirable whatever their interpretation of Gothic architecture. These features are mostly to be seen in central and southern Italy, the Dalmatian coast and central and southern Spain. Colour is used far more than in northern Europe; in marbles, mosaics, and frescoes on the outside as well as the inside of buildings. Window and door openings are smaller to keep the interior cool. The horizontal emphasis is greater than the vertical and, in these countries, it is only in the northern, cooler regions that tall steeples, flying buttresses, traceried large windows and rich, carved decoration in finials and crockets are to be seen. Roof pitches are lower and timber coverings were often preferred to stone vaulting.

Italy

The climate apart, the circumstance which made Italian Gothic architecture different from that in France, Germany or England was the classical tradition. It is sometimes said that there is no Gothic architecture in Italy or that the Italians have never understood the fundamentals of the style. Neither of these statements is true for they exaggerate the reality. Typically Italian Medieval work was still based on Roman or Romanesque designs, examples of both of which existed in quantity all over the country.

The exception is in the north and in monastic structures. The outstanding example is *Milan Cathedral*, as near northern Gothic as the Italians ever reached. Sheathed in white marble (over a brick structure), pinnacled and sculptured, the cathedral has some of the finest stained glass in Europe in its eastern windows. Like Cologne, Milan Cathedral is only really Medieval in its eastern part. Begun here in 1385, the west façade was not completed till the nineteenth century. The majestic polygonal eastern apse is the finest part of the building (**582**). There is a vast quantity of decorative sculpture, carved in white marble and carried out between the fourteenth and nineteenth centuries. Statues and gargoyles on turrets and pinnacles are all over the building, up to the topmost finial. Sculptors came from Italy, France and Germany to carry out this work, but the bulk of the structural and architectural achievement was due to German workers.

ITALIAN GOTHIC CATHEDRALS

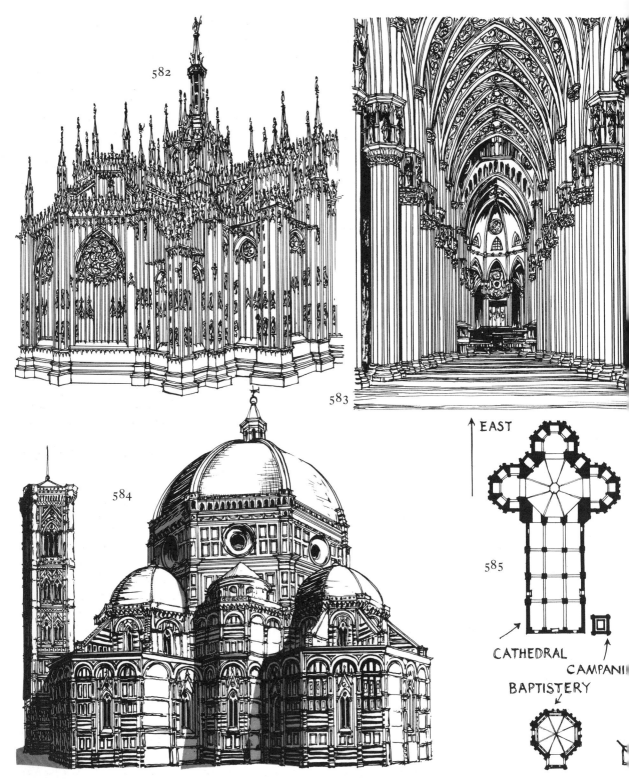

582 *Milan Cathedral from the east, 1387–1410.*
Spire 1750
583 *Milan Cathedral interior, fifteenth century nave*
and choir

584 *Florence Cathedral (Santa Maria del Fiore) from*
the east, 1296–1421. Dome, 1420–37
585 *Florence Cathedral, plan*

EAST

CATHEDRAL

CAMPANI

BAPTISTERY

The cathedral interior (**583**) is lofty and austere in contrast. The nave, especially, is not richly decorated. An unusual ornamental feature is in the niches containing standing, sculptured figures, set above the capitals and below the vault springing. Despite its pinnacles, buttresses and vaults, even Milan Cathedral lacks the northern Gothic verticality; the emphasis is on the horizontal and the design is geometrically based—a fundamental Italian approach.

Some of the abbey churches belonging to the monastic orders follow a traditional Gothic pattern. One is the *Cistercian Abbey* at *Fossanova* in thirteenth century Burgundian style. A more famous example is the early Franciscan double church of *S. Francesco* in *Assisi*. This has a plain traditional Gothic exterior, but inside are mosaic and fresco decoration.

The Italians in general retained the basilican plan to their cathedrals and churches. They built a tall nave arcade and clerestory, but rarely a triforium. They retained the timber roof where possible; if a vault was used, they kept to a square bay compartment over nave and choir. They used brick faced with marbles. Sculpture was more often in relief than in the round. These features, it will be realised, were all Roman or Romanesque practice. The concession to the needs of Gothic design was in the partial use of the pointed arch, the tall campanile and the screen west façade. The screen was indeed, in literal terms, only a façade. Behind its great gable, which masked the aisle roofs, was a church whose construction and interior bore little relationship to its façade. The west wheel window was the chief connecting link between exterior and interior.

Most surviving Medieval work is north of Rome. The Eternal City lay neglected, its Popes in exile in France, while in the south, the long Sicilo-Norman rule and culture gave place to Angevin, centred on Naples not Palermo; Lombard work was still very Romanesque, strongly influenced by its long, powerful tradition. The best Medieval architecture is in Tuscany, south towards Rome and, of completely different derivation, in the expanding empire of Venice. Characteristic are the pointed arch (side by side with the round one), vivid decoration in marble, mosaic and paint, carved white marble tracery and relief sculpture. Ornament and detail were primarily classical; even capitals were Corinthian

more than Gothic, while incorporating Medieval figures and animals. Windows never reached the vast size of northern European ones. The deeply recessed, sculptured portals of France had no counterpart in Italy. Here, the portals were shallower and decorated more by mosaic tympana, relief, bronze door panels and marble sculpture at the sides. The timber nave roofs and lower side aisle vaults needed less abutment and fewer pinnacles. Towers were still separate and a cupola generally covered the crossing.

The finest *cathedrals* are those of *Florence, Siena* and *Orvieto*, all typifying this Tuscan approach. At Florence (**584** and **585**) the original pattern has been altered by later work, the Renaissance dome and the nineteenth century façade. Much of the east end, the plan and parts of the interior are Medieval and the work was in fact begun by Arnolfo di Cambio in 1296. On the exterior, the marble inlay and veneer creates an essentially classical feeling imposed on Gothic apsidal form, while the campanile, designed by Giotto and built 1334–87, is a unique composition in marbled harmony with the group.

Siena cathedral is the most outstanding, clad all over, exterior and interior, in black and white stripes of marble. It is carved richly with white marble and further ornamented with coloured mosaic, bronze sculpture and, on floor and ceiling, marble veneer; it is a glowing, gleaming masterpiece (**588**). The building displays a tremendous sense of space and light inside (**587**). The sculptured pulpit by Nicola and Giovanni Pisano (father and son) stands out even among so much beautiful workmanship (PLATE 68). They were also responsible for much of the façade.

The hill city of *Orvieto* rises abruptly out of a flat plain and its cathedral is sited on top; a glorious colourful building, reminding the visitor of the days of the city's greatness. The three gable façade dominates the piazza in a riot of colour, gilt bronze sculpture and white marble. It is two-dimensional constructively and decoratively. The rest of the exterior is in plain black and white striped marble (**586** and **487**). Inside, the cathedral is simple, spacious and impressive. It is more cohesive than Siena. The magnificent west, rose window is dominant and sheds a golden glow over the whole interior in the evening light.

In contrast is the *Cathedral of Palermo*. Begun in 1185 under Norman Romanesque auspices,

ITALIAN GOTHIC CATHEDRALS

586 *Orvieto Cathedral
from the west, 1290–1600
(façade restored nine-
teenth century)*
587 *Siena Cathedral
interior looking west*
588 *Siena Cathedral,
exterior from the west,
1245–1380*

589

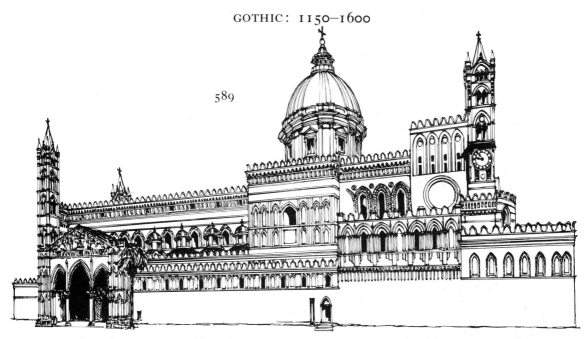

589 Palermo Cathedral, Sicily from the south-east, 1170–85. Porch, 1480 ; cupola, eighteenth century

it was continued till after the end of the four-teenth century. The south façade (**589**) is the prime example of Sicilo-Norman style, richly arcaded and crested. Especially beautiful is the open porch, built *c.* 1480, with its Saracenic style arches and decoration. The west end is more Saracenic in character. It is connected across the street to the Archbishop's Palace. There are two slender minaret towers balancing those at the east end. The interior was rebuilt in 1780 in Baroque style, when the cupola also was added.

Italian Gothic churches are less interesting and many have been altered later. In the Tuscan carved marble, coloured mosaic tradition is the beautiful little *S. Maria della Spina* at *Pisa* (1230–1323). Much plainer brick churches with only marble decoration and facings are the thirteenth century *SS. Giovanni* and *Paolo* and *S. Maria Gloriosa dei Frari* in *Venice*. In *Florence* are *S. Maria Novella*, to which Alberti gave a new façade in 1460 (Vol. 3, p. 5) and *S. Croce*, also both of the thirteenth century. Of interest are the hall churches of Perugia and Todi. The *Cathedral of Perugia* is typical of the hall church pattern, wide and high inside, with nave and aisles of equal height. The interior is darker than is usual with German examples as the aisle windows are much smaller and are all filled with coloured glass. The apse is especially beautiful in the colouring. The quadripartite vault is ornately painted in a later style.

Italy has many Medieval palaces, civic build-ings, castles and bridges. The finest *palaces* are in *Venice*, mainly fronting the Grand Canal, and of these the *Ca' d'Oro* is of the classic pattern (**590**). This can be seen in the white marble ogee arches, the tracery, elegant balconies, arcading and roofline. The *Palazzo Franchetti* is another example (**593**). World famous is the *Doge's Palace*, begun in the ninth century; the present façades to S. Mark's Square and the Grand Canal waterfront date from 1309–1424. In pinkly glowing patterned brickwork and brilliant white carving and arcading, these elevations are the essence of Venetian Gothic architecture at its best. Stylistically they represent a fusion of Constantinople, the Orient, classical Rome and Medieval Gothic, resulting in a unique harmony (**594, 602** and **605**).

Medieval Italy produced a wealth of *town halls*, originally the seats of government for the city states of the peninsula, though the scale varies according to importance. That at Siena (**592**), with its slender, tall tower, castellated roofline and Gothic fenestration is typical. Others include the Palazzo Vecchio, Florence (**591**), the Palazzo dei Priori (or del Municipio), Perugia (1281), the Palazzo dei Priori, Volterra (thirteenth century), the Palazzo Pubblico, Montepulciano and the Palazzo dei Consoli at Gubbio (1332).

Fortified castles and bridges reflect the general western European trend. The *Ponte di Scaligero*

590

591

592

593

590 *Palazzo Ca' d'Oro, Venice, 1421–36*
591 *Palazzo Vecchio, Florence, 1298–1344. Restored*
sixteenth century (viewed from cathedral campanile)

592 *Palazzo Pubblico, Siena, 1288–1309*
593 *Palazzo Franchetti, Venice, c. 1430*

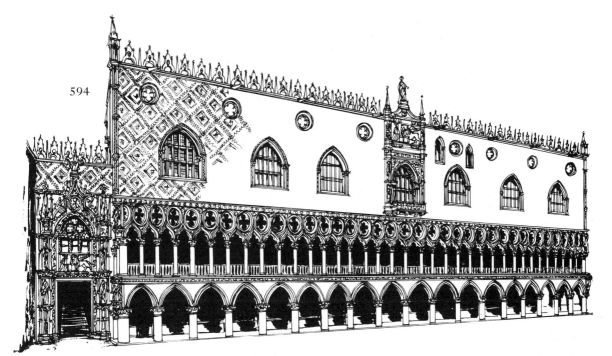

594 Doge's Palace, Venice. Piazza San Marco façade, 1343–1438

at *Verona* is an example (**595**). The *Ponte Vecchio* in *Florence*, over the river Arno, is a civil bridge with houses and shops on it. Two early castles belonged to the Emperor Frederick II, who incorporated Roman military symmetry into the Medieval concentric defence system. One is the *Castel del Monte* in Basilicata (1233–50) which has a classical entrance doorway, and the other the larger, thirteenth century castle at *Prato*. Of the moated, castellated, machicolated, strongly defensive, massive structures, the *Castello degli Estense* in *Ferrara*, is a fine fourteenth century example. There is also the *Castello Nuovo* in *Naples* (1279–83) and the immense, fourteenth

century stronghold on the hill at *Volterra*. In Apulia, at *Lucera*, remains exist of a fortified hill town of brick walls and towers with stone quoins and openings.

Yugoslavia

As in the U.S.S.R., the Medieval work in the southern and inland areas such as Serbia and Macedonia is in Byzantine style. Gothic architecture is to be found down the Dalmatian coast, and this is Venetian owing to the extensive spread of the influence of Venice in this direction. Much of the Gothic work was in continuation of

595 Medieval fortified bridge, Ponte di Scaligero, Verona, 1335

GOTHIC IN YUGOSLAVIA

596 *Ćipiko Palace façade, Trogir,
fifteenth century*
597 *Šibenik Cathedral, south-west
façade, 1440–1540*
598 *Wheel window, Šibenik
Cathedral*
599 *The Rectors' Palace façade,
Dubrovnik, fifteenth century*

GOTHIC ARCHITECTURAL DETAIL

600 Nave capital, Reims Cathedral, France, thirteenth century

601 Cloister capital, Poblet Monastery, Spain, thirteenth century

602 Adam and Eve, Doge's Palace, Venice, Italy, fourteenth century

603 Cloister detail, Jeronimo Monastery, Belém, Portugal, from 1500

604 Cloister Capitals, Convent of Christ, Tomar, Portugal, late Gothic

605 Corner Capital, Doge's Palace, Venice

606 Pier base, Batahla Abbey, Portugal, 1515–34

607 Tomb detail, Cartuja de Miraflores, Spain, from 1500

608 Choir Capital, Lincoln Cathedral, England, from 1256

609 Choir Capitals, Southwell Minster, England, c. 1250

GOTHIC ARCHITECTURAL DETAIL

610 *Apse flying buttresses, Reims Cathedral, France,*
1210

611 *Doorway head, Casa de las Conchas, Salamanca,*
Spain, 1475–83

612 *Nave pier base, Brussels Cathedral, Belgium,*
fifteenth century

613 *Tympanum, S. Elisabeth, Marburg, Germany,*
1257–83

614 *Manoeline Tower window, Belém, Portugal,*
1515–21

615 *Apse flying buttresses. Coutances Cathedral, France,*
thirteenth century

Romanesque schemes; the tower at *Trogir Cathedral*, for example, and the choir stalls at *Zadar*. The work of *Šibenik Cathedral* is of Gothic origin (**597** and **598**), as is the *palace at Trogir* (**596**). In *Dubrovnik*, the local authorities began a new palace for the rectors (**599**). Though restored, this is still an interesting example; particularly noteworthy are the arcade capitals.

Rhodes

Military and fortified domestic Medieval architecture spread through the south-east Mediterranean. The island of Rhodes, near the Turkish coast, was occupied from 1309–1522 by the Knights Hospitallers of S. John of Jerusalem. In the capital (Rhodes) during this time, they built great *mural defences* to the town, especially round the harbour, the *Palace of the Grand Master*, the *cathedral* and the *streets of Inns* of the different countries belonging to the Order. The city was taken by the Turks in 1522. In succeeding years, much of the Gothic work fell into ruin or was destroyed. The Italians, when they occupied the island between 1912–43, restored a number of streets and buildings and rebuilt the destroyed cathedral outside the city walls.

Much still remains to be seen today. There are the city walls, massive gateways (**525**), and the *Hospital of the Knights* (now a museum), with its open courtyard and staircase. On the first floor is a huge room which housed 30 beds. Near each bed was a small room for the servant of the Knight so that he could sleep near his master. The room is well preserved and has a chapel and altar. In the *Street of the Knights* are many Medieval Inns, now restored. There is the Inn of France, of Provence, of Auvergne, of Spain and of Italy. These inns acted as a club for the Knights speaking the appropriate language. Food and drink were provided.

Spain

Development of Gothic architecture in the Iberian Peninsula had something in common with Italy and even more with Germany. The similarities to Italian forms were due to climate, especially in central and southern areas. Here, the large traceried windows and high vaults with consequent flying buttress schemes were unsuitable. Spain preferred smaller windows and larger wall areas to keep out the brilliant sunshine, thick walling, flattish roofs and cloistered shady arcades. As in Italy and Germany, Gothic architecture came late to Spain, partly for the same reason that Romanesque architecture was slow to change but mainly because of the Moorish occupation. In this matter, Iberian development differed from the rest of Europe. The effect of the retreat of the Moors and the advance of the tide of Christianity was discussed on p. 39. This movement affected Gothic development also. Since Moorish occupation of the peninsula did not fully end until the abandonment of Granada in 1492, Gothic architecture in the south was late to evolve.

The most traditional Gothic work developed in the northern region. Here, rather as in Germany, builders found by the thirteenth century that their Romanesque work was internationally out of date and began to adapt themselves to Gothic. But the process started, as in Germany, not as a gentle evolution from national Romanesque, but by an import of fully developed Gothic from France. Monastic orders spread their influence south and west from France and French masons and builders were invited to create imposing cathedrals in Spain. As time passed, German builders also were asked to help, so one can see León Cathedral, for example, on French lines and Burgos nearer German (**616** and **617**).

The Catalan area, around Barcelona, developed a style which had more in common with south-east France. Albi was the inspiration here, with heavy walling, into the thickness of which were built chapels with buttresses between, giving barely any exterior projection.

As in England, Gothic architecture in Spain lingered, but whereas in England the final stage was Perpendicular Gothic, Spanish late Gothic is decorative and richly ornamented and carved. Fifteenth and sixteenth century cathedrals, like Segovia and Salamanca are typical of this. The Spanish love of surface decoration found expression, especially in central and southern areas, in using Moorish forms of ornament. In the final stage of plateresque, whole areas of buildings were covered in surface decoration, both outside and in the interior. The

618

617

616

616 Burgos Cathedral
from the south-west,
begun 1220; façade
towers, 1442–58; central
lantern, 1540–68
617 and 618 View and
plan of Léon Cathedral.
Built mainly 1255–1320

ornament, though rich, was controlled and rarely vulgar. Motifs were predominately Moorish in intricate geometrical and flowing patterns with pierced stone tracery and the use of varied arch shapes. In the south, especially, the horseshoe arch is used, but the pointed arch had been employed here even before it arrived in the Île de France.

Ecclesiastical Building

Cathedrals and Churches

These were nearly all built in stone, a material in ample supply in the mountainous Spanish terrain. Volcanic material was incorporated for polychrome decoration. Also Roman brick construction was employed with wide mortar banding. There was little timber building as forest areas were inadequate. Church plans were usually wider and shorter than in northern Europe, generally on basilican plan but with the *coro* (choir) situated west of the crossing and divided from the altar by an elaborate screen. There were numerous chapels in large ecclesiastical buildings, all round the church. Until 1936, the majority of Medieval cathedrals and churches were in good condition, inside as well as on the exterior, but a tremendous amount of damage was wrought in the Civil War years of 1936–9, particularly in the regions of Madrid, Toledo and Barcelona.

As in France, Spain still possesses a great number of fine cathedrals. Four of the most outstanding, representing different patterns, are León, Burgos, Toledo and Barcelona. *León Cathedral* is on the French model of the best Île de France type. It was built largely in the thirteenth century (**617** and **618**) on a plan similar to Reims. This is in Latin cross form with single aisled nave and double choir, which has a polygonal end and five chevet chapels with double arched flying buttresses. The glass and sculpture make it the Spanish equivalent of Chartres. The façade and transept portals are sculptured. There is some good work, especially in the tympana, but it is not up to French or German standard. The magnificence of the interior is in the vast quantity of coloured glass in the large windows which fill the wall space from vaulting shaft to vaulting shaft. Much of this glass dates from the extensive nineteenth century restoration,

but it is of fine quality and merges well with the original work, presenting a worthy challenge to Chartres. Despite the area of glazing (triforium as well as clerestory) the level of illumination is not high. The impression is of a luminous Byzantine quality in the rich coloured light. The stonework is effectively simple; there is little sculpture or decoration; all the glory is in the glass.

Burgos Cathedral (**616**) is quite different. Whereas León is not impressive on the exterior, lacking the soaring quality of Gothic, Burgos is striking outside, with its classic façade, central lantern and pentagonal, eastern chevet. The building period is a long one and the style of work varies from the early lower part, begun 1221, to the very rich sixteenth century lantern. The cathedral is wide and fairly low, apart from the façade towers which were completed with their fine German style openwork traceried spires in 1486 by Hans of Cologne. The very rich late Gothic *cimborio*, the octagonal central lantern, followed in 1568. Inside this has a magnificent eight-pointed star vault (**472**). The choir is in the usual Spanish position west of the crossing, reducing the nave to a mere vestibule. There are some beautiful late Gothic side chapels, of which the Capilla del Condestable (1482) is superbly ornamented.

Toledo Cathedral, though based on the French model, is very large and very Spanish. It is one of the finest Gothic monuments in Europe. Started in 1226 at the east end, the façade is fifteenth century and later, as is also the unusual and imposing north-west tower (**619**). There are some fine sculptured porches here of different styles and periods; the north with a typical fourteenth-century tympanum, the south, with the richly sculptured, almost plateresque *Puerta de los Leones* (1452) and the triple façade portals on the French pattern. Apart from the façade and interesting cloisters, it is the nave interior which is the glory of the Medieval part of the Cathedral. It is simple, majestic, lofty. The nave arcade has tall multi-shafted piers and foliated capitals carrying the pointed arches. The central shafts rise to the high vault, which is quadripartite. The clerestory windows have geometrical tracery and still a quantity of their original fine glass. There is also a beautiful rose window. The high altar screen is a Gothic masterpiece, representing in hundreds of figures and groups scenes from the life of Christ. The great central space of the cathedral interior is devoted to the choir with its magnificent (later) choir stalls. The whole is enclosed in a Gothic style stone carved screen of great complexity and richness.

Catalan Gothic, which is admirably represented by Barcelona and Gerona Cathedrals, is quite different. The fourteenth century saw the opening of an era of prosperity in Catalonia based on trade with France, Italy and the Balkans, largely through the port of Barcelona. The architectural influence was French from the south-east region and, in particular, examples such as the cathedrals of Albi, Toulouse and Perpignan. The churches are aisleless or with a wide central nave and narrow side aisles. Buttresses are internal, immensely strong and projecting, like those at Albi, inwards into the church. The chapels were built between them.

619 Façade, Toledo Cathedral, Spain, 1400–52

619

The exterior wall was therefore plain and un-interrupted. Inside, Catalan churches are dark. Windows are small, long and narrow, triforia rare and vaults quadripartite.

Gerona Cathedral is based on this pattern. It is immensely wide, with aisleless fifteenth century nave spanned by a 73 foot wide vault. Inside, chapels are situated between the huge internal buttresses which are 20 feet deep and rise to the full height of the building as at Albi. The east end is aisled and has a chevet, a fourteenth century example based on that at Barcelona. The baroque façade rises above a great exterior staircase.

Barcelona Cathedral is the Catalan Gothic masterpiece. On classic Catalan pattern, it was begun in 1298 and largely completed by the early fifteenth century, apart from the façade which is neo-Gothic. The east end is the finest part of the building. It is on the French model of a seven-sided apse with ambulatory and radiating chapels. On the exterior, these chapels are deeply set into the ring of massive buttresses which are connected by flying arches to the clerestory wall, each one set between the circular windows. The cathedral interior is magnificent, giving a vivid impression of Medievalism. It is dark, the light shining in through a quantity of richly coloured glass in windows which are narrow and not very large. The nave arcade is high, with a shallow triforium and clerestory above. There is an octagonal lantern over the crossing. Adjoining the cathedral are the fine mid-fifteenth century cloisters with 22 chapels round them (**513**).

Many Spanish cathedrals still have beautiful *cloisters* and a number of these are of the thirteenth century early Gothic style. Of two particularly interesting examples, one is the *Monastery of Las Huelgas* in *Burgos* (**620**). The work is plain with double columns and foliated capitals, all different from one another. At *Poblet*, near Tarragona, the monastery has recently been restored from a damaged state. The thirteenth century cloisters, however, largely escaped the fire and sack of 1835 and the original work is in fair condition. The ribbed quadripartite vaults extend round the four sides of the cloister. The open arcade is carried on multi-shafted piers with grouped capitals of extraordinary variety and richness (**601**).

The fifteenth and sixteenth centuries in Spain produced many fine late Gothic monuments; among them three great cathedrals: Seville, Segovia and Salamanca. *Seville Cathedral* was the earliest of these, built over a long period beginning in 1402 at the west end. It is the largest Medieval cathedral in Europe and, on a roughly rectangular plan, measures 430 by 247 feet. The cathedral was not finished till *c.* 1520 and much of it is in the late Spanish Gothic style but, since it is in Andalusia where Moorish influence was strong till nearly 1500, both decoration and layout reflect eastern modes. The plan was controlled by its being built on the site of the Moorish mosque and the slender 'giralda' was its minaret. This was built in the twelfth century, of brick, with typical, high quality Moorish brick decoration in trellis patterned panels (**622**). The belfry, which is Renaissance, was added in 1568 and surmounted by the bronze figure which revolves, hence the name 'giralda' from *girar*—to turn round. It is certainly one of the most beautiful bell towers in the world.

Seville Cathedral is impressive, partly because of its immense size. The apsidal end is shown in Fig. **622** and this is the most interesting view. Much of the remainder is restored or altered and the flattish roofs and near horizontal flying buttresses are neither interesting nor very Gothic. Inside, the vista is breathtaking. The nave is very wide, with four broad aisles and surrounding chapels. It also is very high, with a quadripartite vault 130 feet above ground, supported on immense, clustered piers with tiny foliated capitals. There is no triforium, but stained glass clerestory windows with rich curvilinear tracery. The central lantern, rebuilt in 1882 after collapse, has an interior star vault. Despite its long building period and mixture of styles, the interior at least of Seville Cathedral has unity, richness and fine proportions. It represents an imposing penultimate achievement in the Gothic movement. But it was by no means the last.

Both Segovia and Salamanca are sixteenth century buildings and, being in central Spain, are less influenced by Moorish design and decoration. They are purely late Spanish Gothic. *Segovia* was built between 1520 and 1577 on a fine hill site on symmetrical plan. It has a seven-chapel chevet with gently sloping flying buttresses and ornate crocketed pinnacles. The interior is very wide and high with slender, clustered shafts supporting characteristic late Gothic vaulting (**621**).

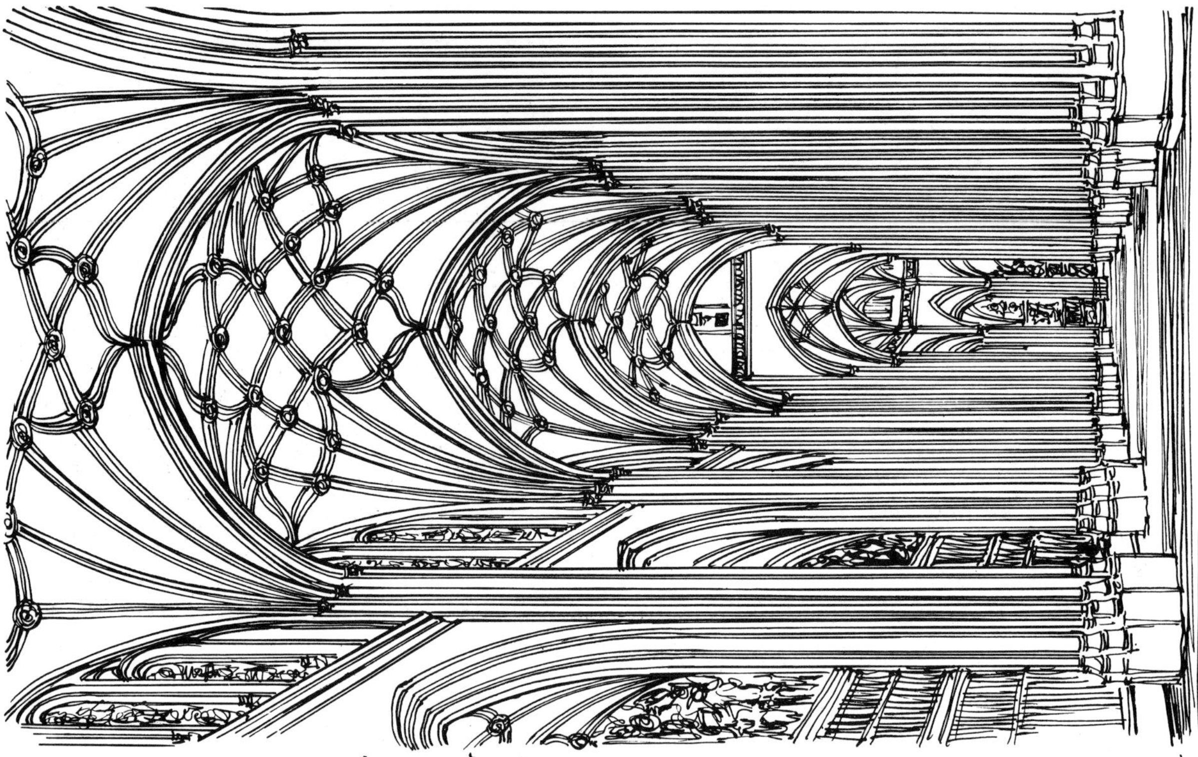

621

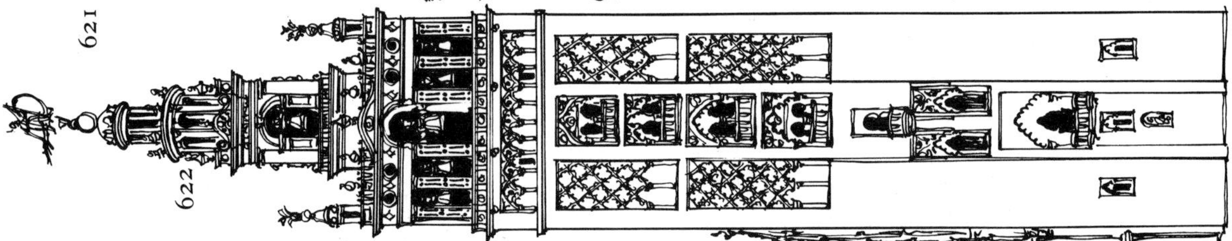

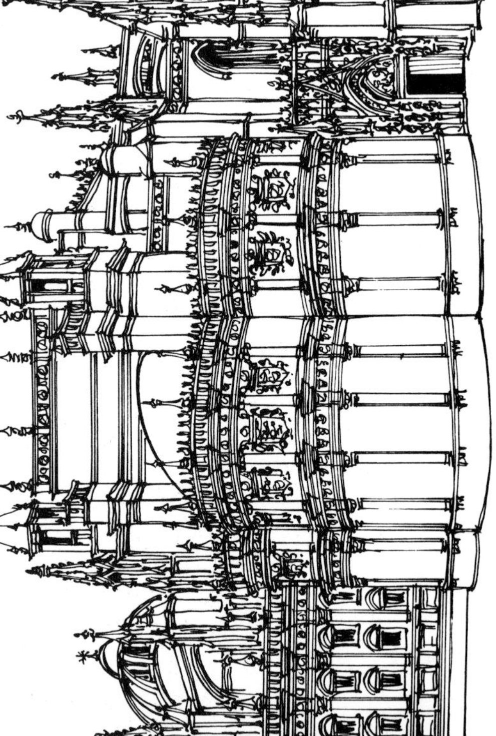

622

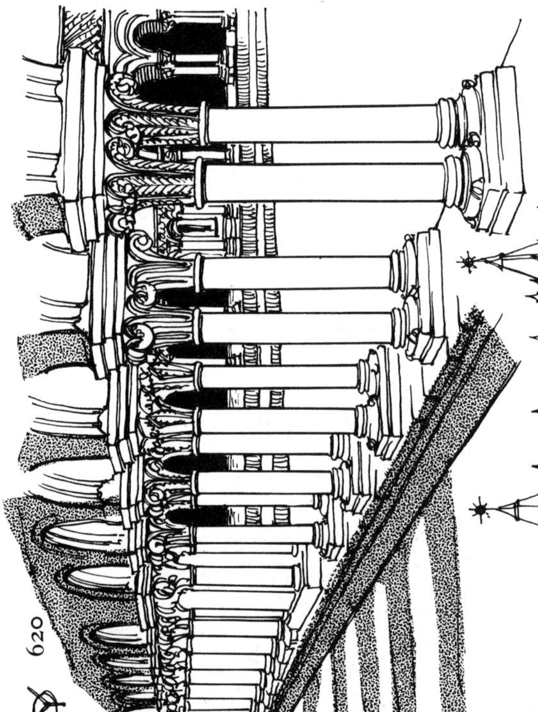

620 Cloisters, Monastery of Las Huelgas, Barcelona, early Gothic

621 South aisle, Segovia Cathedral, 1521–91

622 Seville Cathedral from the east, 1432–67. Tower (the Giralda) 275 feet high, 1184–98 and 1568

620

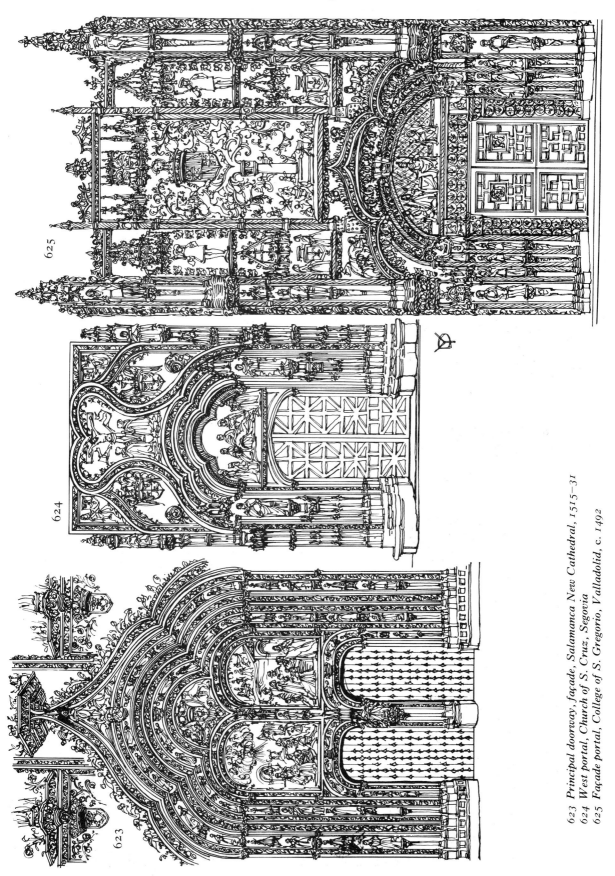

623 Principal doorway, façade, Salamanca New Cathedral, 1515–31
624 West portal, Church of S. Cruz, Segovia
625 Façade portal, College of S. Gregorio, Valladolid, c. 1492

Salamanca Cathedral is exactly contemporary with Segovia. It is built next door to the Romanesque Cathedral (p. 44) on the hill above the river Tormes spanned by the Roman bridge (**165**). It is much like Segovia, especially in its nave and Renaissance-inspired towers with cupolas and lanterns. It has a square east end, though, instead of a chevet and the exterior decoration, especially on the west façade, is of incredible richness (PLATE 64). This is a good example of what is termed *plateresque ornament*. It was named thus, in a later period, as a term if dissapprobation in reference to its affinity with silverwork (*platería*), which was a major Spanish industry at the time. The name emphasises the entirely surface character of the ornament, which had barely any relationship with the architectural form beneath. Indeed, since it

was applied all over doorways, portals, even façades, it tended to blur the architectural lines with a complete carpet of decoration. Motifs, making up this ornamental covering, were varied; they included heraldic forms, Gothic features, human and animal figures, plant and bird life. Sculptural panels, often in high relief, were framed in the total design. The west façade at Salamanca Cathedral, of 1513–31, by Juan Gil de Hontañón, is a prime example (**623** and PLATE 64).

The period of excessive surface ornamentation on both exterior and interior of large buildings lasted through the fifteenth and sixteenth centuries and beyond. It reflected the wealth of the country as well as the love of ostentation and decoration felt by the Spanish people. The academic simplicity of early Gothic or Italian

626 *Cloisters, S. Juan de los Reyes, Toledo, c. 1470*

626

Renaissance was never fully acceptable to Spain. The plateresque form of decorative treatment continued from Gothic into Renaissance; only the motifs changed. Gothic Plateresque is sometimes referred to as Isabelline because the work largely emanates from the reign of Isabella. Other outstanding examples of the style can be seen on the façade of the *Church of S. Cruz* in *Segovia* (**624**) and the amazing façades in *Valladolid* of the *Church of S. Pablo* (PLATES 73 and 74) and the *College of S. Gregorio* (**625**). The last of these is a riot of ornament, with twisted columns, strange figures and Moorish elements.

Among the varied types of *churches* in Spain, one of the most beautiful is *S. Juan de los Reyes* in *Toledo*. Here are magnificent two-storeyed cloisters with traceried openings and sculptured statues in late Gothic style (**626** and **455**) which also prevails on the exterior of the church. Inside

is a fine late star vault under the *cimborio* and some beautiful plateresque decoration on the walls in the choir. The church was a masterpiece by Juan Guäs. Also in *Toledo* is the quite different *S. Maria la Blanca*, which is a five-aisled church on rectangular plan with the roofs at differing levels. The decoration of the capitals and wall arcades as well as the horseshoe arches show strong Moorish influence (**627**).

Further variation in design can be seen in the hall churches of the very late period. These are mostly from the sixteenth and seventeenth centuries and are Gothic buildings with classical décor, like *S. Maria la Redonda* in *Logroño*. There are also the Catalan Gothic types on aisleless plan and with fourteenth and fifteenth century decoration, like *S. Maria del Pino* and *S. Maria del Mar,* both in Barcelona.

627 *S. Maria la Blanca, Toledo. Built twelfth century as a synagogue. Consecrated as a Christian church 1405. Now a national monument*

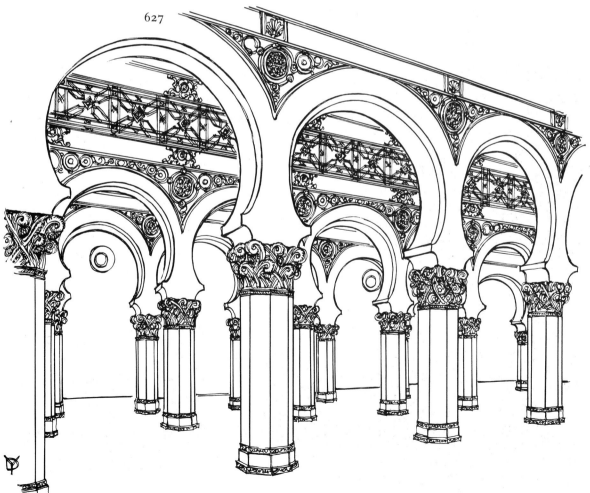

627

SPANISH MEDIEVAL ARCHITECTURE

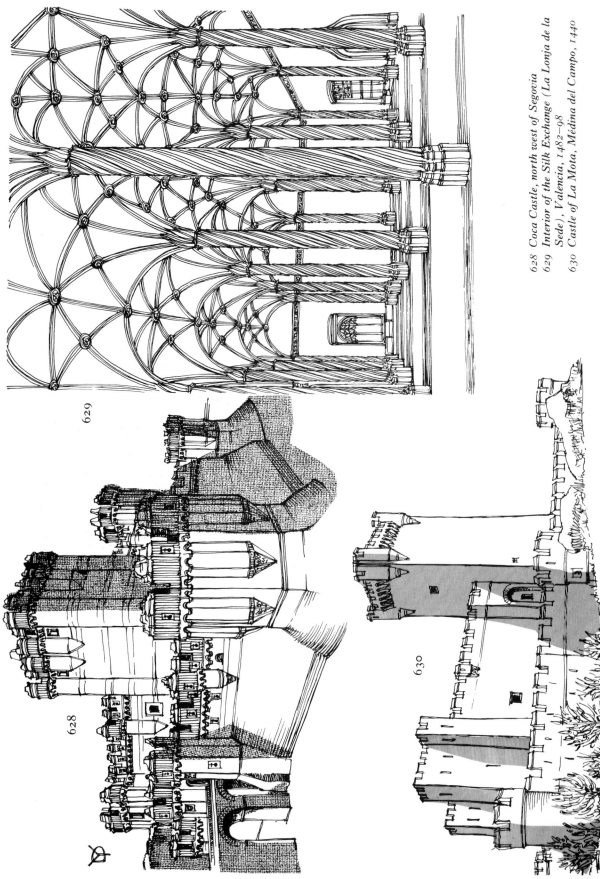

628 *Coca Castle, north west of Segovia*
629 *Interior of the Silk Exchange (La Lonja de la Sede), Valencia, 1482–98*
630 *Castle of La Mota, Medina del Campo, 1440*

629

628

630

Domestic and Civic Buildings

One of the most remarkable palaces in Gothic plateresque style is the *Palacio del Infantado* in *Guadalajara*. This was built 1480–92 by Juan and Enrique Guäs (architects of S. Juan de los Reyes) in an interesting mixture of Gothic and Mujédar forms. The interior, including the picturesque court, was destroyed by bombing in 1936, but the exterior façades remain to the full height of the walls and restoration is now taking place (**465**). There are similar, smaller examples at Baeza in southern Spain. Faceted and decorative stonework façades can still be seen at Segovia and Salamanca. The *Casa de los Picos* in *Segovia* is like the Palazzo dei Diamanti in Ferrara. The

Casa de las Conchas in *Salamanca*, also fifteenth century, is covered in sea-shell decoration. There are also some beautiful windows and grilles (**611** and **459**).

The *Palacio de la Andiencia* in *Barcelona* has been altered, but still retains a Gothic pointed-arched court with exterior stone staircase. There also still exist some of the exchanges which were so typical of Medieval Spain. The *Silk Exchange* in *Valencia* is the finest of these. It has a long, stone façade with rich Gothic fenestration and doorway. Behind is a vaulted hall on hall church pattern, 130 by 75 feet, divided into nave and aisles by spiralled columns (**629**). The *exchange* at *Zaragoza* has now been restored. The exterior is dull but the hall is magnificent. This, like so

631

631 The Exchange (La Lonja), Zaragoza, c. 1550. Gothic with Renaissance detail

Plate 70
The Bamberg Horseman. Bamberg Cathedral,
Germany, c. 1220–30
Plate 71
Cloister detail. Batahla Abbey, Portugal. 14th
and 15th century
Plate 72
S. George and the Dragon. Castle Hill, Prague,
Czechoslovakia. Jiří and Martin of Cluj, 1373

Plates 73 and 74
Façade. Church of S. Pablo, Valladolid, Spain, 1276–1463

632 *Bridge of S. Martín, Toledo, Medieval*

632

many of the sixteenth century exchanges, is a mixture of Gothic and Renaissance forms. The vault is Gothic, with Medieval bosses, but the supporting columns have Ionic capitals and Renaissance putti and shields. The hall is now used for exhibitions (**631**).

Fortified Structures

Spain is more noted for its Medieval castles than any other European country. Castile, the immense area in the centre of the country, had so many that it was named from them (*castillo*). Medieval castles are in all styles: Romanesque, Gothic, Moorish, Renaissance. Many are now ruined, but a number of outstanding examples remain in good condition. One of the best is the *Castillo de la Mota* at *Medina del Campo* (**630**). There is a deep ditch all round, spanned by a bridge, reaching to the double, outer, windowless walls. The castle is austere, large and impressive, built in brick on a hill above the town.

One of the largest castles in Spain is that at *Olite*, near Pamplona, built in 1403. It was damaged by fire in the nineteenth century but 15 vast, mural towers remain. Near the Pyrenean frontier, it was partly of French construction and once had large halls, chambers and extensive gardens. Most of the best remaining castles date from the fifteenth century and are situated in León or Castile. There is the large, interesting example at *Valencia de Don Juan*, ruined and romantically reflected in the waters of the river Esla below; the gaunt 150 foot pile of *Torrelobatón*, an impregnable castle in fine condition; and *Turégano* near Segovia, ruined part castle, part church. Not far away is *Castle Coca* (**628**), an immense mass of pinkish brick towers and turrets set within a deep, enclosing moat.

In large towns it was customary to build an alcázar, a fortified palace. Most of these have been rebuilt, as in Madrid, or much restored. The *Alcázar* at *Segovia* is one of these. It was transformed from a fortress into a fortified palace in 1455 but was rebuilt in more recent times after a disastrous fire in the nineteenth century.

A number of town gateways which were originally part of the city walling have fared better. In good condition are the *Puerta del Sol* at *Toledo*, dating from *c.* 1200 and with horseshoe arches and Moorish decoration, the *Puerta de Serranos* at *Valencia*, 1349, a typical octagonal towered, Gothic structure and the *Puerta de S. Maria* in *Burgos* which is Medieval with Renaissance decoration and sculpture.

Medieval *bridges* in Spain have suffered considerably but the bridge of *S. Martín* at *Toledo* survives (**632**). This is a fine example, spanning the rocky gorge of the River Tagus which almost encircles the town; it has defence gateways at

GOTHIC IN PORTUGAL

633 The façade, Monastery Church, Batahla, 1387–1415

634 Batahla, the cupola vault, Founder's Chapel, 1415–34

635 Interior of the Cistercian Abbey Church of Alcobaça, 1158–1220

636 Batahla, cloister opening

633

634

635

636

637 Façade, church and part of monastery
638 Cloisters

637

638

each end. The *Puente de Pietra* in the centre of *Zaragoza*, a stone example of 1401, has been somewhat altered and spans the river Ebro.

Portugal

Although no geographical barrier separates Spain from Portugal, and although the early history of Moorish occupation was similar in both countries, the artistic development differs. The two peoples are totally dissimilar in character and personality and they have been separate entities for hundreds of years. Not a great deal survives in Portugal from the Gothic era. Partly this is because so much Medieval work was lost in the great earthquake of 1755 which destroyed the city of Lisbon. Three outstanding buildings exist in the pure Gothic style, all abbey churches: Batahla, Alcobaça and Belém.

The *monastery of Batahla*, near Leiria, was founded in 1397. Built mainly in the fifteenth century, it is a fine architectural group. The façade, recently restored and cleaned, is now easy to view as a vast space has been cleared in front of it. The illustration (633) shows the square, richly decorated façade, the flying buttress scheme of nave and choir and, on the left, the remarkable cloister. These have individual and unusual arcade openings (636 and 606) in Manoeline style (PLATE 71). The church itself is cruciform, with apsidal east end and tall lancet windows. The interior is simple, contrasting with the façade and chapels. Its soaring, multi-clustered piers rise to a quadripartite vault. There is a clerestory but no triforium. Very fine, and especially richly decorated, is the octagonal founder's chapel. This has a magnificent star vault (634) carried on an octagonal drum with eight two-light windows and eight piers with cusped arches below. The capitals, like those in Wells and York Cathedrals, are of vine leaf design. It is a tomb chapel and all round the walls are tombs under rich Gothic canopies.

The *Cistercian Abbey Church* of *Alcobaça*, nearby, was built 1158–1223. It now has a Baroque façade in golden stone (Volume 3, p. 117), but its interior presents a contrast. This is a large but simple Medieval hall church in white stone (635). The vaulting shafts of the tall piers are unusual in that they do not descend to the ground but are supported on corbels. (This can also be seen in Fossanova Abbey Church in Italy.) Nave and aisles are of uniform height and vault design. The aisle walls are plain, pierced only by round-headed windows set high, just under the vault. The east end is apsidal with an ambulatory. It has narrow lancet windows and round, Romanesque type columns instead of piers. The whole interior is of one scheme and design.

The *Jeronimo Monastery* at *Belém*, now a suburb of Lisbon, was the last great Portuguese Gothic structure (637). It was built in the early sixteenth century. The church is a rich example of late Gothic work with a fine sculptured portal and ornamental fenestration. Inside, it is again a hall church type. The nave has a remarkable lierne star vault; the remainder is almost a fan design. The columns supporting the nave are carved all over with late Gothic ornament. The window surrounds continue this decorative form. The whole church is in carved stone. As at Batahla, one of the glories of Belém is the cloisters. These are two-storeyed (638 and 603) with traceried, cusped openings and lierne vaults roofing each storey. The carved decoration of column and pier shafts is rich and varied.

Of an earlier Gothic style, in *Lisbon*, are the remains of the *Carmo Convent*, begun in 1385 and partly destroyed in the earthquake, now retained and preserved as the archaelogical museum. The former nave, open to the sky, still shows its fine design and structure. Later Manoeline and Renaissance ornament appear on windows and other details.

The *Manoeline* style represents, to a certain extent, the Portuguese equivalent to Spanish Plateresque. It is so called after Dom Manoel I who reigned 1495–1521, during the period when Portugal was establishing her new sea routes and her great navigators were exploring the world. Manoel was a patron of the arts and helped to encourage the rich decoration of fine buildings. The style, like plateresque, is essentially one of surface decoration. The buildings were late Gothic but rich ornament, chiefly round windows and doorways, was carved in motifs which were a wonderful collection of sea-shells and twisted ropes intermingled with exotic oriental forms. The cloister openings at Batahla are of this type of design, also Belém and some of the doorways at Alcobaça. The *Tower of Belém*, built opposite to the monastery, on the spot at the edge of the Tagus estuary where the navigators sailed from, is a fine example (**523** and **614**). Another building with some fine Manoeline carving is the Templar's Monastery, the *Convent of Christ*, at *Tomar*, north of Lisbon. The monastery is on a hill above the modern town. The round twelfth century church leads into the late Gothic portion which includes the chapter house. There are two remarkable windows here, a circular one on the church and an ornate, rectangular window in the chapter house. This has a frame displaying a riot of decorative forms carved in stone, including all kinds of marine motifs: seaweed, coral, cables, fishing nets mixed up with heraldry and plant life. The window is by Diogo de Arruda (PLATE 69). There are seven cloisters; an interesting Gothic one (**604**), some mixtures of styles and an excellent Renaissance example (Volume 3, p. 163).

Eastern Europe

Rumania

It is difficult for the student to trace specific buildings in eastern Europe as frontiers here have been moved a great deal during the twentieth century and especially since 1939. In consequence, the names of places are completely altered. This is particularly true of Rumania and Hungary. Present day Rumania is much larger than it used to be, and comprises much of what was Hungary, while the U.S.S.R. possesses some of the lands which were Polish and Rumanian. In this book monuments will be found listed under their present day Rumanian nomenclature, not Hungarian, as is common practice.

Rumania today is a large country which possesses a wealth of architecture from the Medieval period. Much of this, as in the U.S.S.R., continued to be Byzantine in form till well into the seventeenth century. This work is described in Volume 1, p. 130. The remainder is derived from differing sources and influences so is varied in style. Buildings are of stone or timber and a few are in brick. The country is partly mountainous and there is an abundance of both stone and wood. The most pure Gothic structures are not very common. They are chiefly of stone and follow mainly a middle period Gothic style

which is not heavily ornamented. The modern main road through Rumania from the Hungarian border at Oradea to Bucharest runs through the Carpathian mountains and also through the towns where most remains are situated: Cluj, Alba Iulia, Sibiu, Braşov, Sinaia. Sighişoara and Bran are not far from this road.

S. Michael's Church in *Cluj* is one of the best examples of pure Gothic design in Rumania. It was built during the fourteenth and fifteenth centuries, but has a nineteenth century tower, and has been excellently restored recently (**640**). It is a hall church with an apsidal ended short chancel which has tall, geometric traceried windows. The graceful piers extend upwards to the quadripartite and star vaults without any interruption from capitals. It is a finely proportioned, simple church of considerable size.

Alba Iulia Cathedral was described on p. 61. It was given a Gothic chancel in 1320–56 which is apsidal with lancet fenestration. There are several Gothic buildings in *Sibiu*, which is a remarkably unspoilt Medieval town. Several town gateways remain, as in the Piata Republica and, nearby in the Piata Grivitá, is the tall, Gothic style church with its six pointed gable façade.

Further east is the larger town of *Braşov* which still possesses a number of Gothic monuments. The *Black Church* is the best known. It is a tall, plain building on the exterior with narrow, geometric traceried windows. The east end is apsidal; at the west is a tall tower. The best view is from the hillside opposite (**639**) as the church is hemmed in in the centre of the town. The interior is in good repair and of unusual design. The nave is two-storeyed with cusped, ogee arches supporting a gallery. The one-storeyed choir rises to the considerable height of the church. Here are tall, octagonal piers with strange voluted capitals set up near to the groined vault. Also in Braşov is the *town hall* (**641**) and the Greek Orthodox *Church* of *S. Nicholas*, begun in 1595 but not completed till 1750.

Also in Gothic style are some of the many fortified structures in Rumania. In the romantic vein of a Carpathian castle are the mountain strong-holds at Bran and Hunedoara. *Bran Castle* is perched on top of a wooded hill, impregnable and difficult of access, not far from Braşov (**545**). Just south of Deva is the fifteenth century *castle* of *Hunedoara*, which is even more unapproachable

GOTHIC IN RUMANIA

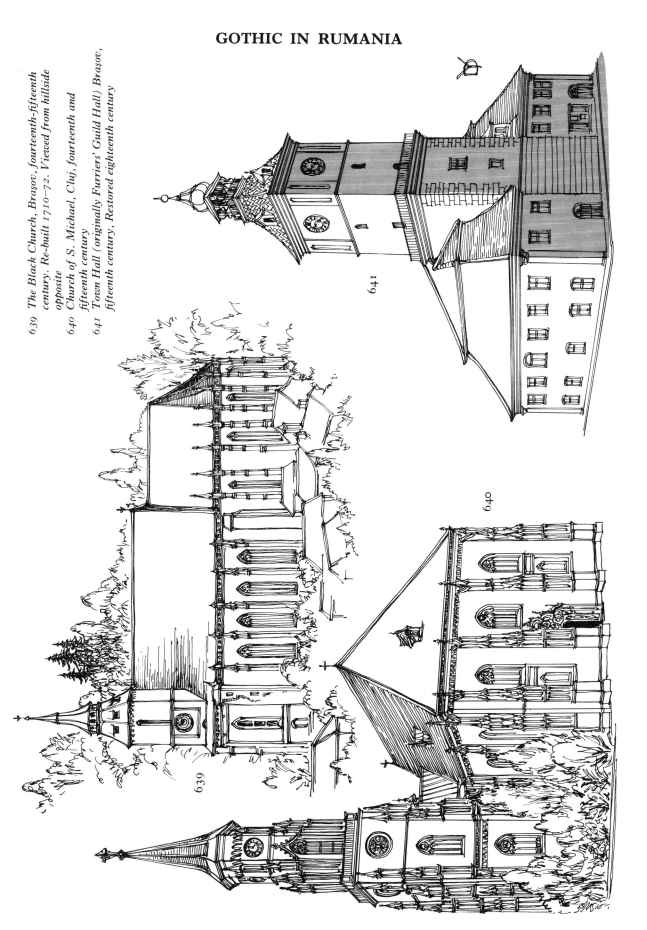

639 The Black Church, Brasov, fourteenth-fifteenth century. Re-built 1710–72. Viewed from hillside opposite
640 Church of S. Michael, Cluj, fourteenth and fifteenth century
641 Town Hall (originally Furriers' Guild Hall) Brasov, fifteenth century, Restored eighteenth century

641

640

639

(548). There is a fine fifteenth century chapel and hall; extensions and alterations were made in the seventeenth and nineteenth centuries. At *Sighişoara*, north-west of Braşov, is the fifteenth century fortified *church*.

The fifteenth and sixteenth centuries also saw the construction of fortified *monastic settlements*. Most of these have been altered or added to in later ages. Especially interesting examples are those of *Dragomirna, Putna* and *Suceviţa*. They are all fortresses as well as monasteries and are surrounded by buttressed walls with mural defence towers. Inside the rectangular court is built the church and other monastic structures. The fortifications are Medieval but the buildings within, good examples of their type, stem from Gothic, Renaissance and Byzantine sources and were added at different periods.

These monasteries are all in *Moldavia* in the north-east part of Rumania, the most remote from centres of population and sharing a border with the U.S.S.R. This is the least known region of the country but, architecturally, the most interesting, for here are the unique Moldavian *painted churches. Suceviţa monastery* contains one of these churches, built 1548. Others include *Voronets* (**644**), *Neamţ* (**642**), *Moldoviţa* and *Humor*. They all stem from the fifteenth and sixteenth centuries and are covered in fresco paintings on the exterior as well as inside. Like the French cathedral portals, they tell the Bible story and are teachers of Christianity to an illiterate population. Apart from their beauty and originality, they are also a mystery. It is still not known how these exterior frescoes have lasted in a severe central European climate for 400 years. The freshness of the colours is remarkable. All that is known is that the lime applied to the walls was kept in pits filled with water for three years before use and that the apprentices daily skimmed a film from the water, removing the impurities from the lime. *Suceviţa* and *Voronets Churches* are the finest examples. They are aglow with glorious colours. Voronets is only a tiny church but Suceviţa is large. On the exterior are frescoes showing vividly Heaven, Earth and Hell in a multitude of figures and scenes. The work is two-dimensional; there is no perspective, yet these are masterpieces of great quality.

In *Iaşi* (Jassy), the ancient capital of Moldavia, is a most original Medieval church, built as late as the seventeenth century, but a Gothic/Byzantine structure with all-over decoration on the exterior of an eastern type reminiscent of the giralda at Seville (**645**). This is the *Church of the Three Hierarchs* and is carved in stone lacework pattern intermingled with Medieval arcading.

There is also the tradition of *timber architecture*, typical of all the heavily forested countries of eastern Europe. These have been mentioned with regard to the U.S.S.R. (p. 149). Rumania possesses more surviving examples of this type of structure than elsewhere and a vast quantity continued to be built until the early nineteenth century in rural areas. Though there are still examples scattered throughout the country, we are indebted for their extensive and varied collection to the magnificent *Village Museum* in *Bucharest*. Here, almost in the centre of the city, in the park surrounding the beautiful Lake Herăstrău, are 15 acres of an open air site. This is planted with trees and shrubs and laid out with grass and paths, with an extensive selection of structures from all over Rumania, re-erected here to their original manner. There are churches, houses, farmsteads, cattle stalls, wells, workshops, portals and many other structures. Mainly they are constructed with solid timber logs, dovetailed and set on a stone or brick base. Roofing is by wooden shingles and these are extended to cover a variety of tall steeples and belfries. Many of the solid wood structures are beautifully carved, for example window frames, furniture, balconies, entrance portals. Some structures are of brick with mud and whitewash facing and many have thatched roofs. Some houses are built with the lower part for animals and the upper for the family. Others are constructed three-quarters underground with a sloping passage downwards from the front door which is at thatched roof level.

The *churches* are the most striking buildings in this medium. The typical layout can be seen in, for example, an eighteenth century church from *Turea* near Cluj and another of 1722 from *Dragomireşti* in Moldavia. Both have a pro-naos, a naos and chancel. Inside, they are subdivided by vast beams of solid timber. The tall steeple is

REGIONAL MEDIEVAL IN MOLDAVIA AND THE CARPATHIANS

642 *Neamț Monastery Church, Moldavia, 1497*

643 *Village timber Church, Rucar, near Brașov, c. 1650. (Church now at Tekirghiol)*

644 *Painted Monastery Church, Voroneț, Moldavia, sixteenth century*

645 *Three Hierarchs Church, Iași, Moldavia, 1639*

set up over the pro-naos. Upright baulks of wood lean slightly inwards towards the narrow steeple, supporting cross beams on an X pattern. Floors are of wood. Wood shingles cover the roofing and steeple. There are wide eaves for heavy snow. In the Dragomireşti Church, the naos is barrel vaulted in wood. The chancel screen is richly carved and all the walls and roof are painted in bright colours. Windows are tiny. The eastern end is apsidal, in pentagonal form. The great timbers are dovetailed into one another to turn the corners.

The example illustrated in Fig. **643** is not in the Museum but in *Tekirghiol*. This is a small spa on the Black Sea near Constantza. The church belonged to the Carpathian mountain village of *Rucar* and was given to Tekirghiol because, in 1930, so many people from Rucar had been cured of their ailments by the waters and mud treatment of the spa at Tekirghiol, that they decided the only thing they could give to express their gratitude was their most precious possession— the village church. It now stands, 400 miles from its birthplace, on the hillside above the restorative Lake Tekirghiol, the only building in the town of any architectural merit. It has been erected in the courtyard of a holiday home for priests of the Greek Orthodox Church. It is a tiny but beautiful example of craftsmanship. In layout it is similar to those in the Village Museum in Bucharest, with pro-naos, naos and chancel and wood partitions between. The chancel is painted all over inside, as is also the naos barrel vaulted roof, with biblical scenes.

U.S.S.R.

There was, as mentioned earlier (p.149), little Gothic architecture in the Soviet Union. Two examples are illustrated; the *Kremlin* at *Rostov* (**562**), which is still largely Byzantine (Volume 3 p. 163) and the remarkable *Church of the Ascension* at *Kolomonskoe* (**560**). This is a building which still defies classification by scholars. It is a brick church, immensely tall, of octagonal structure, bearing a great weight on the lower galleried arcades. It possesses the Gothic quality of verticality but is not Gothic in design or form. It is nearer to the tall, wooden tent churches of northern Russia but, though this has been suggested, concrete evidence is lacking for its dependence, in brick, on these wooden forms. This is a votive church, built in 1532 as part of the Tsar's country residence near Moscow (Basil III). If this unusual and fine building were in western Europe, situated as it is in open country so near to the capital and alongside the river (Moskva), the surroundings would have been landscaped with lawns, flower beds and paths as a place to visit. Here, in addition, are the Church At Dyakova (Volume 1, p. 142) and other later buildings of Byzantine style, but the place is untouched country, undeveloped and visited by few.

Glossary

The reference figures in brackets refer to illustrations in
the text.

Abacus The top member of a capital, usually a square or curved-sided slab of stone or marble (**400**).

Abutment A solid mass of masonry or brickwork from which an arch springs and against which it abuts (**398**).

Alcázar A Spanish word for a castle or fortress (**628**).

Ambulatory A passage or aisle giving access in a church between the choir with high altar and the exterior apse (**544**).

Apse Semicircular or polygonal termination to an church most commonly to be found on the eastern or transeptal elevations (**321**).

Arcade A series of arches, open or closed with masonry, supported on columns or piers (**287**).

Arcuated construction Wherein the structure is supported on arches (**509**).

Articulation The designing, defining and dividing up of a façade into vertical and horizontal architectural members.

Ashlar Hewn and squared stones prepared for building.

Astragal The moulding at the top of a column and below the capital (**404**).

Barbican Outer defence to a city or castle. Generally a double tower over a gate or bridge (**546**).

Barrel vault A continuous vault in semicircular section like a tunnel (**319**).

Basilica A church plan, seen particularly in Italy and France, of rectangular form generally with an apse at one end. Usually such a church was divided internally into nave and aisles by columns or piers which originally supported a timber roof. Earlier examples had no transepts. This plan was based upon the basilica of ancient Rome which was a hall of justice and a centre for commercial exchange. It was adopted by early Christians for their churches and from these the medieval adaptations were made (**268**).

Capital The crowning feature of a column or pier (**604**).

Centering A structure, usually made of wood, set up to support a vault or arch until construction is complete.

Chevet Term given to a circular or polygonal apse when surrounded by an ambulatory from which radiate chapels (**428**).

Chevron ornament Romanesque decoration in zig-zag form (**395**).

Cimborio Spanish term for lantern or fenestrated cupola (**472**).

Clerestory, Clearstory The upper storey in a church generally pierced by a row of windows (**532**).

Conch The domed ceiling of a semicircular apse (**326**).

Corbel table A projecting section of wall supported on corbels (carved blocks of stone or wood) and generally forming a parapet.

Crocket A projecting block of stone carved in Gothic foliage on the inclined sides of pinnacles and canopies (**516**).

Crossing The central area in a cruciform church where the transepts cross the nave and choir arm. Above this space is generally constructed a tower or cupola (**493, 494**).

Cruciform A ground plan based on the form of a cross (**422**).

Cusp Point forming the foliations in Gothic tracery (**457**).

Domical vault A groined or ribbed vault where the diagonal groins or ribs are semicircular in form so causing the centre of the vaulted bay to rise higher than the side arches, as in a low dome.

Finial Ornament finishing the apex of a roof, gable, pinnacle, newel, canopy, etc. (**610**).

Flèche French term for a slender spire commonly to be found over the crossing on a Gothic church (**427**).

Greek cross plan A cruciform ground plan where the four arms of the cross are of equal length.

Hall church One in which the vaulting height of the entire building interior is the same. Such a church has, therefore, no triforium or clerestory. Most commonly found in Gothic design in Italy, Scandinavia and areas of German influence (**522, 538**).

Intersecting vault Where two vaults, either of semicircular or pointed section, meet and intersect at right angles. The most usual instance is in the crossing of a church where transepts cross nave and choir (**315**).

Lantern Structure for ventilation and light. Often surmounting a tower or dome (**622**).

Latin cross plan A cruciform church ground plan where the nave is longer than the other three arms (**423**).

Lierne From the French *lier* = to tie. A short, intermediate rib in Gothic vaulting which is not a ridge rib nor rises from the impost (**468**).

Lintel The horizontal stone slab or timber beam spanning an opening and supported on columns or walls (**398**).

Machicolation A parapet in medieval fortified buildings which has openings in its base between supporting corbels for dropping missiles upon an enemy (**482**).

Manoeline Portuguese decorative style of the early sixteenth century named after Dom Manoel I (1495–1521) (**plate 69**).

Mozarabic A style of architecture in medieval Spain named after the Mozarabs who were Christians owing allegiance to a Moorish King but permitted to practise Christianity (**261**).

Pilaster strip Also known as Lesene, a low relief stone strip with the appearance of a pilaster but with only decorative, not structural purpose (**251**).

Plateresque A form of rich, surface ornament in Spanish architecture used in both Gothic and Renaissance buildings. The term is derived from *plateria* = silverwork (**625**).

Podium A continuous projecting base or pedestal.

Retablo An altar piece or framing enclosing painted panels above an altar. A Spanish word used especially when referring to Spanish architecture.

Relieving arch Is constructed in order to prevent a weight of masonry above it from crushing the lintel below it.

Segmental arch A round arch forming a segment of a circle, its centre below the springing line (**278**).

Set-off A sloping or horizontal member connecting the lower and thicker part of a wall or buttress with the receding upper part (**520**).

Shaft A column between its capital and base (**364**).

Spandrel Triangular space formed between an arch and the rectangle of outer mouldings as in a doorway. Generally decorated by carving (**388**).

Solar Medieval term for an upper room, usually the private sitting room of the owner of the house.

Squinch Arches placed diagonally across the internal angles of a tower to convert the square form into an octagonal base to support a spire.

Stave church Medieval wooden stave or mast churches of Scandinavia constructed in self-contained units. The walls, the stave screens, rest upon the timber sleepers below but do not take weight or thrust. This is taken upon the skeleton framework of poles or masts which are set into the timber ground sills, then attached to the staves (**365, 371**).

Stilted arch A round arch having its springing line higher than the level of the impost mouldings (**300**).

String course A moulding or projecting course set horizontally along the elevation of a building.

Tierceron An intermediate rib in Gothic ribbed vaulting which extends from the vault springing to the ridge rib (**570**).

Tracery The ornamental stonework in the head of a Gothic window (**456**).

Transept The arms of a cruciform church set at right angles to the nave and choir. Transepts are generally aligned north and south (**339**).

Triforium The first floor intermediate stage of a medieval church between the nave arcade and the clerestory. The triforium is usually arcaded and may have a passage behind this which extends all round the church at this level (**293**).

Trumeau A French term which is used to refer to the pier between two openings or, more commonly in Gothic architecture, the pier dividing a large portal into two parts (**plates 56, 61**).

Tympanum The area of walling between the lintel of a doorway and the arch above it. Tympana are generally carved and/or sculptured (**plates 58, 62**).

Undercroft A chamber partly or wholly below ground. In a church this would be a crypt, in a house or castle it would be used for storage (**317**).

Vault An arched roof covering (**581**).

Vaulting bay The rectangular or square area bounded by columns or piers and covered by a stone vault.

Vaulting boss A carved decorative feature set over the intersections of a ribbed vault to hide the junctions (**453**).

Vault springing The point at which the vault ribs spring upwards from the capital, corbel or arch impost (**550**).

Voussoir The wedge-shaped stones which compose an arch (**272**).

Bibliography

A select list of books, classified by country, recommended for further reading.

Europe in General

ALLSOPP, B., *Romanesque Architecture*, Arthur Barker, 1971

ALLSOPP, B., BOOTON, H. W., and CLARK, U., *The Great Tradition of Western Architecture*, A. and C. Black, 1966

ANDERSON, W., *The Rise of the Gothic*, Hutchinson, 1985

BENEVOLO, L., *The History of the City*, The MIT Press, 1986

BRANNER, R., *Gothic Architecture*, Prentice-Hall International, 1961

BUSCH, H., and LOHSE, B., *Gothic Europe*, Batsford, 1959; *Romanesque Europe*, Batsford, 1960

CAMESASCA, E., *History of the House*, Collins, 1971

CICHY, B., *Great Ages of Architecture*, Oldbourne, 1964

CONANT, K. J., *Carolingian and Romanesque Architecture*, Pelican History of Art Series, Penguin, 1979

COPPLESTON, T., Ed., *World Architecture*, Hamlyn, 1963

FLEMING, J. HONOUR, H., and PEVSNER, N., *The Penguin Dictionary of Architecture*, Penguin, 1977

FLETCHER, BANISTER, *A History of Architecture*, Butterworth, 1987

FOSTER, M., *The Principles of Architecture*, Phaidon Press, 1983

FRANKL, P., *Gothic Architecture*, Pelican History of Art Series, Penguin, 1962

GOMBRICH, E., *The Story of Art*, Phaidon Press, 1972

GRODECKI, L., *Gothic Architecture*, Abrams, New York, 1977

HARRIS, J., and LEVER, J., *Illustrated Glossary of Architecture 850–1830*, Faber and Faber, 1966

HARVEY, J., *The Gothic World*, Batsford, 1950

HINDLEY, G., *Castles of Europe*, Hamlyn, 1968

HOAR, F., *European Architecture*, Evans, 1967

HONOUR, H., and FLEMING, J., *A World History of Art*, Macmillan, 1982

JORDAN, R. FURNEAUX, *A Concise History of Western Architecture*, Thames and Hudson, 1969; *European Architecture in Colour*, Thames and Hudson, 1961

KOSTOV, S., *A History of Architecture: Settings and Rituals*, Oxford University Press, 1985

KRINSKY, C. H., *Synagogues of Europe*, The MIT Press, 1986

KUBACH, H. E., *Romanesque Architecture*, Abrams, New York, 1975

KÜNSTLER, G., *Romanesque Art in Europe*, Thames and Hudson, 1969

LINCOLN, E. F., *The Medieval Legacy*, MacGibbon and Kee, 1961

MUSCHENHEIM, W., *Elements of the Art of Architecture*, Thames and Hudson, 1965

NEBOLSINE, G., *Journey into Romanesque*, Weidenfeld and Nicolson, 1969

NORWICH, J. J. Ed., *Great Architecture of the World*, Mitchell Beazley, 1975

NUTTGENS, P., *The Story of Architecture*, Phaidon Press, 1983; *The World's Great Architecture*, Hamlyn, 1980

PEVSNER, N., *An Outline of European Architecture*, Penguin, 1961; *A History of Building Types*, Thames and Hudson, 1984

PLACZEK, A. K., Ed., *Macmillan Encyclopedia of Architects* (4 Vols) Collier Macmillan, 1982

RAEBURN, M., Ed., *Architecture of the Western World*, Orbis Publishing, 1980; *An Outline of World Architecture*, Octopus Books, 1973

RICHARDS, I., *Abbeys of Europe*, Hamlyn, 1968

RICHARDS, J. M., Ed., *Who's Who in Architecture from 1400 to the Present Day*, Weidenfeld and Nicolson, 1977

SAALMAN, H., *Medieval Architecture*, Prentice-Hall International

SCHUERL, W. F., *Medieval Castles and Cities*, 1978

SITWELL, S., *Gothic Europe*, Weidenfeld and Nicolson, 1969

STEWART, C., *Early Christian, Byzantine and Romanesque Architecture* (Simpson's History of Architectural Development), Longmans, Green and Co., 1965; *Gothic Architecture* (Simpson's History of Architectural Development), Longmans, Green and Co., 1965

STIERLIN, H., *Encyclopaedia of World Architecture*, Macmillan, 1983

TRACHTENBERG, M., AND HYMAN, I., *Architecture from Prehistory to Post-Modernism*, Academy Editions, 1986

VERZONE, P., From *Theodoric to Charlemagne: A History of the Dark Ages in the West*, Methuen, 1967

WATKIN, D., *A History of Western Architecture*, Barrie and Jenkins, 1986

YARWOOD, D., *Encyclopaedia of Architecture*, Batsford, 1985; *Chronology of Western Architecture*, Batsford, 1987

Britain

BAKER, J., *English Stained Glass*, Thames and Hudson, 1960

BALCOMBE, G., *History of Building: Styles, Methods and Materials*, Batsford, 1985

BRAUN, H., *Elements of English Architecture*, David and Charles, 1973; *English Abbeys*, Faber and Faber, 1971

BRUNSKILL, R. W., *Traditional Buildings of Britain*, Gollancz, 1982

BRUNSKILL, R. W. and CLIFTON-TAYLOR, A., *English Brickwork*, Ward Lock, 1977

BUTLER, L., and GIVEN-WILSON, C., *Medieval Monasteries of Great Britain*, Michael Joseph, 1979

CLIFTON-TAYLOR, A., *The Pattern of English Building*, Faber and Faber, 1972; *English Parish Churches as Works of Art*, Batsford, 1974; *The Cathedrals of England*, Thames and Hudson, 1967

CLIFTON-TAYLOR, A., and IRESON, A. S., *English Stone Building*, Gollancz, 1983

COOK, O., *The English House Through Seven Centuries*, Whittet Books, 1983

COOK, O., and SMITH, E., *English Abbeys and Priories*, Thames and Hudson, 1960

CRAIG, M., *The Architecture of Ireland*, Batsford, 1982

DUNBAR, J. G., *The Architecture of Scotland*, Batsford, 1978

GIROUARD, M., *Life in the English Country House*, Yale University Press, 1978; *Cities and People*, Yale University Press, 1985

HARVEY, J., *Cathedrals of England and Wales*, Batsford, 1978; *The Mediaeval Architect*, Wayland Publishers, 1972

HEWETT, C. A., *English Cathedral and Monastic Carpentry*, Phillimore, 1985

HILLING, J. B., *The Historic Architecture of Wales*, University of Wales Press, 1976

ISON, I., and W., *English Church Architecture Through the Ages*, Arthur Barker, 1972

JOHNSON, P., *British Castles*, Weidenfeld and Nicolson, 1979; *British Cathedrals*, Weidenfeld and Nicolson, 1980

JONES, E., and WOODWARD, C., *The Architecture of London*, Weidenfeld and Nicolson, 1983

LITTLE, B., *Architecture in Norman Britain*, Batsford, 1985

LLOYD, N., *History of the English House*, The Architectural Press, 1975; *A History of English Brickwork*, Antique Collectors' Club, 1983

PETZCH, H., *Architecture in Scotland*, Longman Group, 1971

PEVSNER, N., and METCALF, P., *The Cathedrals of England*, (2 Vols), Viking, 1986

SAUNDERS, A., *The Art and Architecture of London*, Phaidon, 1984

WEBB, G., *Architecture in Britain in the Middle Ages*, Pelican History of Art Series, Penguin, 1956

WOOD, M., *The English Mediaeval House*, Bracken Books, 1983

WRIGHT, J., *Brick Building in England, Middle Ages to 1550*, John Baker, 1972

YARWOOD, D., *The Architecture of Britain*, Batsford, 1980; *Outline of English Architecture*, Batsford, 1977; *English Interiors*, Lutterworth Press, 1984; *The English Home*, Batsford, 1979

Bulgaria

STAMOV, S., Ed., *The Architectural Heritage of Bulgaria*, State Publishing House Tehnika, Sofia, 1972

Czechoslovakia

KNOX, B., *Bohemia and Moravia*, Faber and Faber, 1962

France

ADAMS, H., *Mont-Saint Michel and Chartres*, Princeton University Press, 1981

BLOMFIELD, R., *A History of French Architecture* (2 Vols), Bell, 1911

BRANNER, R., *Burgundian Gothic Architecture*, Zwemmer, 1985

GOUVION, C. and PHILIPPE, D., *Châteaux of the Loire*, Thames and Hudson, 1986

RODIN, A., *The Cathedrals of France*, Hamlyn, 1965

Germany

BAUM, J., and SCHMIDT-GLASSNER, H., *German Cathedrals*, Thames and Hudson, 1956

Italy

ARSLAM, E., *Gothic Architecture in Venice*, Phaidon, 1972

BERGÈRE, T., and R., *The Story of St. Peter's*, Dodd, Mead, New York, 1966

COARELLI, F., and SANTUCCI, U., *Arte nel Mezzogiorno*, Editalia, Rome, 1966

FRANKLIN, J. W., *The Cathedrals of Italy*, Batsford, 1958

GODFREY, F. M., *Italian Architecture up to 1750*, Tiranti, 1971

GUNTON, L., *Rome's Historic Churches*, Allen and Unwin, 1969

MÂLE, E., *The Early Churches of Rome*, Benn, 1960

WHITE, J., *Art and Architecture in Italy 1250–1400*, Pelican History of Art Series, Penguin, 1966

YARWOOD, D., *The Architecture of Italy*, Chatto and Windus, 1970

Poland

DOBRZYCKI, J., *Cracow: Landscape and Architecture*, Arkady, Warsaw, 1967

JANKOWSKI, S., and ROFALSKI, P., *Warsaw: a Portrait of the City*, Arkady, Warsaw, 1979

KNOX, B., *The Architecture of Poland*, Barrie and Jenkins, 1971

KOSTROWICKI, I. AND J., *Poland*, Arkady, Warsaw, 1980

STANKIEWICZ, J., *Gdansk*, Arkady, Warsaw, 1971

ZACHWATOWICZ, J., *Polish Architecture*, Arkady, Warsaw, 1967

Romania

CIOCULESCU, S., and others, *Romania*, Meridiane, Bucharest, 1967; *Monuments of Religious Art in Romania*, Carpati, Bucharest

Russia (USSR)

BERTON, K., *Moscow*, Studio Vista, 1977

FAENSON, H., and IVANOV, V., *Early Russian Architecture*, Elek, 1975

HAMILTON, G. H., *The Art and Architecture of Russia*, Pelican History of Art Series, Penguin, 1954

IKONNIKOV, A., *Russian Architecture of the Soviet Period*, Raduga Publishers, Moscow (English translation), 1988

VOYCE, A., *The Art and Architecture of Medieval Russia*, University of Oklahoma Press, 1967

Scandinavia

FABER, T., *A History of Danish Architecture*, Det Danske Selskab, 1964

KAVLI, G., *Norwegian Architecture*, Batsford, 1958

RICHARDS, J. M., *800 Years of Finnish Architecture*, David and Charles, 1978

Spain and Portugal

DIETERICH, A., and BOGER, B., *Portrait of Spain*, Oliver and Boyd, 1958

HARVEY, J., *The Cathedrals of Spain*, Batsford, 1957

WEISSMÜLLER, A. A., *Castles from the Heart of Spain*, Barrie and Rockliff, 1967

Index

Buildings are listed under the names of towns or villages. Persons are generally listed under the surname or second name. Line illustrations are printed in bold type.